Lecture Notes in Artificial Ir

Subseries of Lecture Notes in Compute

Edited by J. G. Carbonell, and J. Siekm

T0230167

Lecture Notes in Computer Science

Edited by G. Goos, J. Hartmanis, and J. van Leeuwen

Springer
Berlin
Heidelberg
New York
Barcelona
Hong Kong
London
Milan
Paris
Tokyo

Ron Kohavi   Brij M. Masand
Myra Spiliopoulou   Jaideep Srivastava (Eds.)

WEBKDD 2001 –
Mining Web Log Data
Across All Customers
Touch Points

Third International Workshop
San Francisco, CA, USA, August 26, 2001
Revised Papers

 Springer

Volume Editors

Ron Kohavi
Blue Martini Software
2600 Campus Drive, San Mateo, CA 94403, USA
E-mail: ronnyk@cs.stanford.edu

Brij M. Masand
Data Miners Inc.
77 North Washington Street, Boston, MA 02114, USA
E-mail: bmasand@alum.mit.edu

Myra Spiliopoulou
Leipzig Graduate School of Management
Jahnallee 59, 04109 Leipzig, Germany
E-mail: myra@ebusiness.hhl.de

Jaideep Srivastava
University of Minnesota, 4-192 EECS Building
200 Union St SE, Minneapolis, MN 55455
E-mail: srivasta@cs.umn.edu

Cataloging-in-Publication Data applied for

Die Deutsche Bibliothek - CIP-Einheitsaufnahme

Mining web log data across all customers touch points : third international
workshop ; revised papers ; proceedings / WEBKDD 2001, San Francisco, CA,
USA, August 26, 2001. Ron Kohave ... (ed.). - Berlin ; Heidelberg ; New York ;
Barcelona ; Hong Kong ; London ; Milan ; Paris ; Tokyo : Springer, 2002
    (Lecture notes in computer science ; Vol. 2356 : Lecture notes in
    artificial intelligence)
    ISBN 3-540-43969-2

CR Subject Classification (1998): I.2, H.2.8, H.3-4, K.4, C.2

ISSN 0302-9743
ISBN 3-540-43969-2 Springer-Verlag Berlin Heidelberg New York

Springer-Verlag Berlin Heidelberg New York
a member of BertelsmannSpringer Science+Business Media GmbH

http://www.springer.de

© Springer-Verlag Berlin Heidelberg 2002
Printed in Germany

Typesetting: Camera-ready by author, data conversion by Olgun Computergrafik
Printed on acid-free paper   SPIN 10870091   06/3142   5 4 3 2 1 0

Preface

Workshop Theme

The ease and speed with which business transactions can be carried out over the Web has been a key driving force in the rapid growth of electronic commerce. In addition, customer interactions, including personalized content, e-mail campaigns, and online feedback provide new channels of communication that were not previously available or were very inefficient.

The Web presents a key driving force in the rapid growth of electronic commerce and a new channel for content providers. Knowledge about the customer is fundamental for the establishment of viable e-commerce solutions. Rich web logs provide companies with data about their customers and prospective customers, allowing micro-segmentation and personalized interactions. Customer acquisition costs in the hundreds of dollars per customer are common, justifying heavy emphasis on correct targeting. Once customers are acquired, customer retention becomes the target. Retention through customer satisfaction and loyalty can be greatly improved by acquiring and exploiting knowledge about these customers and their needs.

Although web logs are the source for valuable knowledge patterns, one should keep in mind that the Web is only one of the interaction channels between a company and its customers. Data obtained from conventional channels provide invaluable knowledge on existing market segments, while mobile communication adds further customer groups. In response, companies are beginning to integrate multiple sources of data including web, wireless, call centers, and brick-and-mortar store data into a single data warehouse that provides a multifaceted view of their customers, their preferences, interests, and expectations.

Web mining for e-commerce is the application of web mining techniques to acquire this knowledge for e-commerce. Typical concerns in e-commerce include improved cross-sells, up-sells, personalized ads, targeted assortments, improved conversion rates, and measurements of the effectiveness of actions.

WEBKDD 2001 was the third in the WEBKDD series of workshops, devoted to mining web data. WEBKDD'99 focused on the aspects of web mining related to user profiling, and WEBKDD 2000 focused on Web Mining for E-Commerce.

The URL http://robotics.stanford.edu/~ronnyk/WEBKDD2001 contains the final versions of the workshop papers and the slide presentations.

Papers

The KDD community responded very enthusiastically to the WEBKDD 2001 workshop, and we received a number of requests for attendance. Attendance to the workshop was by invitation only, and requests for attendance were accompanied by short CVs, to allow for discussions among participants with appropriate background and interest. A total of 52 people attended the workshop, which brought together practitioners, tool vendors, and researchers interested in web mining. The paper presentation was divided into three sessions, titled "Predicting User Accesses", "Recommender Systems and Access Modeling", and "Acquiring and Modeling Data and Patterns". A total of 18 papers were submitted to WEBKDD 2001, of which 9 were selected for presentation at the workshop – making it a 50% acceptance rate. The authors of the papers presented at WEBKDD 2001 were invited to submit extended versions of their papers for this special issue. A second round of review was carried out for each paper, and seven papers are included in this book. In this section we summarize each paper.

In her paper titled "Detail and Context in Web Usage Mining: Coarsening and Visualizing Sequences" [1], Berendt illustrates the power of using visualization to better understand the results of web usage mining. Specifically, Berendt shows how visualization can be helpful in understanding long patterns, with little expected structure, that have been mined from the usage logs. Concept hierarchies are presented as a basic method for aggregating web pages, and interval-based coarsening as an approach to representing sequences at different levels of abstraction. A tool, called STRATDYN is described, which uses chi-square test and coarsened stratograms for analyzing differences in support and confidence values. Stratograms with uniform or differential coarsening provide various detail and context views of actual and intended web usage. Relationship to the measures of support and confidence, and methods of analyzing generalized sequences are shown. A case study of an agent-supported e-commerce shopping scenario is used to illustrate the framework.

In "A Customer Purchase Incidence Model Applied to Recommender Services" [2], Geyer-Schulz, Hahsler, and Jahn show how Ehrenberg's theory of repeat-buying can be adapted to the web-based buying environment. Ehrenberg's theory has been successful in describing regularities in a large number of consumer goods and markets. The authors apply the same to show that regularities exist in electronic markets as well, and purchase incidence models provide a theoretically sound basis for recommender and alert services. An empirical validation of the approach, based on data collected from the University of Vienna, is provided.

"A Cube Model and Cluster Analysis for Web Access Sessions" [3] by Huang, Ng, Ching, Ng, and Cheung, show how the application of data cube model and cluster analysis techniques can help in extracting useful e-commerce patterns from web usage data. The cube model organizes session data into three dimensions. The COMPONENT dimension represents a session as a sequence of ordered components, in which the i-th component represents the i-th page visit of the session. Each component is represented by a number of attributes including page ID, category, and time spent. The ATTRIBUTE dimension describes the attributes associated with each component, while the SESSION dimension indexes individual sessions. Irregular sessions are converted into a regular data structure, so that data mining algorithms can be more easily applied. The k-modes algorithms, designed for clustering categorical data and a clustering technique using

Markov transition probabilities is used for the clustering of sequences. An experimental validation of the technique is presented.

In their paper "Exploiting Web Log Mining for Web Cache Enhancement" [4], Nanopoulos, Katsaros, and Manolopoulos show how knowledge gained form mining web usage logs can be used to enhance the performance of better web cache management, thereby reducing the latency perceived by a web user. This is of great value in an e-commerce scenario from a customer experience perspective. The key idea is to use the knowledge extracted to perform better pre-fetching, based on the development of a good page access prediction model. The proposed scheme achieves a good balance between caching and pre-fetching. The pre-fetched documents are placed in a dedicated part of the cache, to avoid the drawback of replacing requested documents with the ones whose access is only speculative. Experimental evaluation of the proposed scheme is presented.

Tan and Kumar, in their paper entitled "Mining Indirect Associations in Web Data" [5], introduce the concept of indirect associations and show how it is applicable to web usage mining. An indirect association between items A and B is said to exist if the direct association between them is quite weak, but there exists item-set X such that the association between A and X is strong and the association between X and B is also strong. The application of this idea to web usage data enables the identification of groups of users with distinct interests. Such patterns may not be discernible using traditional approaches, unless these user groups are known a priori. The approach is validated using data from an academic site as well as a commercial site.

In "A Framework for Efficient and Anonymous Web Usage Mining Based on Client Side Tracking" [6], Shahabi and Bannaei-Kashani describe an approach to using web usage mining for personalization applications. The claim is that for on-line and anonymous personalization to be effective, web usage mining must be carried out in real-time, and with high accuracy. In addition, the approach must allow a tradeoff between accuracy and speed. They introduce the distributed web-tracking approach for accurate, efficient, and scalable collection of usage data. An approach called Feature Matrices (FM) model is proposed to capture and analyze usage patterns. With FM various features of the usage data can be captured with flexible precision, so that accuracy and scalability can be traded off based on application requirements. Additionally, low model complexity allows FM to adapt to user behavior changes in real time. A new similarity measure, designed for capturing partial navigational patterns, is presented. Experimental validation with synthetic and real-life data sets is presented.

In their paper "LOGML: Log Markup Language for Web Usage Mining" [7], Punin, Krishnamoorthy, and Zaki introduce an XML-based language for representing objects of use in the web log mining domain. As per the authors, while extracting simple information from web logs is straightforward, identifying complex knowledge is very challenging. In addition, data cleaning and pre-processing are very complex and demanding tasks. This paper presents two new ideas, namely XGMML and LOGML, to ease this task. The former is a graph description language, while the latter is a web-log report description language.

The web robot of the WWWPal system is used to generate the XGMML graph of a web site. Web-log reports, in LOGML format, are generated from web usage data, and the XGMML graph of a site. Examples illustrate how the combination of XGMML and LOGML can be used to easily capture the web mining process for a particular web site. This make it easy to reuse the various components of the analysis – providing much better leverage for the effort spent in creating the analysis.

Conclusion

WEBKDD 2001 turned out to be a very successful workshop by all measures. A number of people showed interest in the workshop and over 50 attended it. The quality of papers was excellent, the discussion was lively, and a number of interesting directions of research were identified. This is a strong endorsement of the level of interest in this rapidly emerging field of inquiry.

Acknowledgements: We would like to acknowledge the Program Committee members of WEBKDD 2001 who invested their time in carefully reviewing papers for this volume: Jonathan Becher (Accrue/Neovista Software, Inc.), Bettina Berendt, (HU Berlin, Germany), Ed Chi (Xerox Parc, USA), Robert Cooley (KXEN, USA), Johannes Gehrke (Cornell Univ., USA), Joydeep Ghosh (Univ. of Texas, USA), Oliver Guenther (HU Berlin, Germany), Vipin Kumar, (AHPCRC-University of Minnesota, USA), Yannis Manolopoulos (Aristotle Univ., Greece), Llew Mason (Blue Martini Software, USA), Ann Milley (SAS Institute Inc., USA), Bamshad Mobasher (De Paul Univ., USA), Rajeev Rastogi (Bell Labs, Lucent, USA), Alex Tuzhilin (NYU/Stern School of Business, USA), Mohammed Zaki (Rensellaer Polytechnic Institute, USA) and Zijian Zheng, Blue Martini Software, USA.

We would also like to thank others that contributed to WEBKDD 2001, including the original PC members who reviewed the first set of workshop papers. We are grateful to the KDD 2001 organizing committee, especially Roberto Bayardo (workshops chair) and Jeonghee Yi (Registration chair), for their help in bringing the WEBKDD community together. Finally we would like to thank the many participants who brought their ideas, research, and enthusiasm to the workshop and proposed many new directions for the WEBKDD research to continue.

June 2002

Ronny Kohavi
Brij Masand
Jaideep Srivastava
Myra Spiliopoulou

References

1. B. Berendt, "Detail and Context in Web Usage Mining: Coarsening and Visualizing Sequences", pp. 1–24, this book.
2. Geyer-Schulz, Hahsler, and Jahn "A Customer Purchase Incidence Model Applied to Recommender Services", pp. 25–47, this book.
3. Huang, Ng, Ching, Ng, and Cheung, "A Cube Model and Cluster Analysis for Web Access Sessions", pp. 48–67. This book.
4. Nanopoulos, Katsaros, and Manolopoulos, "Exploiting Web Log Mining for Web Cache Enhancement", pp. 68–87, this book.
5. Tan and Kumar, "Mining Indirect Associations in Web Data", pp. 145–166, this book.
6. Shahabi and Bannaei-Kashani, "A Framework for Efficient and Anonymous Web Usage Mining Based on Client-Side Tracking", pp. 113–144, this book.
7. Punin, Krishnamoorthy, and Zaki, "LOGML: Log Markup Language for Web Usage Mining", pp. 88–112, this book.

Table of Contents

Detail and Context in Web Usage Mining:
Coarsening and Visualizing Sequences 1
  Bettina Berendt

A Customer Purchase Incidence Model Applied
to Recommender Services 25
  Andreas Geyer-Schulz, Michael Hahsler, and Maximillian Jahn

A Cube Model and Cluster Analysis for Web Access Sessions 48
  Joshua Zhexue Huang, Michael Ng, Wai-Ki Ching, Joe Ng,
  and David Cheung

Exploiting Web Log Mining for Web Cache Enhancement 68
  Alexandros Nanopoulos, Dimitrios Katsaros, and Yannis Manolopoulos

LOGML: Log Markup Language for Web Usage Mining 88
  John R. Punin, Mukkai S. Krishnamoorthy, and Mohammed J. Zaki

A Framework for Efficient and Anonymous Web Usage Mining
Based on Client-Side Tracking 113
  Cyrus Shahabi and Farnoush Banaei-Kashani

Mining Indirect Associations in Web Data 145
  Pang-Ning Tan and Vipin Kumar

Author Index 167

Detail and Context in Web Usage Mining:
Coarsening and Visualizing Sequences

Bettina Berendt

Humboldt University Berlin, Faculty of Economics, Institute of Information Systems,
Spandauer Str. 1, D-10178 Berlin, Germany
berendt@wiwi.hu-berlin.de
http://www.wiwi.hu-berlin.de/~berendt

Abstract. As Web sites begin to realize the advantages of engaging users in more extended interactions involving information and communication, the log files recording Web usage become more complex. While Web usage mining provides for the syntactic specification of structured patterns like association rules or (generalized) sequences, it is less clear how to analyze and visualize usage data involving longer patterns with little expected structure, without losing an overview of the whole of all paths. In this paper, concept hierarchies are used as a basic method of aggregating Web pages. *Interval-based coarsening* is then proposed as a method for representing sequences at different levels of abstraction. The tool STRATDYN that implements these methods uses χ^2 testing and *coarsened stratograms*. Stratograms with uniform or differential coarsening provide various detail-and-context views of actual and intended Web usage. Relations to the measures support and confidence, and ways of analyzing generalized sequences are shown. A case study of agent-supported shopping in an E-commerce site illustrates the formalism.

Keywords: Web usage mining, sequence mining, visualization, statistical methods, abstraction, agent communication

The way users navigate a Web site can be used to learn about their preferences and offer them a better adapted interface, from improving site design [43] to offering dynamic personalization [33].

However, behavior is complex and can exhibit more 'local' and more 'global' regularities. This becomes particularly important in a site where meaningful behavioral patterns, i.e. episodes [48], may extend over longer periods of time. Episodes are becoming longer as Web sites go from offering information, online catalogs, and purchasing options to utilizing the full power of interactivity and communication. For example, E-commerce sites start to employ agents that offer users support along their way through the site and engage them in a sales dialogue. This kind of dialogue, along with the option to abandon it and/or restart it at any time, provides a rich, semi-structured interface, leading to more extended user interaction, and more knowledge to be discovered.

R. Kohavi et al. (Eds.): WEBKDD 2001, LNAI 2356, pp. 1–24, 2002.

Much of the information contained in an interaction process is sequential. Sequence mining investigates the temporal characteristics of Web usage (e.g., [2,7,22,31,34,44,46]). Queries and result representation focus on statistical measures like the frequency of sequences, and in addition may allow the specification and visual inspection of alternative paths taken through a site to reach a given goal page from a given start page [40].

The powerful techniques available for the identification of patterns often lead to huge result sets. The mining challenge is to combine openness and little specification to be able to find unexpected patterns with enough structure to easily find meaningful results, i.e. interesting patterns.

One approach is to *select* patterns, e.g. by filtering based on numerical criteria like support thresholds or more sophisticated mechanisms [14], or query languages to constrain patterns syntactically, e.g., [2,40].

Another approach is to *abstract* from details by classifying accessed pages or paths. Concept hierarchies treat a number of Web pages as instances of a higher-level concept, based on page content (as in market basket analysis [23]), or by the kind of service requested, for example, the query options that a user employs to search a database [6]. Generalized sequences [40] are used to define pattern templates that summarize a number of different sequences of requests. For example, $[A_1, [0; 5], A_2]$ matches all sequences found in user paths that start with a request for a page A_1 and end with a request for a page A_2, with up to 5 further arbitrary requests in between. A generalized sequence thus abstracts sequences by declaring parts of user paths to be of secondary interest. One problem of this kind of aggregation is that the paths in between the specified pages are either lost in the representation of results (if only the support and confidence of a pattern are given), or are represented in very fine detail (e.g., as the disjunction of all the different paths actually taken [40]). The latter necessitates the visual inspection and formulation of new, abstract or specific, hypotheses to be tested. If these in-between paths are of interest, and there is not enough information or prior expectation to specify them syntactically, a mechanism appears desirable that presents a large number of paths in a compact way.

Visualizations can be regarded as supporting abstraction *per se*, because they utilize the human capabilities of quickly recognizing patterns that may not stand out in a non-pictorial representation of the data. Different kinds of visualizations of web usage have been proposed, which emphasize different aspects of Web usage. The present paper uses *stratograms*, first introduced in [3,4], as a way of combining these visualization approaches. It extends this basic idea by introducing *coarsening* as an abstraction along the temporal dimension, as measured by the order of requests. The proposed method, *interval-based coarsening*, deals with binary as well as n-ary sequences, and it can be used to analyze generalized sequences. Relations to the standard Web usage mining measures support and confidence are shown. *Coarsened stratograms* are presented as powerful visualizations that allow the results to be easily communicated to non-experts. This may allow local *and* global patterns to be detected. A coarse first overview of the data can also help the analyst to quickly concentrate on areas of the data that contain interesting patterns.

The paper starts with an overview of visualization methods (section 1) and shows how this relates to the semantic modeling of the analyzed site (section 2). Sections 3 and 5 describe stratogram visualizations and coarsening. Throughout, a case study introduced in section 4 is used. Section 6 presents the statistical background, pattern discovery and comparison using type hierarchies. Algorithms to compute stratograms based on type hierarchies are described, and extensions discussed. Section 7 discusses stratograms as tools for describing and comparing intended with actual usage. Section 8 concludes the paper.

1   Visualizations of Web Usage

Different kinds of visualizations emphasize different aspects of Web usage. Due to the focus on sequential behavior, we only consider visualizations that analyze *transitions* between two pages visited in succession, or *paths* of arbitrary length[1]. (Visualizations that focus on the properties of single HTTP requests include access log analyzers[2], Starfield displays [24], or glyphs located on the nodes of a web site graph, as in [11,18].)

The tool of [28] computes measures of actual and intended usage, derived from requests or paths. It plots these against each other. While this is very useful for easily identifying divergences from intended usage, the reduction to numerical values means that progress along user paths cannot be investigated.

In [13], longest repeating subsequences (LRPs, aggregations of several users' paths) are overlaid on a site graph. A *site graph* is a directed graph whose nodes are pages and whose edges are the hyperlinks between pages. Such *site-based layout* may reveal possible inadequacies of the space provided for navigation, but it can also be very space-consuming and thus quickly become cluttered. *Usage-based layout* displays only those pages of the site that were actually visited. While the combination of site-based and usage-based layout can be very helpful in detecting relevant associations in behavior, the display of paths in site graphs, or in the graphs defined by usage, poses a problem for visual interpretation. Since each transition in each LRP is shown as a straight line between two nodes, it can become difficult to differentiate different LRPs (or repetitions of the same transition), and to visually track progress.

This becomes easier when the visited nodes are plotted against time. These plots usually contain multiple representations of pages that were revisited along the displayed path. One example are the navigation patterns of WUM [40,41], which are paths specified by grammatical and statistical constraints and joined together at their common prefixes to form a tree.

VisVIP [17] displays each path as a spline overlaid on the site graph. This makes it easier to distinguish different paths and to inspect them in detail. However, only a small number of paths can stand out in their entirety; tracking the

---

[1] Throughout the paper, *page* is used as synonymous with *page view*, and with *URL*. I.e., it is assumed that the required preprocessing steps have been taken (filtering out images, identifying pageviews of framesets, renaming alternative URLs, etc.).

[2] compilation at http://www.uu.se/Software/Analyzers/Access-analyzers.html.

progress of different paths can become increasingly difficult with their number. The same is the case for the "individualized site maps" of [5].

In WebQuilt [25,26], individual paths are overlaid on a 2D site graph. The line thickness of an edge $(A \rightarrow B)$ increases with the support of the transition from A to B. Focusing on the immediate precursors and successors of a specified node, this can be generalized to the analysis of many sessions (cf. the Visual Insights visitor flow visualization [18]). Color is used to encode the average time of a transition, and to show intended paths.

When the site, or the subsite defined by usage, is treated as a graph, node position bears no meaning beyond a page's identity. A node's position is governed by graph layout algorithms, which aim to maximize clarity and minimize edge crossings [10]. Layout algorithm may also order pages visited after a given start page by support [13], or by time of first visit [5]. This may reveal unexpected relations.

An alternative is to treat the pages as points in a *state space*. The coordinates of points describe page properties. Usually, the state space will be discrete (for example, the group of products that are the content of this page, the level of detail of description, the media or MIME type of the page, etc.). The sequence of requests in a path then becomes a sequence of points in that state space, which, in the visualization, may be joined by connecting lines to resemble a trajectory. Here, position bears meaning: the value of a page along the different dimensions. For example, in [36], the pages containing proof steps generated by students in a hypermedia logics learning program are ordered by increasing degrees of concreteness, i.e., by how many variables are instantiated.

Regardless of whether a graph or a state space is employed, the *multiplicity of individual pages' locations* utilizes human perceptual capabilities in different ways. A unique page location, as used in site graph representations, ensures an "identity of place", which corresponds to the perception of pages as locations comparable to places in the physical world. *Alignment* is the repetition of an axis at a different position in the space [9]. In a 2D representation of paths, alignment means that the plotting of nodes along the y axis is repeated at different time steps along the x axis. This is a popular method in displays of individual paths: Pages or groups of pages can be enumerated along the y axis as in [27,38], or ordered as in [36,35].

Stratograms integrate ideas of several of the previous approaches. They merge trees of multiple paths into directed acyclic graphs, embedding these in a state space. The visual variables area and color (grey value in black/white displays) encode support, and shape encodes different actions (transitions vs. exits). They allow the display of many as well as of individual paths [39]. A formal definition of stratograms will be given in section 3, and an example in section 4.

In the visualization approaches discussed, abstraction methods are generally restricted to support thresholds or, more generally, the selection of certain nodes, requests, transitions, or paths. Stratograms provide these options, and extend them by employing coarsening. Rather than (de-)selecting data, coarsening represents them at a different degree of granularity. Stratograms provide a state space as *context*, and navigation at different levels of *detail* (cf. [30]). This will be elaborated in section 5. The degree of detail can be uniform across the whole display, or different to provide selective zooming.

2   Modeling Site Semantics

A second kind of abstraction employed by stratograms utilizes the site's semantics: At first glance, a navigation path (individual or aggregated) is only a sequence of distinguishable nodes, or a path through a (metaphorically physical) space which may involve recurrent visits to distinguishable places.

In order to *understand* a path, the analyst can define and investigate quantitative measures such as the path's length as an indicator of the ease of traversing it [28]. To understand it at a qualitative level, however, the site's semantics need to be taken into account. This can be done by annotating the path textually. Annotations can consist of the visited pages' names (this is done in most visualization approaches), and they may indicate the number of times this page has been visited before in the current session [40]. This can only be understood by an analyst able to associate page name with content. An analysis program may aid the analyst in this task by automatically extracting terms from the document constituting the page, and presenting these as a content summary. This allows the analyst to derive the likely "information scent" that was followed and thus caused this path [13,12].

More knowledge can be discovered if a model underlying the site's pages is available (e.g., [20]) or can be constructed (semi-)automatically (e.g., [6,16]). Ontologies that are concept hierarchies [23], possibly extended by more information [19], may reveal relations on subsequently visited pages (such as a common topic matter that is not indicated by common terms at the linguistic surface).

Ontologies that allow the analyst to *order* pages or groups of pages by some abstract criterion are particularly interesting for knowledge discovery by visualization. As an example, consider an online shop with a canonical event sequence for a purchase: searching/browsing, selecting an item, adding it to the shopping cart, and payment (cf. [32]). This event sequence defines an order on groups of pages of the site. Sites like the online bookstore Amazon use a similar order on the shopping process explicitly to help *the user* navigate, displaying a 'process bar' of icons at the top of pages, with the current stage visually highlighted.

In the running example used in the present paper, a similar idea is employed to help *the analyst* understand site usage. The general idea, to specify a site model that allows an ordering on groups of pages accessed, can be employed for different types of sites [4]. Examples investigated in that paper include online catalogs and educational software [36].

3   Basic Stratograms

A basic stratogram rests on the relative frequencies of transitions, i.e., binary sequences, in a log. The log can be a Web server log, a log collected at the client's computer, etc., and all standard pre-processing steps such as data cleaning and sessionizing are assumed to have been completed [45]. For each session s from a total of S sessions, all requests after an offset are considered. The offset may be the first request in a session, or it may be the (first) request for a certain page. $s.(o_s+t)$ denotes the tth request, or step, in session s after the offset o_s. A *node* is an individual page or a page concept that encompasses several pages according to a concept hierarchy. The *normalized frequency* of the transition from a node A_1 to a node A_2 at the tth step after the respective session offsets o_s is[3]

$$f(A_1, A_2, t) = \frac{|\{s \mid s.(o_s+t)=A_1 \wedge s.(o_s+t+1)=A_2\}|}{S} . \qquad (1)$$

The offset can be specified by the user. Its purpose is to disregard irrelevant requests before an event of interest. Also, choosing the right value for the offset can make patterns stand out more clearly, because it leads to a grouping of requests depending on their distance from a chosen event. Therefore, a significant event should be chosen as offset (cf. the template specification of the first request when mining for sequences using template languages [40,2]).

Since the number of all transitions between t and $t+1$ is at most S (it may be less because some sessions may end earlier than $t+1$ steps after their respective offsets), each normalized frequency is at most 1, and their sum is at most 1.

In addition to frequencies, a stratogram requires a function v that maps the visited pages from the set *pages* to numerical values N according to some interpretation of the site's structure and content[4]. This may be a 'degree of specificity' in a search, or some other scale along which pages may be ordered for the analysis question at hand, as discussed in section 2 above. To be able to identify a transition's frequency with that of its associated numerical values, it is assumed for simplicity that the function v is bijective, i.e. that pages are not further summarized by v. Each session is augmented by a request for the special page "end" after its last request.

Definition 1. *A basic stratogram strat is defined as*

$$strat = \langle pages, st, v, tr, \theta_1, \theta_2 \rangle \quad with$$
$$st = \{0, \ldots, max_s(|s| - 2)\}, v : pages \mapsto N,$$
$$tr = \{f(A_1, A_2, t) \mid A_1 \in pages, A_2 \in pages \cup \{end\}, t \in st\} , \qquad (2)$$

where the θ are support thresholds.

A basic stratogram visualization *consists of (1) for each t, A_1, A_2 s.t. $A_2 = end$ and $f(A_1, A_2, t) \geq \theta_1$: a circle with center $(t, v(A_1))$ and radius increasing with $f(A_1, A_2, t)$, and (2) for each other t, A_1, A_2 s.t. $A_2 \neq end$ and $f(A_1, A_2, t) \geq \theta_2$: a line from $(t, v(A_1))$ to $(t + 1, v(A_2))$, with thickness increasing with $f(A_1, A_2, t)$.*

---

[3] The concepts and measures used in this paper are relative to a log and a page classification. To simplify notation, both will be assumed given and not included as extra arguments.

[4] More complex stratograms that make v depend on the page and the previous requests are discussed in [4].

In the following, "stratogram" and "stratogram visualization" will be used interchangeably when clarified by the context.

The number of steps is bounded above by the number of nodes in the longest session minus 1, so t ranges from 0 to $max_s(|s|-2)$, where $|s|$ is the length of s.

The stratogram is normalized by support levels either found in the data or imposed by the analyst, i.e. there are support thresholds, $sup_i^{min} = \theta_i, i = 1, 2$.

4   Example: Agent-Supported Shopping in an Online Store

The Web site used in the case study is an online store developed at the Institute of Information Systems of Humboldt University Berlin, in cooperation with a German retail chain. After selecting a product category and going through an introductory phase, users are encouraged to answer up to 56 questions related to the product they intend to purchase. This communication is initiated by an anthropomorphic shopping agent. At any time, the agent can be asked to determine the current top 10 products out of the shop's offers, based on the user's preferences as stated in the answers given so far. From the top 10 page, information on each product can be obtained. From there, further information is available, and the product can be placed into the shopping cart and purchased. From the top 10 page, users can also go back to continue answering questions, or to revise given answers. Exit without purchasing is possible at any time. Apart from the questions tailored to the product category and the products on offer (but parallelized according to sales strategy, see [1]), the shopping interface is identical for different products.

Here as in many other analyses of Web usage, the initial analysis questions were "What did users do in this site? When? And how often?". A first, incomplete conceptual sketch of possible activities in the site is shown in Fig. 1 (a).

The analyst's first task is to design a scheme for the classification of each URL and the distinction of relevant activities. The result is shown in Fig. 1 (b).

The URLs of the main shopping phase were generated dynamically. URLs were classified as follows: "Q(uestion) categories" is an overview page containing seven groups of questions of different content, visible to the user. For the analysis, the questions were classified into four categories ordered by decreasing relatedness to the product and judged by independent raters as decreasingly legitimate and relevant in the shopping context. This manipulation was an intentional part of the shopping process designed to find out in how far shoppers let themselves be involved in a communication that elicits privacy-relevant information [1]. The remaining pages were ordered by increasing closeness to a decision for a product: "top 10", "product info", "more product info", "product info with purchase option", and "purchase". This gives rise to an order on pages defined by *closeness to the product*, increasing from top to bottom.

The present analysis used the navigation data of participants of an experiment with a choice of two product categories, compact cameras and winter

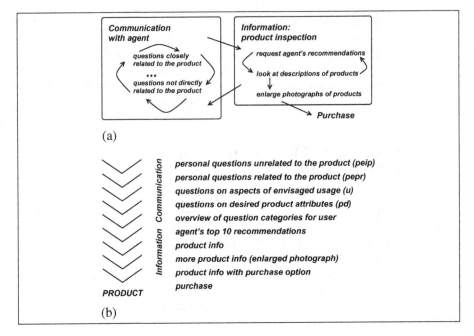

Fig. 1. Activities/requests in the example site: (a) related to one another in an initial sketch, (b) ordered by increasing closeness to product

jackets. Buying decisions were binding for participants (for details, see [39] and http://iwa.wiwi.hu-berlin.de).

Figure 2 shows stratograms aggregating the paths taken by 152 camera shoppers and 50 jacket shoppers through the store. The analysis focused on behavior after the (highly structured) introductory phase. So requests prior to a user's first request for the question categories page are not shown. In the phase shown, users were free to explore the site.

Each segment along the x axis denotes one step in the original logs. The two numbers at the right hand side of the figure both denote the maximal number of steps considered. Lines between a point (t, v) and another point $(t + 1, v')$ denote the frequencies of transitions according to Definition 1. Some lines are close enough to one another and/or thick enough to generate a visual 'block', e.g., those at the bottom right between "top 10" and "product info".

To find *interesting* patterns, pages have been abstracted using a concept hierarchy. To also find *unexpected* patterns, all paths through the site are investigated in their total length.

The figures show the unexpected result that two phases emerged in user behavior: a 'communication phase' (top left) and an 'information phase', in which products were inspected (bottom right), and that their distinctness changes with product category. Commonalities and differences in behavior are easily seen: First, most users have answered most of the questions, regardless of legitimacy /

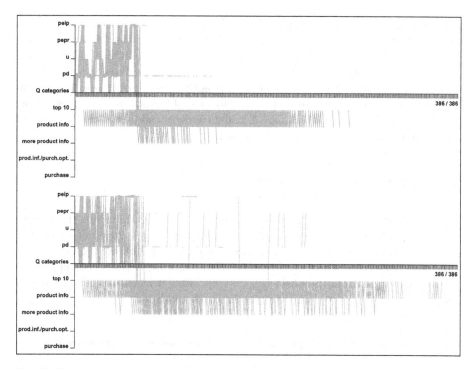

Fig. 2. Basic stratograms of camera shoppers (top) and jacket shoppers (bottom). $\theta_1 = \theta_2 = 0.05$

relevance, in the order suggested by the site. This is shown by the relatively few, thick lines at the top left. However, camera shoppers followed the sequence of questions even more closely before entering the information phase. In contrast, jackets were inspected already during the communication phase (see bottom left), and answers corrected, resulting in a longer communication phase. Also, in the information phase, "more product info" was requested more often (see bottom right), and the information phase lasted longer. Statistical analysis showed that conversion efficiency, the ratio of the number of buyers to the number of all shoppers, was higher for cameras (55%) than for jackets (24%) ($\chi_1^2 = 14.75, p <$ 0.01). In particular, conversion efficiency over short paths was higher (35% vs. 10%, $\chi_1^2 = 11.37, p < 0.01$). Paths were classified as "short" if they were shorter than half the maximal length of purchasing sessions. These results suggest that the design of the online store and its shopping agent may be more suited to selling search goods like cameras, i.e. products that may be judged by examining a range of technical details. Online selling of experience goods like jackets, on the other hand, may require further interface developments, offering better substitutes for the 'experience' of fabric and fit typically required to judge these products.

As this example has shown, stratograms address all three of the initial analysis questions. The ordering of pages along the y axis makes the nature of sequences of activities visible, e.g., "remaining within communication", "engaging in prolonged information-seeking behavior", or "changing / alternating between communication and information". This addresses the question "What did users do in the site?". The ordering of requests along the x axis makes the temporal characteristics of sequences of activities visible, e.g., the division into a communication and an information phase. This addresses the question "When did users do something in the site?". The distribution of transitions along the x axis, together with the relative thickness of visual elements, addresses the question of "how often" certain activities were pursued.

5   Interval-Based Coarsening

The visualization of longer episodes in basic stratograms harbors the danger that one may 'not see the wood for the trees' in the fine resolution of single-step actions. Also, actions that do occur frequently around, but not exactly at the same step, will not stand out as frequent. For example, actions that appear at different distances from the offset (e.g., 3 steps after it in one session, 4 steps in another one) will not be grouped together by the addition.

5.1   Coarsened Frequency Tables and Coarsened Stratograms

Interval-based coarsening summarizes transitions in consecutive, disjoint intervals of a size $g \geq 1$, starting from the respective offset. The *normalized frequency* of the transition from a node A_1 to a node A_2 in the tth interval after the respective session offsets o_s is

$$f_g(A_1, A_2, t) = \sum_{x=t \times g}^{(t+1) \times g - 1} f(A_1, A_2, x) \, . \tag{3}$$

This measure may count a given session several times if it contains more than one transition between A_1 and A_2 between steps tg and $(t+1)g$. However, each binary transition in the log is still counted exactly once.

The frequencies as defined in Equation (3) can be tabulated, e.g. in a table with one row per transition (A_1, A_2), or transitions differentiated by product, and one column per interval t. The resulting table represents a coarsening of the table corresponding to Equation (1). Frequency tables aggregated in this way can be tested for statistically significant differences between single cells or groups of cells using χ^2 tests ([4], see [37] for generalizations to higher-order frequency tables).

Note that each cell can be interpreted as the *support* of that sequence in that interval. Adding cells, $\sum_{A_2} f_g(A_1, A_2, t)$ gives the support of node A_1 in that interval, allowing the *confidence* of each sequence to be calculated.

The visual equivalent of coarsened frequency tables is given by

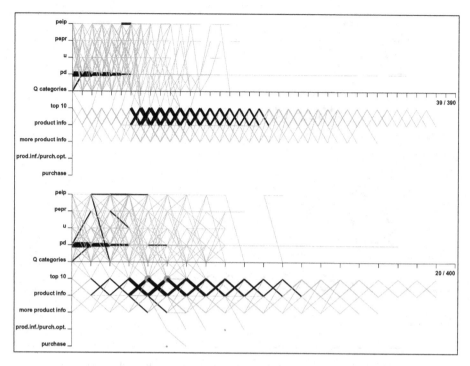

Fig. 3. Cameras, $g = 10$ (top), $g = 20$ (bottom). $\theta_1 = \theta_2 = 0.05$

Definition 2. *A* coarsened stratogram $strat_g$ *with degree of coarsening g is defined as*

$$strat_g = \langle pages, st, v, tr, \theta_1, \theta_2, g \rangle \quad with$$
$$st = \{0, \ldots, int(\frac{max_s(|s| - 2)}{g})\}, v : pages \mapsto N,$$
$$tr = \{f_g(A_1, A_2, t) \mid A_1 \in pages, A_2 \in pages \cup \{end\}, t \in st\}, \quad (4)$$

where the θ are support thresholds.

A coarsened stratogram visualization *is defined analogously to a basic stratogram visualization.*

In a coarsened stratogram, the set of all transitions between t and $t + 1$ includes g steps, so their number is at most $g \times S$. Therefore, a normalized frequency may be larger than 1. This can only be the case if in at least one session, the transition under consideration occurred more than once. So this transition may be considered as 'more characteristic' of this interval than others. Therefore, these transitions are displayed not only as thicker to indicate their higher frequency, but also in a darker color (black vs. grey) to indicate this qualitative difference. Since each user leaves exactly once, the cumulation of frequencies does not apply for the circles denoting exits, so there is only one kind (color) of circles. Figures 3 and 4 show examples of coarsened stratograms.

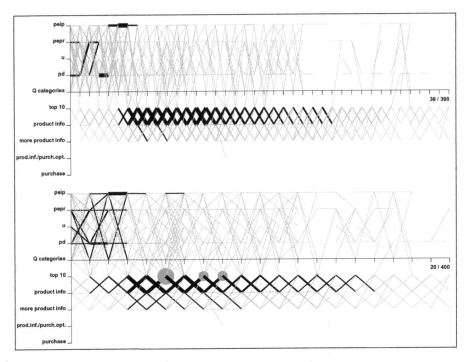

Fig. 4. Jackets, $g = 10$ (top), $g = 20$ (bottom).$\theta_1 = \theta_2 = 0.05$

A value t along the x axis should be read as the $(tg)^{th}$ step in the original log, as shown by the two numbers at the right hand side of the figures.

Basic stratograms are one limiting case of coarsened stratograms ($g = 1$). The opposite limiting case, $g \to \infty$, considers only one interval $[t, t+1] = [0, 1]$, which comprises all transitions anywhere between the first step ($0 \times g$) and the last step of each session after its respective offset ($1 \times g$). For each transition, the support over the whole log is shown. An example is shown in Fig. 5.

5.2   Visual Operations and Newly Emerging Patterns

Coarsened stratograms summarize behavior that may occur in roughly the same shape, but start at different offsets, see Figures 2 to 4. They also allow the analyst to first gain a summary view and then 'zoom in' by decreasing the value of g.

Figure 6 illustrates the use of another zoom / unzoom operation: increasing the support thresholds reduces the number of transitions shown, increasing visual clarity. The figure shows that behavior in the communication phase was more homogeneous in the first of the four distinct 'spiky' parts than in the rest.

Another advantage is that new regularities become visible. For example, Figures 3 and 4 show that camera shoppers more often went from 'innocuous' pd questions to other pd questions, while jacket shoppers were more at risk of not

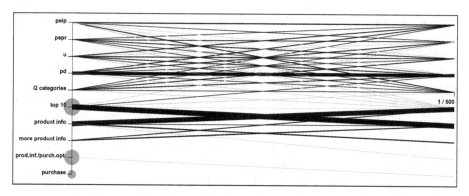

Fig. 5. Camera shoppers, $g = 500$. $\theta_1 = 0.05; \theta_2 = 0.2$

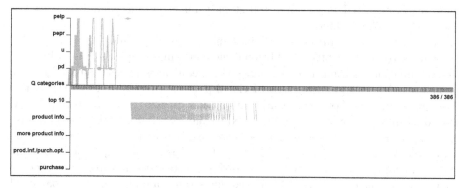

Fig. 6. Basic stratograms of camera shoppers, $\theta_1 = \theta_2 = 0.15$

only answering *one* personal peip question, but proceed directly to the next one, and that these patterns occurred at different stages of the whole navigation history. This is not visible in the basic stratograms in Fig. 2, and the information would be lost in a standard analysis considering support across the whole session (cf. also Figure 5). Statistical analysis comparing the frequencies of these two transitions with those of other question transitions confirmed the visual impression ($\chi_2^2 = 422.71, p < 0.001$) [5].

While 'directly repetitive patterns' thus show up as thick horizontal lines, a new kind of regularity also becomes visible: cyclic behavior. This is shown by thick X-shaped crossings between one step and the next. To understand why, consider the meaning of the two legs of an X: one marks a frequent transition, in the respective interval, from a node A_1 to a node A_2, while the other marks a frequent transition, in the same interval, from A_2 to A_1. This kind of cyclic

---

[5] The post hoc analysis should include α error corrections. However, in contrast to the shorter episodes analyzed in [4], the fine-grained analysis presented here allows for, and the visualizations encourage, a very large number of post hoc tests. Therefore, testing the hypotheses with a different dataset than the one used for exploratory analysis is advisable, and will be the subject of future work.

behavior is not restricted to $[A_1, A_2, A_1, A_2, ...]$ sequences, but may involve in-between visit to other nodes. Figures 3 and 4 show clearly that there was a marked tendency for all shoppers to cycle between top 10 and product info pages, although this occurred earlier for camera shoppers than for jacket shoppers. The figures also show that cycling between product info and photo enlargement pages was much less pronounced. Both cycles went on for a much larger number of steps for jacket shoppers than for camera shoppers. (top 10, info) transitions are a characteristic part of this pattern. The occurrence of these transitions in the first 60 steps, the 200 steps after that, and the rest were highly different between products ($\chi_2^2 = 49.75, p < 0.001$).

Moreover, patterns of leaving the site become clearer. In the example, a clearer pattern emerges in the $g = 20$ stratograms concerning where and when a majority of shoppers leave the site. Statistical analysis showed that for cameras, more exits occurred in the first 100 steps than after that, and vice versa for jackets ($\chi_1^2 = 7, p < 0.05$).

In general, coarsening causes all lines and circles to become thicker, and some grey lines to become black. Additional elements may appear. This is because the summation in Equation (3) makes the frequencies at each step t increase monotonically with g. Also, series of visual patterns are reduced to fewer items. For example, every two consecutive X-shaped crosses between "top 10" and "product info" in Fig. 3 (top) are reduced to one cross in Fig. 3 (bottom) because $g_2 = 2 \times g_1$. However, coarsening is usually combined with an increase in support thresholds. This has the reverse effect on the shape of the graph: Lines become thinner, change from black to grey, or disappear altogether. Circles are affected analogously. The exact changes between one stratogram and another, coarsened one will therefore depend on the interaction of data, degree of coarsening, and adaptation of the support thresholds.

5.3   Differential Coarsening

Once a general overview of user behavior has been gained, it may be desirable to investigate only a particular part of the process of Web usage in detail, for example the final information phase, in order to be able to trace the decision-making during that phase. The rest of the process should remain visible to provide context. In STRATDYN, this is realized as *differential coarsening*, i.e., a specification of different degrees of granularity for different regions.

Figures 7 (a) and (b) show stratograms with differential coarsening of the regions identified in the previous section (the first 60 steps, the 200 steps after that, and the remaining steps). Figure 7 (b) is then transformed into Fig. 7 (c) by maximally coarsening the irrelevant communication-centered first 60 steps, and simultaneously refining the second part of the information phase which characterizes jacket shoppers. All stratograms are aligned to show steps at the same x position, with the numbers on the right specifying the number of intervals displayed / maximal number of atomic steps in log. In contrast to (b), (c) shows that cycling between product info and more product info became less frequent,

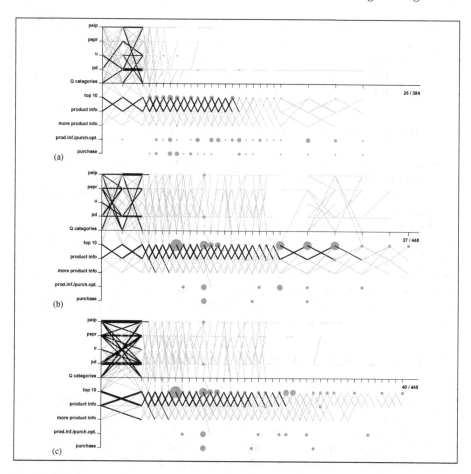

Fig. 7. (a) Camera shoppers: $g = 30$ in $[0, 60]$, $g = 10$ in $[60, 260]$, $g = 40$ afterwards; (b) Jacket shoppers: $g = 30$ in $[0, 60]$, $g = 10$ in $[60, 260]$, $g = 40$ afterwards; (c) Jacket shoppers: $g = 60$ in $[0, 60]$, $g = 10$ afterwards. $\theta_1 = 0.005$, $\theta_2 = 0.075$

so that cycling between top 10 and product info constituted the main activity during the latest steps performed by undecided jacket shoppers.

In accordance with the step-based nature of interval-based coarsening, the regions are at present specified by lower and upper bounds on the step number. In an interactive setting of stratogram generation and inspection, this is easy to specify because an interesting region will be identified by its position, i.e. step numbers, anyway. Specifications like "from the first request for page X onwards" are a straightforward extension and a subject of further work.

Because of the high dependence both on the characteristics of the data and the question of the analysis, there is no generally applicable procedure for choosing, or for changing, values of g; rather, the tool aims to encourage the analyst to iterate through several mining cycles. One general strategy is to start from a high value of g and then zoom in by comparatively large decrements (e.g., in steps of 10 for sessions as long as in the present example). If, during this process, the display gets too cluttered (or too sparse), the θs can be increased (decreased). When interesting patterns emerge, they can be investigated in more detail using differential coarsening.

6   Pattern Representation and Discovery

According to Definitions 1 and 2, the patterns sought consist of a *type* of the transition described by a pair of nodes or page concepts $[A_1, A_2]$, and a step number t. To save space, only those tuples $\langle A_1, A_2, t, f_{[g]} \rangle$ should be stored whose frequency counter $f_{[g]}$ is strictly greater than 0.

These types give rise to *type hierarchies* that allow the discovery and statistical comparison of patterns independently of visualization. All types $[A_i, A_j]$ and $[A_i, end]$ are subtypes of the type $[A_i]$, and all types $[A_i]$ are subtypes of the generic "any type". Since all of the entities thus classified are disjoint and counted only once, the frequency counters allow one to use χ^2 tests to determine, for example, whether there were significantly more sessions that went from the initial *question categories* page to a *pd* page than to a *peip* page.

6.1   Two Algorithms to Produce Coarsened Stratograms

To produce a stratogram, an algorithm is needed that traverses the log, classifies the transitions, and determines their frequencies. In the following algorithm, the procedure `classify(a1,t)` reads a request from the log into a local variable a2. If in the frequency table, an entry for `(a1,a2,t,f)` exists, it increments `f` by 1. Otherwise, it creates an entry `(a1,a2,t,1)`. It then returns a2.

The variable a1 can take any value from *pages*, and a2 can take any value from *pages* $\cup \{end\}$.

Requests prior to the specified offset are not processed. A counter i is maintained to ensure that basic steps in the log are counted towards the (possibly coarsened) correct step t.

```
(1)  determine_frequencies_1 (g)
(2)     create empty frequency table;
(3)     for each session do
(4)        repeat
(5)           read(a1);
(6)        until ((is_offset(a1)) or (end-of-session));
(7)        t := 0; i := 1;
(8)        while (not end-of-session) do
(9)           a1 := classify(a1,t);
(10)          i++;
(11)          t := div(i,g);
```

Let L be the size of the log, i.e., the total number of requests. Let $T = |pages|$. In the example, $T = 10$. Each request in each session (i.e., each request in the whole log) is read exactly once. Step (9) reads each request after the first, regards it as the second node of the binary transition, and therefore has to test it against $T+1$ possibilities. So the time complexity is $O(L \times T)$, and since T is constant for a given analysis, this means that the algorithm is linear in the size of the log. As discussed above, it is useful to classify pages using concept hierarchies, such that T will typically be small compared to L. The space complexity is determined by the frequency table constructed; this is bounded above by the minimum over (i) the number of possible transitions defined by the chosen types and the t_{max} investigated steps $(T(T+1) \times t_{max})$, and (ii) the fact that there can be no more different transitions in the log than there are transitions (maximally $L - 1$). So space complexity is $O(min(T^2 \times t_{max}, L))$. For a given log, let nfc be the resulting number of (non-zero) frequency counters for $g = 1$.

Alternatively, coarsened stratograms can be computed incrementally from their corresponding basic stratogram. As can be seen from Equation (3), only the type hierarchy, and not the whole log, needs to be parsed:

```
(1) determine_frequencies_2 (g)
(2)    initialize all f_g(A1,A2,t):=0;
(3)    for each A1 do
(4)       for each A2 do
(5)          x:=0; t:=0;
(6)          while (x <= t_max) do
(7)             f_g(A1,A2,t) += f(A1,A2,x)
(8)             x++;
(9)             if (x >= (t+1)*g) then
(10)               t++;
```

This involves reading each of the nfc original frequency counters once. As pointed out above, $nfc \leq min(T(T + 1) \times t_{max}, L - 1)$. This is (usually much) smaller than $(L \times T)$, the number of steps needed for **determine_frequencies_1**. (In the running example, $L \times T = 355860$ and $nfc = 6119$). Space complexity is determined by the size of the resulting frequency table, which is $\frac{nfc}{g}$.

When repeated coarsening is performed with g growing in geometric progression with a base b, e.g., with $g = 1, 2, 4, 8, \ldots$ or $g = 1, 3, 9, 27, \ldots$, the idea of **determine_frequencies_2** can be utilized to compute the frequencies for $g = b^{(i+1)}$ from those for $g = b^i$, $i \geq 1$. This will further reduce the number of steps needed.

Differential coarsening requires the splitting of line (6) of **determine_frequencies_2** into an outer loop that executes n times for n regions of granularity, and an inner loop that executes the main body from the current region's lower to its upper bound (analogous changes can be made to **determine_frequencies_1**).

6.2   Extensions: n-ary Sequences and Generalized Sequences

The methods described above focus on binary transitions, or sequences of length 2. For some applications, it is relevant to investigate sequences of arbitrary lengths, or generalized sequences.

The investigation of longer sequences can also help to avoid possible misinterpretations of stratograms. Consider a stratogram with a 'thick' line between (t, A_1) and $(t + 1, A_2)$, and a 'thick' line between $(t + 1, A_2)$ and $(t + 2, A_3)$. This indicates that the transition from A_1 to A_2 was frequent at step t, and that the transition from A_2 to A_3 was frequent at step $(t + 1)$. It bears no information about the frequency of either of the sequences $[A_1, A_2, A_3]$ or $[A_1, *, A_3]$. However, the *Gestalt* principles of connectedness and (if the two lines have the same slope) continuity [47] can lead to the perception of a 'thick curve' from A_1 via A_2 to A_3. To differentiate between these cases, visual investigations of the frequencies of n-ary sequences like $[A_1, A_2, A_3]$ or generalized sequences like $[A_1, *, A_3]$ are useful.

The first step needed for the analysis of n-ary and/or generalized sequences is an algorithm for identifying them in a log and determining their respective frequencies. This requires a definition of *types* that are n-ary and/or generalized sequences. A corresponding type definition, and a procedure `classify` that extends the one presented above accordingly, are presented in [4]. The algorithm presented there classifies each session exactly once, according to the first of the distinguished types counted in that session. For the present purposes, this classification is repeated until the end of the session is encountered. This yields a set of type instances that can be regarded as episodes, where one session may contain one or more of these episodes. All counted episodes are disjoint, so these frequencies can be analyzed using χ^2 tests.

The generalization of stratograms to n-ary sequences is straightforward: An n-ary sequence, like a binary sequence, is counted only once, in the interval containing its first node. The procedure developed in the previous sections requires the following adaptations:

1. The frequency definition in expression (3) is extended to produce $f_g(A_1, A_2, \ldots, A_n, t)$. The changes to the right hand side of the definition, as well as to Definition 2, are straightforward.

2. Within each interval $[t, t+1]$, $n-1$ subintervals are marked by the stratogram drawing routine, for example by vertical grid lines.

3. To ensure that lines do not obscure one another, a data structure is added that maintains a vertical offset for each grid point (i.e. each pair of a vertical grid line and a v value). Whenever one n-ary pattern has been drawn that traverses a grid point, the offset is incremented, such that the next line traversing the point will be drawn a little higher. It must be ensured that the vertical distance between different values of v is sufficiently large compared to the number of lines that can traverse a grid point. This technique thereby avoids the occlusions that are a consequence of the present use of the alignment technique.

Generalized sequences have a fixed number of nodes, for example, the generalized sequence $[A * B * C]$ has three nodes, and wildcard path specifications in between that allow an arbitrary number of nodes. A generalized sequence with n nodes can be treated like an n-ary sequence by the algorithm and visualization. An annotation to the visualization should remind the analyst of the fact that a line from (t, A_1) to $(t + 1, A_2)$ indicates users who went *from A_1 to A_2 via some path* that is not shown.

Setting $g = \infty$ allows one to derive an overall *support* and *confidence* value for a generalized sequence. For example, for an association rule defined as a generalized sequence with 2 fixed nodes $[A_1 * A_2]$, the frequency of non-overlapping occurrences of paths $[A_1, ..., A_2]$ in the whole log is given by $f_\infty(A_1, A_2, 0) = sup(A_1, A_2)$. The confidence of that generalized sequence can be computed analogously (cf. section 5.1).

7   Using Abstraction to Specify Intended Usage

The preceding discussion has illustrated how stratograms can help the site analyst communicate results on actual usage to the site owner. However, the communication from site owner to site analyst (and site designer) is of equal importance, and this too should happen in terms of 'business objects' rather than technical page accesses (cf. [14,28] for discussions of the importance of specifying intended usage and ways of comparing it to actual usage).

Stratograms offer a simple way of specifying intended usage: draw the 'best trajectory' into the stratogram. This trajectory can be treated as an (inexact) sketch and compared to actual usage based on visual inspection. Alternatively, it can be treated as an (exact) specification and automatically transformed into a null hypothesis to be tested statistically (this is most suitable for short intended paths like the "3-click rule" below).

As in any specification of intended usage for direct comparison with actual usage, the interpretation of the best trajectory sketch must correspond to the interpretation of the mined patterns: For binary transitions, only the intended frequency of transitions between two subsequent pages can be specified. For n-ary and/or generalized sequences, the meaning of the sketch and its parts changes accordingly.

Fig. 8 (a) shows an example sketch of two kinds of intended behavior. It uses a canonical event model for E-commerce sites [32], which subsumes the "information phase" of the model used in the current paper. The first is more "vertical"; it assumes that users should proceed to checkout quickly. The second is more "horizontal"; it concedes that an environment that encourages users to "spend time on the premises", i.e. a site with high stickiness during the search/browse phase, can be more agreeable and lead to more purchases.

Fig. 8 (b) and (c) show the actual usage of two search options in an online catalog ordered by information concreteness (1–3 search parameters specified, or 4=goal) [4]. The overlaid intended path represents the "3-click-rule": start page with search options → list matching the chosen search criteria → goal. (Because the list page was chosen as offset, the start page is not shown.)

How can this knowledge be made actionable? In the example, a site with the "intended usage 1" of Fig. 8 (a) could improve service for camera shoppers by pointing out superior search options that may help them discover a desired item fast, thus supporting their pre-existing "vertical" preferences. The shopping

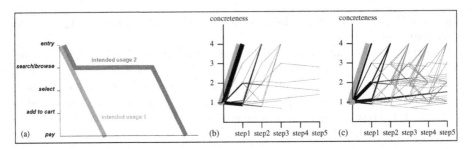

Fig. 8. (a) Intended usage of an online store; (b) efficient search option in an online catalog; (c) inefficient search option in an online catalog

time of jacket shoppers does not seem to be dominated by searching, but by an undecided cycling between product selection and the inspection of further products. They may be encouraged to proceed to checkout faster if given special offers at the point of product selection, like discounts that are only available for a limited time. In contrast, a site with "intended usage 2" could try to keep users in the store by providing interesting offers (like "related items") or entertainment items as the analogy of comfortable surroundings, coffee shops, etc. in a physical store.

8   Conclusions and Outlook

The current paper has presented interval-based coarsening, and its inverse zooming, as a technique to mine Web usage at different levels of abstraction. Basic and coarsened stratograms, together with differential coarsening, have been proposed to visualize Web usage at different degrees of detail. Using a case study of online shopping with an anthropomorphic agent, we have demonstrated that this kind of abstraction offers new possibilities of understanding complex paths through a semi-structured, interaction-rich environment.

In principle, the methods presented in the current paper are independent of site modeling. However, the *grouping of pages by concept hierarchies* is useful to ensure a tractable number of page concepts, in the visualization a tractable number of values along the y axis, thus reducing clutter. The arrangement of these concepts in a *meaningful order* is useful to create a diagram that is simpler to understand, and in which "movement", i.e., the orientation of the lines representing transitions and paths, becomes interpretable. This allows one to analyze sites with hundreds or thousands of different pages like that used in the case study. Conversely, when little abstraction is used and pages are grouped into a large number of concepts, or not grouped at all, and when no meaningful order is identified, the clarity of the display may suffer. Note, however, that even then 'hot spots' and behavioral tendencies can be detected, cf. [27].

Therefore, one of our current research directions is a semantic analysis of different types of sites. This also includes the development of ordering heuristics for sites that do not immediately suggest an order. Also, the analyst should be supported by tools that aid in semantic data preprocessing. Visual patterns that emerge in the absence of a meaningful ordering are also explored. As an example, consider the X-shaped patterns in the figures above. Provided these patterns are sufficiently frequent to not be obscured by in-between lines, they will also be visually prominent when the two concepts are far apart on the y axis. Usage-based layout similar to [13] may provide a bottom-up, automated complement to these methods by suggesting usage-defined orders on page subsets.

A second main aim of future work is to find further ways of abstraction. One research direction concerns extensions of the expressive power of the pattern representation language, for example by including timestamp information and allowing for more complex grammatical expressions [37,21].

An important factor for abstraction is the number of pages visited, and the number of pages distinguished T. The aggregation of pages by concept hierarchies employed here can be regarded as a clustering of requests, or pages, along the stratograms' y axis: a user navigates from one cluster (e.g., a question page) to another cluster (e.g., a top 10 page). Interactive enhancements of stratograms could allow the analyst to delve into this cluster and distinguish which individual URLs were visited at this step by individual users. Requests / pages could also be clustered along the temporal dimension, i.e., along the x axis. This would show navigation between clusters, e.g., from questions to top 10 pages, without internal differentiation regarding how many question pages were visited. For example, navigation from the question cluster to the top 10 page would be a sequence $[question, question*, top10]$, with $*$ denoting an arbitrary number of pages of the given category. This abstraction requires the corresponding extension of the path specification concept.

Yet another option for stratogram simplification is to filter the log to exclude all requests that are not instances of a concept, or set of concepts, of interest. For example, analysis may concentrate on "shopping" activities in a site that also offers "search" and "communication" facilities. These activities will then be comprised of requests for a smaller number of subconcepts (comparable to those in the running example of this paper) that can be ordered meaningfully and give rise to interpretable stratograms.

Acknowledgements

I thank the IWA team for supplying a highly useful data set, and my reviewers and the WebKDD'01 participants for helpful comments and suggestions.

References

1. Annacker, D., Spiekermann, S., & Strobel, M. (2001). Private consumer information: A new search cost dimension in online environments. In B. O'Keefe, C. Loebbecke, J. Gricar, A. Pucihar, & G. Lenart (Eds.), *Proceedings of 14th Bled Electronic Commerce Conference* (pp. 292–308). Bled, Slovenia. June 2001.

2. Baumgarten, M., Büchner, A.G., Anand, S.S., Mulvenna, M.D.& Hughes, J.G. (2000). User-driven navigation pattern discovery from internet data. In [42] (pp. 74–91).

3. Berendt, B. (2000). Web usage mining, site semantics, and the support of navigation. In [29] (pp. 83–93).

4. Berendt, B. (2002). Using site semantics to analyze, visualize, and support navigation. *Data Mining and Knowledge Discovery, 6,* 37–59.

5. Berendt, B. & Brenstein, E. (2001). Visualizing Individual Differences in Web Navigation: STRATDYN, a Tool for Analyzing Navigation Patterns. *Behavior Research Methods, Instruments, & Computers, 33,* 243–257.

6. Berendt, B. & Spiliopoulou, M. (2000). Analysis of navigation behaviour in web sites integrating multiple information systems. *The VLDB Journal, 9,* 56–75.

7. Borges, J. & Levene, M. (2000). Data mining of user navigation patterns. In [42] (pp. 92–111).

8. Brin, S., Motwani, R., & Silverstein, C. (1997). Beyond market baskets: Generalizing association rules to correlations. In *ACM SIGMOD International Conference on Management of Data* (pp. 265–276).

9. Card, S.K., Mackinlay, J.D., & Shneiderman, B. (1999). Information visualization. In S.K. Card, J.D. Mackinlay, & B. Shneiderman (Eds.), *Readings in Information Visualization: Using Vision to Think* (pp. 1–34). San Francisco, CA: Morgan Kaufmann.

10. Chen, C. (1999). *Information Visualisation and Virtual Environments.* London: Springer.

11. Chi, E.H. (1999). *A Framework for Information Visualization Spreadsheets.* University of Minnesota, Computer Science Department: Ph.D. Dissertation. http://www-users.cs.umn.edu/~echi/phd

12. Chi, E.H., Pirolli, P., Chen, K., & Pitkow, J. (2001). Using information scent to model user information needs and actions on the Web. In *Proceedings of ACM CHI 2001 Conference on Human Factors in Computing Systems* (pp. 490–497). Amsterdam: ACM Press.

13. Chi, E.H., Pirolli, P., & Pitkow, J. (2000). The scent of a site: a system for analyzing and predicting information scent, usage, and usability of a web site. In *Proceedings of ACM CHI 2000 Conference on Human Factors in Computing Systems* (pp. 161–168). Amsterdam: ACM Press.

14. Cooley, R. (2000). *Web Usage Mining: Discovery and Application of Interesting Patterns from Web Data.* University of Minnesota, Faculty of the Graduate School: Ph.D. Dissertation. http://www.cs.umn.edu/research/websift/papers/-rwc_thesis.ps

15. Cooley, R., Tan, P.-N., & Srivastava, J. (2000). Discovery of interesting usage patterns from web data. In [42] (pp. 163–182).

16. Craven, M., DiPasquo, D., Freitag, D., McCallum, A., Mitchell, T., Nigam, K., & Slattery, S. (2000). Learning to Construct Knowledge Bases from the World Wide Web. *Artificial Intelligence, 118,* 69–113.

17. Cugini, J., & Scholtz, J. (1999). VISVIP: 3D Visualization of Paths through Web Sites. In *Proceedings of the International Workshop on Web-Based Information Visualization (WebVis'99)* (pp. 259–263). Florence, Italy: IEEE Computer Society.

18. Eick, S.G. (2001). Visualizing online activity. *Communications of the ACM, 44 (8),* 45–50.

19. Fensel, D. (2000). *Ontologies: Silver Bullet for Knowledge Management and Electronic Commerce.* Berlin: Springer.

20. Fernández, M., Florescu, D., Levi, A., & Suciu, D. (2000). Declarative specification of Web sites with STRUDEL. *The VLDB Journal, 9*, 38–55.
21. Fu, W.-T. (2001). ACT-PRO Action Protocol Analyzer: a tool for analyzing discrete action protocols. *Behavior Research Methods, Instruments, & Computers, 33*, 149–158.
22. Gaul, W., & Schmidt-Thieme, L. (2000). Mining web navigation path fragments. In [29] (pp. 105–110).
23. Han, J., & Kamber, M. (2001). *Data Mining: Concepts and Techniques.* San Francisco, LA: Morgan Kaufmann.
24. Hochheiser, H., & Shneiderman, B. (1999). *Understanding Patterns of User Visits to Web Sites: Interactive Starfield Visualizations of WWW Log Data.* College Park: University of Maryland, Technical Report TR_99-3. http://www.isr.umd.edu/TechReports/ISR/1999/TR_99-3/TR_99-3.pdf
25. Hong, J.I., Heer, J., Waterson, S., & Landay, J.A. (in press). WebQuilt: A Proxy-based Approach to Remote Web Usability Testing. *ACM Transactions on Information Systems.* http://guir.berkeley.edu/projects/webquilt/pubs/acmTOIS-webquilt-final.pdf
26. Hong, J., & Landay, J.A. (2001). WebQuilt: A Framework for Capturing and Visualizing the Web Experience. In *Proceedings of The Tenth International World Wide Web Conference,* Hong Kong, May 2001.
27. Jones, T. & Berger, C. (1995). Students' use of multimedia science instruction: Designing for the MTV generation? *Journal of Educational Multimedia and Hypermedia, 4*, 305–320.
28. Kato, H., Nakayama, T., & Yamane, Y. (2000). Navigation analysis tool based on the correlation between contents distribution and access patterns. In [29] (pp. 95–104).
29. Kohavi, R., Spiliopoulou, M., Srivastava, J. & Masand, B. (Eds.) (2000). *Working Notes of the Workshop "Web Mining for E-Commerce – Challenges and Opportunities." 6th ACM SIGKDD International Conference on Knowledge Discovery and Data Mining.* Boston, MA. August 2000.
30. Lamping, J., Rao, R., & Pirolli, P. (1995). A focus+context technique based on hyperbolic geometry for visualizing large hierarchies. In *Proceedings of ACM CHI 1995 Conference on Human Factors in Computing Systems* (pp. 401–408). New York: ACM Press.
31. Mannila, H. & Toivonen, H. (1996). Discovering generalized episodes using minimal occurrences. In *Proceedings of the 2nd ACM SIGKDD International Conference on Knowledge Discovery and Data Mining* (pp. 146–151).
32. Menascé, D.A., Almeida, V., Fonseca, R. & Mendes, M.A. (1999). A Methodology for Workload Characterization of E-commerce Sites In *Proceedings of the ACM Conference on Electronic Commerce,* Denver, CO, November 1999.
33. Mobasher, B., Cooley, R., & Srivastava, J. (2000). Automatic personalization based on web usage mining. *Communications of the ACM, 43(8),* 142–151.
34. Nanopoulos, A., & Manolopoulos, Y. (2001). Mining patterns from graph traversals. *Data and Knowledge Engineering, 37*, 243–266.
35. Niegemann, H.M. (2000, April). *Analyzing processes of self-regulated hypermedia-supported learning: On the development of a log-file analysis procedure.* Paper presented at the Annual Meeting of the American Educational Research Association, New Orleans, LA.
36. Oberlander, J., Cox, R., Monaghan, P., Stenning, K., and Tobin, R. (1996). Individual differences in proof structures following multimodal logic teaching. In *Proceedings COGSCI'96* (pp. 201–206).

37. Olson, G.M., Herbsleb, J.D., & Rueter, H. (1994). Characterizing the sequential structure of interactive behaviors through statistical and grammatical techniques. *Human-Computer Interaction, 9,* 427–472.
38. Schellhas, B., & Brenstein, E. (1998). Learning strategies in hypermedia learning environments. In T. Ottmann & I. Tomek (Eds.), *Proceedings of ED-MEDIA and ED-TELEKOM 98:* (pp. 1922-1923). Charlottesville, VA: Association for the Advancement of Computing in Education.
39. Spiekermann, S., Grossklags, J., & Berendt, B. (2001). E-privacy in 2nd generation E-Commerce: privacy preferences versus actual behavior. In *Proceedings of the ACM Conference on Electronic Commerce (EC'01).* Tampa, FL. October 2001.
40. Spiliopoulou, M. (1999). The laborious way from data mining to web mining. *International Journal of Computer Systems, Science & Engineering, 14,* 113–126.
41. Spiliopoulou, M. (2000). Web usage mining for site evaluation: Making a site better fit its users. *Communications of the ACM, 43 (8),* 127–134.
42. Spiliopoulou, M. and Masand, B. (Eds.) (2000). *Advances in Web Usage Analysis and User Profiling.* Berlin: Springer.
43. Spiliopoulou, M. & Pohle, C. (2001). Data Mining for Measuring and Improving the Success of Web Sites. *Data Mining and Knowledge Discovery, 5,* 85–14.
44. Srikant, R. & Agrawal, R. (1996). Mining sequential patterns: Generalizations and performance improvements. In *EDBT* (pp. 3–17). Avignon, France, March 1996.
45. Srivastava, J. Cooley, R., Deshpande, M., & Tan, P.-N. (2000). Web usage mining: discovery and application of usage patterns from web data. *SIGKDD Explorations, 1,* 12–23.
46. Wang, K. (1997). Discovering patterns from large and dynamic sequential data. *Intelligent Information Systems, 9,* 8–33.
47. Ware, C. (2000). *Information Visualization. Perception for Design.* San Diego,CA: Academic Press.
48. World Wide Web Committee Web Usage Characterization Activity. (1999). *W3C Working Draft: Web Characterization Terminology & Definitions Sheet.* www.w3.org/1999/05/WCA-terms/

A Customer Purchase Incidence Model Applied to Recommender Services

Andreas Geyer-Schulz[1], Michael Hahsler[2], and Maximillian Jahn[2]

[1] Universität Karlsruhe (TH), D-76128 Karlsruhe, Germany
andreas.geyer-schulz@em.uni-karlsruhe.de
[2] Wirtschaftsuniversität Wien, A-1090 Wien, Austria
Michael.Hahsler@wu-wien.ac.at

Abstract. In this contribution we transfer a customer purchase incidence model for consumer products which is based on Ehrenberg's repeat-buying theory to Web-based information products. Ehrenberg's repeat-buying theory successfully describes regularities on a large number of consumer product markets. We show that these regularities exist in electronic markets for information goods, too, and that purchase incidence models provide a well founded theoretical base for recommender and alert services.

The article consists of two parts. In the first part Ehrenberg's repeat-buying theory and its assumptions are reviewed and adapted for web-based information markets. Second, we present the empirical validation of the model based on data collected from the information market of the Virtual University of the Vienna University of Economics and Business Administration from September 1999 to May 2001.

1 Introduction

In this article we concentrate on an anonymous recommender service of the correlation-type made famous by Amazon.com applied to an information broker. It is based on consumption patterns for information goods (web-sites) from market baskets (web-browser sessions) which we treat as consumer purchase histories with unobserved consumer identity. In Resnick and Varian's design space [25] this recommender service is characterized as:

1. The contents of a recommendation consists of links to web-sites.
2. It is an implicit service based on observed user behavior.
3. The service is anonymous.
4. The aggregation of recommendations is based on identifying outliers with the help of a stochastic purchase incidence model.
5. A sorted list of recommended related web sites is offered to the user of a web site (see figure 1).

This recommender service is part of the first educational and scientific recommender system integrated into the Virtual University of the Vienna University of Economics and Business Administration (http://vu.wu-wien.ac.at) since September 1999. A full description of all recommender services of this educational and scientific recommender system can be found in Geyer-Schulz et al. [16].

R. Kohavi et al. (Eds.): WEBKDD 2001, LNAI 2356, pp. 25–47, 2002.
© Springer-Verlag Berlin Heidelberg 2002

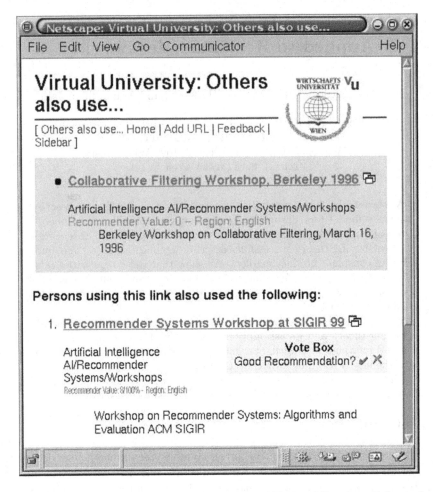

Fig. 1. An Anonymous Recommender Based on "Observed Purchase Behavior".

For example, figure 1 shows the recommended list of web-sites for users inter-ested in web-sites related to the `Collaborative Filtering Workshop 1996 in Berkeley`. The web-site (in figure 1 the `Collaborative Filtering Workshop 1996 in Berkeley`) in the yellow box (gray in print) is the site for which re-lated web-sites have been requested. For every recommended web-site a Vote Box allows users to evaluate the quality of this recommendation.

In Geyer-Schulz et al. [15] we have presented the architecture of an informa-tion market and its instrumentation for collecting data on consumer behavior. We consider an information broker with a clearly defined system boundary and web-sites consisting of one or more web-pages as information products. The infor-mation broker contains only meta-data on the information products (including an external link to the home page of each information product). Clicking on an external link (which leaves the information broker and leads to the home page of a web-site) is equated as "purchasing an information product". In marketing, we assume that a consumer will only repeatedly purchase a product or a product combination if he is sufficiently content with it. The rationale that this analogy holds even for *free* information products stems from an analysis of the transaction costs of a user of an information broker. Even *free* information products burden the consumer with search, selection and evaluation costs. Therefore, in this article we derive recommendations from products which have been used (= purchased) together in a session repeatedly across different sessions (= buying occasions) (see Böhm et al. [8]). Data collection (logging) is restricted entirely to the information broker, only clicking on an external link is logged. This implies that on the one hand in the logs of the information broker usage behavior for information products can not be observed (and is in fact completely irrelevant as far as repeat-buying theory is concerned) and that on the other hand almost no preprocessing is necessary to obtain sessions. Without such an instrumented architecture the purchase incidence model may still be of use in combination with web-usage mining approaches as e.g. the sequence miner WUM of Spiliopoulou [28]. For a recent survey of work on this area see Srivastava et al. [29].

Such recommendations are attractive for information brokers for the following reasons:

- Observed consumer purchase behavior is the most important information for predicting consumer behavior. For offline behavior this has been known for a long time (see Ehrenberg [11]), for online behavior see Bellmann et al. [6] for a recent study.
- In traditional retail chains, basket analysis shows up to 70 percent cross-selling potential (see Blischok [7]). Such recommendations facilitate "repeat-buying" which is one of the main goals of e-commerce sites as reported in Bellmann et al. [6].
- Most important in a university environment is that such recommendations are not subject to several incentive problems found in systems based on explicit recommendations (as e.g. free-riding, bias, ...) which are analyzed by Avery and Zeckhauser [5]. The transaction cost of faking such recommendations is high, because only one co-occurrence of products is counted per user-session as usual in consumer panel analysis (see Ehrenberg [11]). Free-riding is impossible because by using the information broker each user contributes usage data for the recommendations. The user's privacy is preserved.
- And, last but not least, the transaction costs for the broker are low since high-quality recommendations can be generated without human effort. No editor, no author, no web-scout is needed.

Recently the problem of generating personalized recommendations from anonymous sessions (or market basket data) and user sessions (or consumer panels with individual purchase histories) has attracted considerable attention. Personalization is achieved by taking the user's current navigation history into account. Mobasher has studied two variants of computing recommendations from anonymous session data, namely PACT (profile aggregation based on clustering transactions) and ARHP (association rule hypergraph partitioning) in [23] and [24]. Lawrence et al. [21] report on a hybrid recommender based on clustering association rules from purchase histories combined with the product taxanomy and the profit contribution of a product. Gaul and Schmidt-Thieme [14] construct recommender systems from frequent substructures of navigation histories. Lin et al. [22] develop an association rule mining algorithm with adaptive support for a collaborative recommender system.

However, anonymous recommendations based on consumption or usage patterns nevertheless have the following two problems which we address in this article with the help of Ehrenberg's repeat-buying theory [11]:

- Which co-occurrences of products qualify as non-random?
- How many products should be recommended?

Ehrenberg's repeat-buying theory provides us with a reference model for testing for non-random outliers, because of the strong stationarity and independence assumptions in the theory discussed in section 2. What makes this theory a good candidate for describing the consumption behavior for information products is that it has been supported by strong empirical evidence in several hundred consumer product markets since the late 1950's. Ehrenberg's repeat-buying theory is a descriptive theory based on consumer panel data. It captures how consumers behave, but not why. Several very sophisticated and general models of the theory (e.g. the Dirichlet model by Goodhardt et al. [18]) exist and have a long tradition in marketing research. However, for our purposes, namely identifying non-random purchases of two information products, the simplest model – the logarithmic series distribution (LSD) model – will prove quite adequate. In this setting the LSD model removes all random co-purchases from the recommendation lists. It acts like a filter for noise. For a survey on stochastic consumer behavior models, see e.g. Wagner and Taudes [32].

One of the main (conceptual) innovations of this paper is that we explain how we can apply a theory for analyzing purchase histories from consumer panels to mere market baskets.

2 Ehrenbergs Repeat-Buying Theory and Bundles of Information Products

Of the thousand and one variables which might affect buyer behavior, it is found that nine hundred and ninety-nine usually do not matter. Many aspects of buyer behavior can be predicted simply from the penetration and the average purchase frequency of an item, and even these two variables are interrelated. A.S.C. Ehrenberg (1988) [11].

In purchasing a product a consumer basically makes two decisions: when does he buy a product of a certain product class (purchase incidence) and which brand does he buy (brand choice). Ehrenberg claims that almost all aspects of

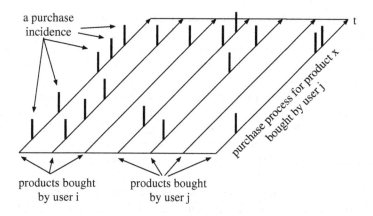

a purchase
incidence

products bought
by user i

products bought
by user j

t

purchase process for product x
bought by user j

Fig. 2. Purchase Incidences as Independent Stochastic Processes.

repeat-buying behavior can be adequately described by formalizing the purchase incidence process for a single brand and by integrating these results later (see figure 2).

In a classical marketing context Ehrenberg's repeat-buying theory is based on purchase histories from consumer panels. The *purchase history* of a consumer is the sequence of the purchases in all his market baskets over an extensive periods of time (a year or more) for a specific outlet. For information products, the purchase history of a consumer corresponds e.g. to the sequence of sessions of a user in a personalized environment of a specific information broker. Note, however, a purchase history could be a sequence of sessions recorded in a cookie, in a browser cache, or in a personal persistent proxie-server, too.

A *market basket* is simply the list of items (quantity and price) bought in a specific trip to the store. In a consumer panel the identity of each user is known and an individual purchase history can be constructed from market baskets. For information products the corresponding concept is a session which contains records of all information products visited (used) by a user. In anonymous systems (e.g. most public web-sites) the identity of the user is not known. As a consequence no individual purchase history can be constructed.

Very early in the work with consumer panel data it turned out that the most useful unit of analysis is in terms of purchase occasions, not in terms of quantity or money paid. A *purchase occasion* is coded as yes, if a consumer has purchased one or more items of a product in a specific trip to a store. We ignore the number of items bought or package sizes and concentrate our attention on the frequency of purchase. For information products we define a purchase occasion as follows: a purchase occasion occurs if a consumer visits a specific information product at least once in a specific session. We ignore the number of pages browsed, repeat visits in a session, amount of time spent at a specific information product, ... Note, that this definition of counting purchases or information product usage is basic for this article and crucial for the repeat-buying theory to hold. One of the earliest uses of purchase occasions is due to L. J. Rothman [30].

Analysis is carried out in distinct time-periods (such as 1-week, 4-week, quarterly periods) which ties in nicely with other standard marketing reporting practices. A particular simplification from this time-period orientation is that most repeat-buying results for any given item can be expressed in terms of penetration and purchase frequency.

The *penetration b* is the proportion of people who buy an item at all in a given period. Penetration is easily measured in personalized recommender systems. In such systems it has the classical marketing interpretation. For this article, penetration is of less concern because in anonymous public Internet systems we simply cannot determine the proportion of users who use a specific web-site at all.

The *purchase frequency w* is the average number of times these buyers buy at least one item in the period. The mean purchase frequency w is itself the most basic measure of repeat-buying in the Ehrenberg's theory [11] and in this article.

In the following we consider anonymous market baskets as consumer panels with **unobserved consumer identity** – and as long as we work only at the aggregate level (with consumer groups) everything works out fine as provided that Ehrenberg's assumptions on consumer purchase behavior hold.

Figure 2 shows the main idea of purchase incidence models: a consumer buys a product according to a stationary Poisson process which is independent of the other buying processes. Aggregation of these buying processes over the population under the (quite general) assumption that the parameters μ of the Poisson distributions (the long-run average purchase rates) follow a truncated Γ-distribution results in a logarithmic series distribution (LSD) as Chatfield et al. [9] have shown.

The logarithmic series distribution (LSD) describes the following frequency distribution of purchases (see Ehrenberg [11]), namely the probability that a specific product is bought a total of 1, 2, 3, ..., r times without taking into account the number of non-buyers.

$$P(r \quad \text{purchases}) = \frac{-q^r}{r \ln(1 - q)}, \quad r \geq 1 \tag{1}$$

$$\text{Mean purchase frequency} \quad w = \frac{-q}{(1 - q) \ln(1 - q)} \tag{2}$$

The variance is:

$$\sigma^2 = \frac{w}{(1 - q)} - w^2 = \frac{-q \left(1 + \frac{q}{\ln(1-q)}\right)}{(1 - q)^2 \ln(1 - q)} \tag{3}$$

One important characteristic of the LSD is that $\sigma^2 > w$. For more details on the logarithmic series distribution, we refer the reader to Johnson and Kotz [19]. The logarithmic series distribution results from the following assumptions about the consumers' purchase incidence distributions:

1. The share of never-buyers in the population is not specified. In our setting of an Internet information broker with anonymous users this definitely holds.

2. The purchases of a consumer in successive periods follow a Poisson distribution with a certain long-run average μ. The purchases of a consumer follow a Poisson distribution in subsequent periods if a purchase tends to be independent of previous purchases (as is often observed) and a purchase occurs in such an irregular manner that it can be regarded as if random (see Wagner and Taudes [32]).

3. The distribution of μ in the population follows a truncated Γ-distribution so that the frequency of any particular value of μ is given by $(ce^{-\mu/a}/\mu)d\mu$, for $\delta \leq \mu \leq \infty$, where δ is a very small number, a a parameter of the distribution, and c a constant, so that $\int_\delta^\infty (ce^{-\mu/a}/\mu)d\mu = 1$.
A Γ-distribution of the μ in the population may have the following reason (see Ehrenberg [11, p. 259]): If for different products $P, Q, R, S, \ldots$ the average purchase rate of P is independent of the purchase rates of the other products, and $\frac{P}{(P+Q+R+S+\ldots)}$ is independent of a consumer's total purchase rate of buying all the products, then it can be shown that the distribution of μ must be Γ. These independence conditions are likely to hold approximately in practice (see e.g. [4], [10], [26], [27]).

4. The market is in equilibrium (stationary). This implies that the theory does not hold for the introduction of new information products into the broker.

Next, we present Chatfield's proof in detail because the original proof is marred by a typesetting error:

1. The probability p_r that a buyer makes r purchases is Poisson distributed:

$$\frac{e^{-\mu}\mu^r}{r!}$$

2. We integrate over all buyers in the truncated Γ-distribution:

$$p_r = c\int_\delta^\infty \left(\frac{e^{-\mu}\mu^r}{r!}\right)\left(\frac{e^{-\mu/a}}{\mu}\right)d\mu$$

$$= \frac{c}{r!}\int_\delta^\infty e^{-(\mu+\mu/a)}\mu^{r-1}d\mu$$

$$= \frac{c}{r!}\int_\delta^\infty e^{-(1+1/a)\mu}\frac{(1+1/a)^{r-1}}{(1+1/a)^{r-1}}\mu^{r-1}d\mu$$

$$= \frac{c}{r!(1+1/a)^{r-1}}\int_\delta^\infty e^{-(1+1/a)\mu}((1+1/a)\mu)^{r-1}d\mu$$

$$= \frac{c}{r!(1+1/a)^{r-1}}\int_\delta^\infty e^{-(1+1/a)\mu}((1+1/a)\mu)^{r-1}\frac{1}{(1+1/a)}d(1+1/a)\mu$$

$$= \frac{c}{r!(1+1/a)^{r}}\int_\delta^\infty e^{-(1+1/a)\mu}((1+1/a)\mu)^{r-1}d(1+1/a)\mu$$

Since δ is very small, for $r \geq 1$ and setting $t = (1+1/a)\mu$ this is approximately

$$p_r = \left(\frac{c}{r!(1+\frac{1}{a})^r}\right) \int_\delta^\infty e^{-t} t^{r-1} dt$$

$$\approx \left(\frac{c}{r!(1+\frac{1}{a})^r}\right) \Gamma(r)$$

$$= \frac{c}{(1+\frac{1}{a})^r r}$$

$$= c\frac{q^r}{r}$$

$$= q p_{r-1}(r-1)/r$$

with $q = \frac{a}{1+a}$.

3. If $\sum p_r = 1$ for $r \geq 1$, by analyzing the recursion we get $p_1 = \frac{-q}{\ln(1-q)}$ and $p_r = \frac{-q^r}{r\ln(1-q)}$. (However, this is the LSD. q.e.d.)

Next, consider for some fixed information product x in the set X of information products in the broker the purchase frequency of pairs of (x, i) with $i \in X \setminus x$. The probability $p_r(x \wedge i)$ that a buyer makes r purchases of products x and i together in the same session in the observation period which follow independent Poisson processes with means μ_x and μ_i is [20]: $p_r(x \wedge i) = \frac{e^{-\mu_x}\mu_x^r}{r!}\frac{e^{-\mu_i}\mu_i^r}{r!}$. For our recommender services for product x we need the conditional probability that product i has been used under the condition that product x has been used in the same session. Because of the independence assumption it is easy to see that the conditional probability $p_r(i \mid x)$ is again Poisson distributed by

$$p_r(i \mid x) = \frac{p_r(x \wedge i)}{p_r(x)}$$

$$= \frac{\frac{e^{-\mu_x}\mu_x^r}{r!}\frac{e^{-\mu_i}\mu_i^r}{r!}}{\frac{e^{-\mu_x}\mu_x^r}{r!}}$$

$$= \frac{e^{-\mu_i}\mu_i^r}{r!} = p_r(i)$$

This is not the end of the story. In our data, sessions do not contain the identity of the user – it is an unobserved variable. However, we can identify the purchase histories of sets of customers (market segments) in the following way: For each information product x the purchase history for this segment contains all sessions in which x has been bought. For each pair of information products x, i the purchase history for this segment contains all sessions in which x, i has been bought. The stochastic process for the segment (x, i) – n customers which have bought product x and an other product i – is represented by the sum of n independent random Bernoulli variables which equal 1 with probability p_i, and 0 with probablity $1 - p_i$. The distribution of the sum of these variables tends to a Poisson distribution. For a proof see Feller [12, p. 292]. (And to observe this aggregate process at the segment level is the best we can do.) If we assume that the parameters μ of the segments' Poisson distributions follow a truncated Γ-

distribution, we can repeat Chatfields proof and establish that the probability of r purchases of product pairs (x,i) follow a logarithmic series distribution (LSD).

However, we expect that non-random occurrences of such pairs occur more often than predicted by the logarithmic series distribution and that we can identify non-random occurrences of such pairs and use them as recommendations. For this purpose we estimate the logarithmic series distribution for the whole market (over all consumers) from market baskets, that is from anonymous web-sessions. We compute the mean purchase frequency w and solve equation 2 for q, the parameter of the LSD. By comparing the observed repeat-buying frequencies with the theoretically expected frequencies we identify outliers and use them as recommendations.

The advantage of this approach is that the estimation of the LSD is computationally efficient and robust. The limitation is that we cannot analyze the behavior of different types of consumers (e.g. light and heavy buyers) which would be possible with a full negative binomial distribution model (see Ehrenberg [11]).

What kind of behavior is captured by the LSD-model? Because of the independence assumptions the LSD-model estimates the probability that a product pair has been used at least once together in a session by chance r-times in the relevant time period. This can be justified by the following example: Consider that a user reads – as his time allows – some Internet newspaper and that he uses an Internet-based train schedule for his travel plans. Clearly, the use of both information products follows independent stochastic processes. And because of this, we would hesitate to recommend to other users who read the same Internet newspaper the train schedule. The frequency of observing this pair of information products in one session is as expected from the prediction of the LSD-model. Ehrenberg claims that this describes a large part of consumer behavior in daily life and he surveys the empirical evidence for this claim in [11].

Next, consider complementarities between information products: Internet users usually tend to need several information products for a task. E.g. to write a paper in a foreign language the author might repeatedly need an on-line dictionary as well as some help with LaTeX, his favorite type-setting software. In this case, however, we would not hesitate to recommend a LaTeX-online documentation to the user of the on-line dictionary. And the frequency of observing these two information products in the same session is (far) higher than predicted by the LSD-model.

A *recommendation* for an information product x simply is an outlier of the LSD-model – that is an information product y that has been used more often at least once together in the same session with product x in the observation period as could have been expected from independent random choice acts. A recommendation reveals a complementarity between information products.

The main purpose of the LSD-model in this setting is to separate non-random co-occurrences of information products (outliers) from random co-occurrences (as expected from the LSD-model). We use the LSD-model as a benchmark for discovering regularities.

Table 1. Algorithm for computing recommendations.

---

1. Compute for all information products x in the market baskets the frequency distributions for repeat-purchases of the co-occurrences of x with other information products in a session, that is of the pair (x, i) with $i \in X \setminus x$. Several co-occurrences of a pair (x, i) in a single session are counted only once.
2. Discard all frequency distributions with less than l observations.
3. For each frequency distribution:
    (a) Compute the **robust** mean purchase frequency w by trimming the sample by removing x percent (e.g. 2.5%) of the high repeat-buy pairs.
    (b) Estimate the parameter q for the LSD-model from
        $w = \frac{-q}{(1-q)(\ln(1-q))}$ with either a bisection or Newton method.
    (c) Apply a χ^2-goodness-of-fit test with a suitable α (e.g. 0.01 or 0.05) between the observed and the expected LSD distribution with a suitable partitioning.
    (d) Determine the outliers in the tail. (We suggest to be quite conservative here: Outliers at r are above $\sum_{r}^{\infty} p_r$.)
    (e) Finally, we prepare the list of recommendations for information product x, if we have a significant LSD-model with outliers.

Table 1 shows the algorithm we use for computing recommendations. In step 1 of the algorithm repeated usage of two information products in a single session is counted once as required in repeat-buying theory. In step 2 of the algorithm we discard all frequency distributions with a small number of observations, because no valid model can be estimated. This implies that in this case no recommendations are given. For each remaining frequency distribution, in step 3, the mean purchase frequency, the LSD parameter and the outliers are computed.

Note that high repeat-buy outliers may have a considerable impact on the mean purchase frequency and thus on the parameter of the distribution. By ignoring these high repeat-buy outliers by trimming the sample (step 3a) and thus computing a robust mean we considerably improve the chances of finding a significant LSD-model. This approach is justified by the data shown in column V of table 4 as discussed in section 4.1.

In step 3d outliers are identified by the property that they occur more often as predicted by the cumulated theoretically expected frequency of the LSD-model. Several less conservative options for determining the outliers in the tail of the distribution are discussed in the next section. These options lead to variants of the recommender service which exhibit different first and second type errors.

3 A Small Example: Java Code Engineering & Reverse Engineering

In figure 3 we show the first 16 candidates for recommendations of the list of 117 web-sites generated for the site Java Code Engineering & Reverse Engineering by the algorithm described in table 1 in the last section. Table 2 shows

```
Java Code Engineering & Reverse Engineering

Persons using the above web-site used the following web-sites too:

 1. Free Programming Source Code
 2. Softwareentwicklung: Java
 3. Developer.com
 4. Java-Einfuehrung
 5. The Java Tutorial
 6. JAR Files
 7. The Java Boutique
 8. Code Conventions for the Java(TM) Programming Language
 9. Working with XML: The Java(TM)/XML Tutorial
10. Java Home Page
11. Java Commerce
=== Cut =================================================
12. Collection of Java Applets
13. Experts Exchange
=== Cut =================================================
14. The GNU-Win32 Project
15. Microsoft Education: Tutorials
16. HotScripts.com
...
```

Fig. 3. List of web-sites with cuts.

the statistics for this recommendation list. In the table as well as in the following we denote with $nf(x_{obs})$ the observed frequency distribution for r repeat-buys, by $f(x_{obs})$ the observed relative frequency distribution, by $f(x_{exp})$ the density function of the estimated LSD-model, by $F(x_{obs})$ the cumulative relative frequency distribution and by $F(x_{exp})$ the distribution function of the estimated LSD-model. For a sample of n observations, the expected number of observations with r repeat buys is $nf(x_{exp}, r)$, the expected number of observations with at least r repeat buys is $nF(x_{exp}, j \geq r) = n \sum_{j=r}^{\infty} f(x_{exp}, j)$.

The observed mean purchase frequency in table 2 is 1.564. After trimming the highest 2.5 percentile (ignoring two observations with 7 and 8 repeat-buys, respectively), the robust mean purchase frequency is 1.461 and the estimated parameter q of the LSD-model is 0.511. Visual inspection of figures 4 and 5 shows that the estimated LSD-model properly describes the empirical data. This impression is supported by comparing the columns $nf(x_{obs})$ and $nf(x_{exp})$ in table 2 as well as looking at the χ^2-values in the second part of table 2. The χ^2 goodness-of-fit test for the trimmed data is highly significant with a χ^2-value of 1.099 which is considerably below 3.841, the critical value at $\alpha = 0.05$.

Table 2 also shows, that fitting a LSD-model to the original, untrimmed data results in a higher parameter q (0.567) and leads to a model with a higher χ^2-value (2.369) than the model obtained from the trimmed data. This indicates that ignoring high repeat-buy outliers improves the fit of the LSD-model. However, experimentation with several trimming percentiles in the range from 1.0 to 10 % indicated that ignoring 2.5 % of the observations contributed to an improved model fit, whereas ignoring additional observations did not lead to further improvement. In addition, in the evaluation the quality of recommendations proved rather insensitive to trimming. Our current experience suggests that 2.5 % of trimming is a robust choice for this parameter. However, additional experience with different data sets would be welcome.

All outliers whose observed repeat-purchase frequency is above the theoretically expected frequency are candidates to be selected as recommendations. In figure 5 (with a logarithmic y-axis) we explore three options of determining the cut-off point for such outliers:

Option 1. Without doubt, as long as the observed repeat-purchase frequency is above $F(x_{exp}, j \geq r)$, we have detected outliers. Look for $nf(x_{obs}, r) > n(1 - F(x_{exp}, r))$ in table 2. In our example, this holds for all co-purchases with more than 3 repeat-buys which correspond to the top 11 sites shown as recommendations in figure 3. For $r = 3$ $nf(x_{obs}, r) = 2$ is less than $n(1 - F(x_{exp}, r)) = 12.080$ in table 2, so we can not expect outliers in this class. This is the most conservative choice. Inspecting these recommendations shows that all of them are more or less directly related to Java programming, which is probably the task in which students use the example site.

Option 2. Discounting any model errors, as long as the observed repeat-purchase frequency $nf(x_{obs}, r)$ is above the theoretically expected frequency $nf(x_{exp}, r)$ is a less conservative option. For the example, we select all co-purchases with more than 3 occurrences as recommendations. Here this coincides with the option described above. See the top 11 sites in figure 3.

Option 3. If we take the cut, where both cumulative purchase frequency distributions cross, we get 13 recommendations regarding all co-purchases occurring more than twice as nonrandom – see the top 13 sites in figure 3. However, it seems, that web-sites 12 and 13, namely `Collection of Java Applets` and `Experts Exchange` seem to be not quite so related to Java programming.

The last three web-sites shown in figure 3 are not used as recommendations by any of the three explored options. And in fact they seem to be of little or no relevance for Java programming.

We have implemented the most conservative approach, namely option 1, in the recommender service based on a check of the face validity of the recommendations for a small sample of information products (25 products). We think that, at least in cases with a considerable number of candidates for the recommendation list, this is a suitable approach.

Instead of the 3 simple cutoff algorithms described above we consider the following error threshold procedure. We can determine for each class of products with r repeat-buys individually the probability of recommending a random website by dividing the theoretically expected number of occurrences by the observed

Table 2. Statistics for web-site Java Code Engineering & Reverse Engineering.

```
# Web-site: wu01_74 (Mon May  7 16:48:37 2001)
# Heuristic: Distr=NBD - Case 4: NBD heuristic var>mean
# Total number of observations: 117
# Sample mean=1.56410256410256 and var=1.64456233421751
# Estimate for q=0.566835385131836
#
# Robust estimation: Trimmed begin: 0 / end: 0.025 (2 observations)
# Robust estimation: Number of observations: 115
# Robust mean=1.46086956521739
# Robust estimate for q=0.511090921020508

# Plot:
# r repeat-buys  nf(x_obs)  nf(x_exp)  n(1-F(x_obs,r))  n(1-F(x_exp,r))
   1             87         83.565     117              117
   2             17         21.355      30               33.435
   3              2          7.276      13               12.080
   4              5          2.789      11                4.804
   5              3          1.140       6                2.015
   6              1          0.486       3                0.874
   7              1          0.213       2                0.389
   8              1          0.095       1                0.176

# Identifying non-random co-occurrences:
# Option 1: mixed intersection (f(x_obs) with 1-F(x_exp) at:
#     3 (leaves 11 nonrandom outliers)
# Option 2: f(x) intersection at: 3 (leaves 11 nonrandom outliers)
# Option 3: 1-F(x) intersection at: 2 (leaves 13 nonrandom outliers)

# Chi-square test (q=0.566835385131836; 117 observations):
# Class  obs      exp         chi-square
# 1      87       79.269      0.754
# 2      17       22.466      1.330
# 3      13       15.071      0.285
#                            -------
# Chi-square value:           2.369

# Chi-square test (robust) (q=0.511090921020508; 115 observations):
# Class  obs      exp         chi-square
# 1      87       82.137      0.288
# 2      17       20.990      0.758
# 3      11       11.794      0.053
#                            -------
# Chi-square value:           1.099

# Chi-square test threshold with alpha=0.01 w/1 d.f.: 10.828
# Chi-square test threshold with alpha=0.05 w/1 d.f.:  3.841
# -> LSD with alpha=0.05
```

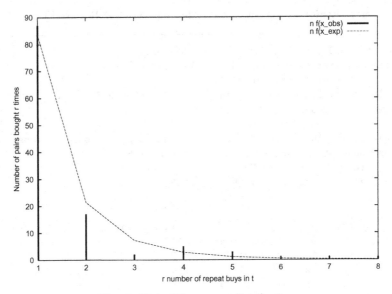

Fig. 4. Plot of frequency distribution.

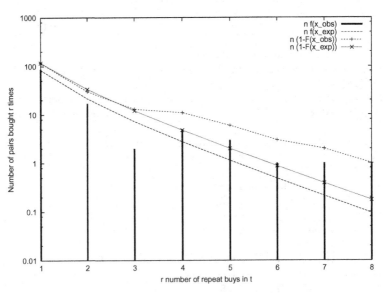

Fig. 5. Plot of log frequency distribution.

number of occurrences ($f(x_{exp})/f(x_{obs})$ in table 2). If this quotient exceeds 1 the probability is 1. Consider, for example, the number of product combinations which have been bought 8 times together in table 2. Theoretically, we would expect that this is a chance event roughly in one out of ten cases (0.095). Now, we have observed 5 product combinations with 4 repeat-buys. Unfortunately,

Table 3. Finding classes with less than 0.40 random observations.

r repeat-buys	$nf(x_{obs})$	$nf(x_{exp})$	$f(x_{exp})/f(x_{obs})$	Class shown
1	87	83.565	0.961	0
2	17	21.355	1.256	0
3	2	7.276	3.638	0
4	5	2.789	0.558	0
5	3	1.140	0.380	1
6	1	0.486	0.486	0
7	1	0.213	0.213	1
8	1	0.095	0.095	1

```
Java Code Engineering & Reverse Engineering

Persons using the above web-site used the following web-sites too:

1. Free Programming Source Code
2. Softwareentwicklung: Java
4. Java-Einfuehrung
5. The Java Tutorial
6. JAR Files
```

Fig. 6. List of web-sites selected by class.

theoretically 2.789 product combinations can be expected from pure chance. In this class we observe now a mixture of random product combinations and non-random product combinations, but we are not able to distinguish them. However, we can specify a threshold for the chance of falsely presenting a random co-occurrence, e.g. below 0.40. Table 3 summarizes this procedure. That is we pick only those classes with r observed repeat-buys where the probability of falsely presenting an outlier is below $\theta = 0.40$.

In the example, we would then present the web-sites in classes 5, 7, and 8, but not the web-site in class 6. That is, we would present web-sites 1, 2, 4, 5, and 6 as shown in figure 6. Web-site 3 (Developer.com, a site definitely not exclusively devoted to Java programming) and others from figure 3 are not shown because of the high probability of presenting random web-sites.

Considering the theoretically expected number of occurrences $f(x_{exp})$ of a class as the error to give a recommendation for a random co-occurrence (the type II error) leads to a thresholding strategy based on the specification of acceptable expected type II error β: We add to the recommender products from the tail of the distribution as long as the expected type II error of the recommender is smaller than β. If there is more than one product in a class r, the type II error of this class is divided by the number of products in the class and products in a class may be picked in arbitrary sequence. This strategy has been implemented and used for the evaluation of the recommender in section 4.3.

Table 4. Detailed results for observation period 1999-09-01 – 2001-05-07.

	I q undef.	II no χ^2 (< 3 classes)	III Sign. $\alpha = 0.05$	IV Sign. $\alpha = 0.01$	V Sign. (trim)	VI Not sign.	$\sum$
A Obs.< 10	1128 (0)	66 (63)	0 (0)	0 (0)	0 (0)	0 (0)	1194 (63)
B $\bar{x} = 1$	1374 (0)	0 (0)	0 (0)	0 (0)	0 (0)	0 (0)	1374 (0)
C $\bar{x} > \sigma^2; r \leq 3$	2375 (0)	0 (0)	0 (0)	0 (0)	0 (0)	0 (0)	2375 (0)
D $\bar{x} > \sigma^2; r > 3$	201 (0)	617 (605)	105 (105)	46 (46)	15 (15)	372 (145)	1356 (916)
E $\sigma^2 > \bar{x}$	3 (0)	86 (86)	222 (222)	194 (194)	93 (93)	253 (253)	851 (848)
$\sum$	5081 (0)	769 (754)	327 (327)	240 (240)	108 (108)	625 (398)	7150 (1827)

(x) indicates x lists with at least 1 outlier.

In the analysis of outliers there is still room for improvement as e.g. by developing statistical tests for identifying outliers. For example, the choice of the threshold value should be analyzed in terms of the tradeoff between errors of type I and II for a sample of co-occurrence lists all of whose entries have been completely evaluated by experts with regard to their usefulness as recommendations.

4   First Empirical Results

To establish that a recommender service based on Ehrenberg's repeat buying-theory is supported by empirical evidence, we proceed as follows:

1. In section 4.1 we investigate how well the LSD-model explains the actual data for 7150 information products.
2. However, that the LSD-model fits the data well does not yet mean that the outliers we have identified are suitable recommendations for a user. In section 4.2 we present the results of a first small face evaluation experiment whose result suggests that these outliers are indeed valuable recommendations.

The data set used for the example given in section 3 and in this section is from the anonymous recommender services of the Virtual University of the Vienna University of Economics and Business Administration (http://vu.wu-wien.ac.at) for the observation period from 1999-09-01 to 2001-03-05. Co-occurrences have been observed for 8596 information products. After elimination of web-sites which ceased to exist in the observation period co-occurrences for 7150 information products remain available for analysis.

4.1 Fit of Data to LSD-Models

Table 4 summarizes the results of applying the algorithm for computing recommendations presented in table 1. If the sample variance is larger than the sample mean this may indicate that a negative binomial distribution (NBD)-model (and thus its LSD-approximation) is appropriate (see Johnson and Kotz [19, p.138]). This heuristic suggests 851 candidates for an LSD-model (see table 4, row E).

The rows of the table represent the following cases:

A The number of observations is less than 10. In this row we find co-occurrence lists either for very young or for very rarely used web-sites. These are not included into the further analysis. Cell (A/II) in table 4 contains lists which have repeated co-occurrences despite the low number of observations. In this cell good recommendation lists may be present (4 out of 5).

B No repeat-buys, just one co-occurrence. These are discarded from further analyses.

C Less than 4 repeat-buys and trimmed sample mean larger than variance. Trimming outliers may lead to the case that only the observations of class 1 (no repeat-buys) remain in the sample. These are discarded from further analyses.

D More than 3 repeat-buys and trimmed sample mean larger than variance. In cell (D/I) after trimming only class 1 web-sites remain in the trimmed sample (no repeat-buys). As a future improvement, the analysis should be repeated without trimming. In cell (D/II) the χ^2-test is not applicable, because less than 3 classes remain.

E (Trimmed) sample variance larger than sample mean. For cell (E/I) we recommend the same as for cell (D/I). For cell (E/II) we observe the same as for cell (D/II).

The columns I – VI of table 4 have the following meaning:

I The parameter q of the LSD model could not be estimated. For example, only a single co-occurrence has been observed for some product pairs.

II The χ^2 goodness-of-fit test could not be computed, because of lack of observations.

III, IV The χ^2 goodness-of-fit test is significant at $\alpha = 0.05$ or $\alpha = 0.01$, respectively.

V The χ^2 goodness-of-fit test is significant at $\alpha = 0.01$ using the trimmed data. All high repeat-buy pairs in the 2.5 percentile have been excluded from the model estimation.

VI The χ^2-test is not significant.

Table 5. Summary of results for observation period 1999-09-01 – 2001-05-07.

	n	%
Information products	9498	100.00
Products bought together with other products	7150	75.28
Parameter q defined	2069	21.78
Enough classes for χ^2-test	1300	13.69
LSD with $\alpha = 0.01$ (robust)	675	7.11
LSD not significant	625	6.58
LSD fitted, no χ^2-test	703	7.40
$n < 10$ and no χ^2-test	66	0.69

As summarized in table 5 we tested the fitted LSD-model for the frequency distributions of co-occurrences for 1300 information products. For 675 information products, that is more than 50 percent, the estimated LSD-models pass a χ^2 goodness-of-fit test at $\alpha = 0.01$.

4.2   Face Validation of Recommendations

In order to establish the plausibility of the recommendations identified by the recommender service previously described we performed a small scale face validation experiment. The numbers in parenthesis in table 4 indicate the number of lists for which outliers were detected. From these lists 100 lists of recommendations were randomly selected. Each of the 1259 recommendations in these lists was inspected for plausibility. Plausible recommendations were counted as good recommendations by pressing the affirmative symbol (a hook) in the Vote Box shown in figure 1 in the introduction of this paper.

This small scale face validation experiment of inspecting recommendations for plausibility led to a quite satisfactory result:

– For the 31 lists for which a significant LSD-model could be fitted, 87.71 % of the recommendations were judged as good recommendations.
– 25 lists for which an LSD model was not significant contained 89, 45 % good recommendations.
– Only 75.74 % good recommendations were found in the 44 lists for those LSD-models where no χ^2 test could be computed which is a significantly lower percentage.

Surprisingly, the class of models where the LSD model was not significant contains a slightly higher number of recommendations evaluated as good. However, a number of (different) reasons may explain this:

- First, we might argue that even if the LSD-model is insignificant, it still serves its purpose, namely to identify non-random outliers as recommendations.
- A close inspection of frequency distributions for these lists revealed the quite unexpected fact that several of these frequency distributions were for information products which belong to the oldest in the data set and which account for many observations. The reasons for this may be explained e.g. by a shift in user behavior (non-stationarity) or too regular behavior as e.g. for cigarettes in consumer markets (see Ehrenberg [11]). If too regular behavior is the reason that the LSD-model is insignificant, again, we still identified the non-random outliers.
- Another factor which might contribute to this problem is that several web-sites in this group belong to lists integrated in the web-sites of other organizational units. These lists, at least some of them, contain web-sites which have been carefully selected by the web-masters of these organizational units for their students. For example, the list of web-sites for student jobs is integrated within the main web-site of the university. The recommendations for such lists seem to reflect mainly the search behavior of the users. A similar effect is known in classic consumer panel analysis, if the points of sale of different purchases are not cleanly separated. This implies that e.g. purchases in a supermarket are not distinguished from purchases from a salesman. In our analysis, the purchase occasions are in different web-sites, namely the broker system and the organizational web-site with the embedded list. Ehrenberg's recommendation is to analyse the data separately for each purchase occasion.

Also, the fact that the data set contains information products with different age may explain some of these difficulties. However, to settle this issue further investigations are required.

4.3 A First Comparison with a Simple Association Rule Based Recommender System

Compared to several other recently published recommender systems (e.g. [21], [24], [23]) which combine several data mining techniques, most noteably association-rule mining algorithms and various clustering techniques, the recommender system discussed here is very simple. Computing the frequency distribution corresponds exactly to the identification of frequent itemsets in association-rule mining algorithms whose most famous representative is Agrawal's a-priori algorithm ([2], [3]) with support and confidence of 0. Recent improvements of these algorithms include TITANIC of Stumme et al. [31] for highly correlated data sets, the association rule mining algorithm with adaptive support of Lin et al. [22], a graph-based approach for association rule mining by Yen and Chen [33], and a new approach for the online generation of association rules by Aggrawal and Yu [1]. TITANIC efficiently exploits the concept lattice and is based on concept analysis (see Ganter and Wille [13]).

The difference between our system and the association rule framework is in the way, "significant" item pairs are identified. In our model "significant" item

Table 6. Comparison of LSD-model with no trim and an acceptable expected type II error rate of 0.1 and with association rules with a support of 0.00015 and a confidence of 0.01.

No. of	LSD-model	Association Rules
produced recommendations	145	154
correct recommendations	96	100
unknown recommendations	35	38
false recommendations (type II error)	14	16
missed recommendations (type I error)	465	461

pairs are outliers with regard to the LSD model, in association rule approaches "significant pairs" have more than a specified amount of support and more than a specified amount of confidence.

We have evaluated these two simple recommender systems on the VU data set for the observation period of 2001-01-01 to 2001-06-30. For the purpose of comparing our recommender system with a simple association rule based recommender system we have randomly drawn association lists for 300 information products with a total of 1966 pairs of information products. For each pair (x, i) a member of our research group answered with yes or no to the following question "Is i a good recommendation for x?". For 561 pairs the answer was yes, for 1100 pairs the answer was no. Unfortunately, however, for 305 pairs no expert evaluation could be done, because the web-site for i ceased to exist.

This evaluation approach differs from the usual machine learning methodology of splitting the data set in a training and a testing data set for testing the capability of the algorithm to extract patterns. In addition we test whether frequent co-purchase (or co-usage) is a suitable indicator for recommendations.

Table 6 shows a first result for the two suitably parametrized models. A rough comparison indicates that the LSD-model is at least as good as the association rule approach. However, a complete analysis of the trade-off of the type I and II error over the parameter range of the two models and a sensitivity analysis with regard to misspecification of parameters is still on the todo-list. With regard to parametrization, the type II error threshold is the only parameter of the LSD-model based algorithm. This parameter is independent of the size of the data set. The support and confidence parameters of association rule algorithms seem to depend on the data set size.

5   Further Research

The main contribution of this paper is that Ehrenberg's classical repeat-buying models can be applied to market baskets and describe – despite their strong independence and stationarity assumptions – the consumption patterns of information products – at least for the data set analyzed – surprisingly well. For e-commerce sites this implies that a large part of the theory developed for consumer panels may be applied to data from web-sites, too, as long as the analysis remains on the aggregate level.

For anonymous recommender services they seem to do a remarkable job of identifying non-random repeated-choice acts of consumers of information products as we have demonstrated in section 3. The use of the LSD-model for identifying non-random co-occurrences of information products constitutes a major improvement which is not yet present in other correlation-type recommender services.

However, establishing an empirical base for the validity of repeat-buying models in information markets as suggested in this article still requires a lot of additional evidence and a careful investigation of additional data sets. We expect that such an empirical research program would have a good chance to succeed because to establish Ehrenberg's repeat-buying theory a similar research program has been conducted by Aske Research Ldt., London, in several consumer product markets (e.g. dentifrice, ready-to-eat cereals, detergents, refrigerated dough, cigarettes, petrol, tooth-pastes, biscuits, color cosmetics, ...) from 1969 to 1981 (see Ehrenberg [11]).

The current version of the anonymous recommender services (and the analysis in this article) still suffers from several deficiencies. The first is that new information products are daily added to the information broker's database so that the stationarity assumptions for the market are violated and the information products in the data set are of non-homogenous age. The second drawback is that testing the behavioral assumptions of the model, e.g. by testing the behavioral assumptions with data from the personalized part of the VU, as well as validation either by studying user acceptance or by controlled experiments, still has to be done. Third, for performance reasons the co-occurrence lists for each information product do not contain time-stamps. Therefore, the development of time-dependent e.g. alert systems has not been tried, although Ehrenberg's theory is in principle suitable for this task.

We expect Ehrenberg's repeat-buying models to be of considerable help to create anonymous recommender services for recognizing emerging shifts in consumer behavior patterns (fashion, emerging trends, moods, new subcultures, ...). Embedded in a personalized environment Ehrenberg's repeat-buying models may serve as the base of continuous marketing research services for managerial decision support which provide forecasts and classical consumer panel analysis in a cost efficient way.

Acknowledgment

We acknowledge the financial support of the Jubiläumsfonds of the Austrian National Bank under Grant No. 7925 without which this project would not have been possible. For the evaluation of the system we acknowledge support of the DFG for the project "Scientific Libraries in Information Markets" of the DFG program SPP 1041 "V3D2: Verteilte Verarbeitung und Vermittlung digitaler

Dokumente". Thanks to Anke Thede and Andreas Neumann for correcting the final versions of this contribution and to one of the anonymous reviewers whose constructive critic helped us to improve this contribution considerably.

References

1. Aggrawall, C.C., Yu, P.S.: A New Approach to Online Generation of Association Rules. IEEE Trans. on Knowledge Eng. **13(4)** (2001) 527-540
2. Agrawal, R., Imielinski, T., Swami, A.: Mining Association Rules between Sets of Items in Large Databases. Proc. of the 1993 ACM SIGMOD Int'l Conf. on Management of Data (1994) 207-216
3. Agrawal, R., Srikant, R.: Fast Algorithms for Mining Association Rules. Proc. 20th Int'l Conf. on Very Large Databases (1994) 478-499
4. Aske Research: The Structure of the Tooth-Paste Market. Aske Research Ltd., London (1975)
5. Avery, C., Zeckhauser, R.: Recommender Systems for Evaluating Computer Messages. CACM **40(3)** (1997) 88–89
6. Bellmann, S., Lohse, G.L., Johnson, E.J.: Predictors of Online Buying Behavior. CACM **42(12)** (1999) 32–38
7. Blischok, T.J.: Every Transaction Tells a Story. Chain Store Age Executive **71(3)** (1995) 50–62
8. Böhm, W., Geyer-Schulz, A., Hahsler, M., Jahn, M.: Repeat Buying Theory and its Application for Recommender Services. In: Opitz, O. (Ed.): Studies in Classification, Data Analysis, and Knowledge Organization, Springer, Heidelberg (to appear)
9. Chatfield, C., Ehrenberg, A. S. C., Goodhardt, G. J.: Progress on a Simplified Model of Stationary Purchasing Behavior. J. of the Royal Stat. Society A **129** (1966) 317–367
10. Charlton, P., Ehrenberg, A. S. C.: Customers of the LEP, Appl. Statist. **25** (1976) 26-30.
11. Ehrenberg, A. S. C.: Repeat-Buying: Facts, Theory and Applications. Charles Griffin & Company Limited, London (1988)
12. Feller, W.: An Introduction to Probability Theory and Its Applications. Vol. 2. John Wiley & Sons, New York (1971)
13. Ganter, B., Wille, R.: Formal Concept Analysis: Mathematical Foundations. Springer, Heidelberg (1999)
14. Gaul, W., Schmidt-Thieme L.: Recommender Systems Based on User Navigational Behavior in the Internet. Behaviormetrika **29(1)** 2002 to appear.
15. Geyer-Schulz, A., Hahsler, M., Jahn, M.: myVU: A Next Generation Recommender System Based on Observed Consumer Behavior and Interactive Evolutionary Algorithms. In: Gaul, W., Opitz, O., Schader, M. (Eds.): Data Analysis – Scientific Modeling and Practical Applications, Studies in Classification, Data Analysis, and Knowledge Organization, Vol. 18, Springer, Heidelberg (2000) 447-457
16. Geyer-Schulz, A., Hahsler, M., Jahn, M.: Educational and Scientific Recommender Systems: Designing the Information Channels of the Virtual University. Int. J. of Engineering Education **17(2)** (2001) 153-163
17. Geyer-Schulz, A., Hahsler, M., Jahn, M.: Recommendations for Virtual Universities from Observed User Behavior. In: Gaul, W., Ritter, G., Schader, M. (Eds.): Studies in Classification, Data Analysis, and Knowledge Organization, Springer, Heidelberg (to appear)

18. Goodhardt, G.J., Ehrenberg, A.S.C., Collins, M.A.: The Dirichlet: A Comprehensive Model of Buying Behaviour. J. of the Royal Stat. Society A **147** (1984) 621-655
19. Johnson, N.L., Kotz, S.: Discrete Distributions. Houghton Mifflin, Boston (1969)
20. Johnson, N.L., Kotz, S., Balakrishnan, N.: Discrete Multivariate Distributions. John Wiley & Sons, New York (1997)
21. Lawrence, R.D., Almasi, G.S., Kotlyar, V., Viveros, M.S., Duri, S.S.: Personalization of Supermarket Product Recommendations. Data Mining and Knowledge Discovery **5** (2001) 11–32
22. Lin, W., Alvarez, S.A., Ruiz, C.: Efficient Adaptive-Support Association Rule Mining for Recommender Systems. Data Mining and Knowledge Discovery **6(1)** (2002) 83-105
23. Mobasher, B., Cooley, R., Srivastava J.: Automatic Personalization Based on Web Usage Mining. CACM **43(8)** (2000) 142–151
24. Mobasher, B., Dai, H., Luo, T., Nakagawa, M.: Discovery and Evaluation of Aggregate Usage Profiles for Web Personalization. Data Mining and Knowledge Discovery **6** (2002) 61–82
25. Resnick, P., Varian, H.R. (1997): Recommender Systems. CACM **40(3)** (1997) 56–58
26. Powell, N., Westwood, J.: Buyer-Behaviour in Management Education. Appl. Statist. **27** (1978) 69-72
27. Sichel, H. S.: Repeat-Buying and the Poisson-Generalised Inverse Gaussion Distributions. Appl. Statist. **31** (1982) 193-204
28. Spiliopoulou, M.: Web Usage Mining for Web Site Evaluation. CACM **43(8)** (2000) 127–134
29. Srivastava, J., Cooley, R., Deshpande, M., Tan P.-N.: Web Usage Mining: Discovery and Applications of Usage Patterns from Web Data. SIGKDD Explorations **1(2)** (2000) 1–12
30. S.R.S.: The S.R.S. Motorists Panel. S.R.S. Sales Research Service, London (1965)
31. Stumme, G., Taouil, R., Bastide Y., Pasquier N., Lakhal L.: Computing Iceberg Concept Lattices with TITANIC. J. on Knowledge and Data Engineering to appear.
32. Wagner, U., Taudes, A.: Stochastic Models of Consumer Behaviour. Europ. J. of Op. Res. **29(1)** (1987) 1–23
33. Yen, S.J., Chen, A.L.P.: A Graph-Based Approach for Discovering Various Types of Association Rules. IEEE Trans. on Knowledge Eng. **13(5)** (2001) 839-845

A Cube Model and Cluster Analysis for Web Access Sessions

Joshua Zhexue Huang[1], Michael Ng[2], Wai-Ki Ching[2],
Joe Ng[1], and David Cheung[1]

[1] E-Business Technology Institute
The University of Hong Kong
jhuang,kkng,dcheung@eti.hku.hk
[2] Department of Mathematics
The University of Hong Kong
mng,wkc@maths.hku.hk

Abstract. Identification of the navigational patterns of casual visitors is an important step in online recommendation to convert casual visitors to customers in e-commerce. Clustering and sequential analysis are two primary techniques for mining navigational patterns from Web and application server logs. The characteristics of the log data and mining tasks require new data representation methods and analysis algorithms to be tested in the e-commerce environment. In this paper we present a cube model to represent Web access sessions for data mining. The cube model organizes session data into three dimensions. The COMPONENT dimension represents a session as a set of ordered components $\{c_1, c_2, ..., c_P\}$, in which each component c_i indexes the ith visited page in the session. Each component is associated with a set of attributes describing the page indexed by it, such as the page ID, category and view time spent at the page. The attributes associated with each component are defined in the ATTRIBUTE dimension. The SESSION dimension indexes individual sessions. In the model, irregular sessions are converted to a regular data structure to which existing data mining algorithms can be applied while the order of the page sequences is maintained. A rich set of page attributes is embedded in the model for different analysis purposes. We also present some experimental results of using the partitional clustering algorithm to cluster sessions. Because the sessions are essentially sequences of categories, the k-modes algorithm designed for clustering categorical data and the clustering method using the Markov transition frequency (or probability) matrix, are used to cluster categorical sequences.

1 Introduction

Web server log is a primary data source in Web mining [7][17]. A Web server log records transactions of connections to the Web server [18]. Each transaction presents an interaction between the Web server and a client machine a user used to visit the Website. Standard data elements in a Web log file include *Host*,

R. Kohavi et al. (Eds.): WEBKDD 2001, LNAI 2356, pp. 48–67, 2002.
© Springer-Verlag Berlin Heidelberg 2002

Ident, Authuser, Time, Request, Status and *Bytes* [25]. Additional elements such as *Referrer, Agent* and *Cookie* can also be found in some log files. Details of these Web log data elements are given in [16]. At some popular Web sites, such as www.amazon.com and www.yahoo.com, millions of transactions are being generated daily in their log files. Managing and mining the huge Web data source has become a big challenge to many online organizations.

In Web mining, objects of different abstraction levels, such as *Users, Server Access Sessions, Episodes, Clickstreams and Page Views* [23] [16], are usually identified from Web log files for different mining tasks. Preprocessing techniques for extracting these objects are discussed in [6]. Among others, server access sessions (or sessions for short) are very important for *Web structure mining, Web usage mining* [17], and *path traversal patterns mining* [5]. Web usage mining is related to the problems of discovery of Web access patterns, online customer behavior analysis, Web personalization, and design and building of adaptive Web sites [15]. Clustering and sequential analysis of Web access sessions play a key role in solving these problems [10]. For instance, Banerjee and Ghosh [1] have used weighted longest common subsequences in clickstream clustering.

A Web server session is defined by W3C as a collection of user clicks to a single Web server during a user session or visit [26]. A simple view of a session is a sequence of ordered pages $\{P_1, P_2, P_3, P_4, P_3, P_5, \cdots, \}$ where P_i is a unique id for a page URL in the Web site. The discussion of session exploration can be found in [3]. A session database can be viewed as a set of such sequences. Because different numbers of pages often occur in different sessions, this simple representation of sessions does not satisfy the input data requirement of many existing data mining algorithms. Adding more page information such as the time spent and total hits further complicates the session representation. Different approaches have been adopted to represent sessions for different mining tasks. In [19], a set of sessions is encoded as a set of N_U-dimensional binary attribute vectors in which each attribute represents a URL and its value is "1" if the URL appears in a session and "0" otherwise. This representation satisfies many existing data mining algorithms. The major concern is the lost of page orders. By using the attribute-oriented induction method [9], sessions with different numbers of pages can be generalized into vectors in the same dimensions based on the page hierarchy [8]. Regular vectors can be obtained after sessions are aggregated up to a certain level so clustering algorithms such as BIRCH [28] can be applied to the generalized sessions. One problem is again the lost of page orders. Another problem is the lost of information on the low level pages in the page hierarchy which are probably more interesting to users. The WUM system uses the sophisticated aggregate tree model to represent sessions which supports user initiative queries to discover navigation patterns using an SQL like query language MINT [22]. Such a structure can speed up the query process. However, data-driven mining process is not supported.

In this paper, we introduce a cube model for representing sessions to effectively support different mining tasks. The cube model organizes session data into three dimensions. The *Component* dimension represents a session as a set of ordered components $\{c_1, c_2, .., c_p\}$, in which each component c_i indexes the ith visited page in the session. Each component is associated with a set of attributes describing the page indexed by it. The attributes associated with each component are defined in the *Attribute* dimension of the cube model. Depending on the analysis requirements, different attributes can be defined in the Attribute dimension such as Page ID, Page Category and View Time spent at a page. The *Session* dimension indexes individual sessions. The details of the cube model are given in the next section. In comparison with other representation methods mentioned before, the cube model has the following advantages: (1) it represents sessions in a regular data structure to which many existing data mining algorithms can be applied; (2) it maintains the order of the page sequences and (3) it can easily include more page attributes for different analysis purposes. Simple operations can be defined to extract necessary data from the model for different mining operations and produce reports for summary statistics and frequency counts of page visits. Therefore, the model can be used as an efficient and flexible base for Web mining.

We present a result of using the k-modes algorithm [11] to cluster sessions described as sequences of page URL IDs. Since the URL IDs should be treated as categorical values, clustering such categorical sessions is clearly a challenge to some numeric only algorithms such as CLARANS [20] and BIRCH [28] which are incapable as pointed out by other researchers [14]. Our result has shown that the k-modes algorithm is efficient and effective in discovering interesting clusters with strong path patterns. We will present cluster analysis on two Web log files and some interesting clusters identified using the criteria of average distance of sessions to cluster centers and the size of clusters. We also propose a Markov transition frequency (or probability) matrix approach to clustering sessions and show some initial results. We remark that Cadez et al. [4] have also considered to use Markov models for clustering.

This paper is organized as follows. In Section 2, we describe the cube model and some basic operations. In Section 3, we discuss the basis of the k-modes algorithm. In Section 4, we present a new approach of using the Markov transition frequency (or probability) matrix to cluster and analyze categorical sequences. In Section 5, we show some initial clustering results of two Web log files using the two clustering algorithms. We draw some conclusions and present our future work in Section 6.

2   A Cube Model to Represent User Sessions

2.1   Session Identification

We consider a Web log as a relation table T that is defined by a set of attributes $\mathcal{A} = \{A_1, A_2, ..., A_m\}$. Usual attributes include *Host, Ident, Authuser, Time, Request, Status, Bytes, Referrer, Agent* and *Cookie*. Assume that transactions generated by different users are identified by a subset of attributes $S \subset \mathcal{A}$. Let U be a set of user ids and $F : S \to U$ a function that maps each unique combination of values of S to a user id of U. Let A_t be the Time attribute. Time attribute does not belong to S. We first perform the following two operations on T:

1. Use $A_U = F(S)$ as a derived ID atttribute.
2. Sort T on A_U and A_t.

T is transformed to T' after the two operations. Let $A_k(t_i)$ be the value of attribute A_k in the ith transaction of T'. We then identify sessions according to the following definition:

Definition 1. *A session s is an ordered set of transactions in T' which satisfy $A_U(t_{i+1}) = A_U(t_i)$ and $A_t(t_{i+1}) - A_t(t_i) < \tau$ where $t_{i+1}, t_i \in s$ and τ is a given time threshold (usually 30 minutes).*

Host IP address or Domain Name is often used in S to identify users [21] [22] but host IP address alone can result in ambiguity in user identification caused by firewalls and proxy servers. In fact, Cookies and/or registration are needed for reliable user identification. More attributes such as Referrer and Agent can also be used to resolve this problem [6]. In [2], Berendt et al. measured the accuracy of sessionizers for Web usage analysis.

2.2 The Cube Model

Conceptually, a session defined Definition 1 is a set of ordered pages viewed in one visit by the same visitor. We define the number of viewed pages in a session as the length of the session. Each page identified by its URL is described by many attributes, including

- Page ID,
- Page_Category – a classification of pages in a Web site based on the context of the page contents,
- Total_Time – the total time spent at a page,
- Time – the time spent at a page in a session,
- Overall_Frequency – the total number of hits at a page,
- Session_Frequency – the number of hits at a page in a session.

The values of these attributes can be computed from particular Web log files. A particular page in a session is characterized by its attribute values while the set of ordered particular pages characterizes a session.

Let P_{max} be the length of the longest session in a given Web log file. For any session with a length $P < P_{max}$, we define the pages of the session between $P + 1$ and P_{max} as missing pages identified with the missing value "-". As such, we can consider that all sessions in a given Web log file have the same length.

Given the above considerations, we define a cube model for representing sessions as follows:

Definition 2. *A cube model is a four tuple $< S, C, A, \mathcal{V} >$ where S, C, A are the sets of indices for three dimensions (Session, Component, Attribute) in which*

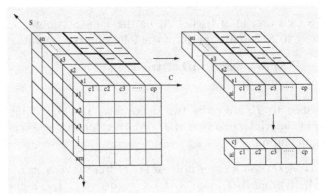

Fig. 1. The cube model (left) and some operations (right).

1. S *indexes all identified sessions* $s_1, s_2, ..., s_n$,
2. C *consists of* p_{max} *ordered indices* $c_1, c_2, .., c_{p_{max}}$ *identifying the order of components for all sessions,*
3. A *indexes a set of attributes,* $A_1, A_2, ..., A_m$, *each describing a property of sessions' components, and*
4. $\mathcal{V}$ *is a bag of values of all attributes* $A_1, A_2, ..., A_m$.

Figure 1 (left) illustrates the cube model. The order of session components is very important in the cube model while the orders of dimensions S and A are irrelevant. Each index $a_i \in A$ is associated with a pair $<AttributeName, DataType >$. In this figure, we assume that sessions are sorted on the value of Length(s_i) where function Length(s_i) returns the real length of session s_i.

Definition 3. *Let F be a mapping from $< S, C, A >$ to $\mathcal{V}$ that performs the following basic operations on the cube model:*

1. $F(s, c, a) = v$ *where* $s \in S, c \in C, a \in A$ *and* $v \in \mathcal{V}$,
2. $F(s_k, ., a_i) = V_{s_k, a_i}$ *where* V_{s_k, a_i} *is session* s_k *represented by attribute* a_i,
3. $F(., ., a_i) = V_{a_i}$ *where* V_{a_i} *is a* $p \times n$ *matrix,*
4. $F(., [c_i, c_{i+z}], a_i)$ *returns a* $z \times n$ *matrix which represents a set of partial sessions.*

Definition 4. *Let "$|$" be a cancatenation operator.* $F(s_k, ., a_i) \mid F(s_{k+1}, ., a_i)$ *attaches session* s_{k+1} *to session* s_k.

With these basic operators defined on the cube model, data preparation for different analysis tasks can be greatly simplified. For example, we can use $F(., ., a_i)$ to take a slice for cluster analysis (Figure 1 (right)) and use $F(s_k, ., a_i)$ to obtain a particular session described by a particular attribute for prediction (Figure 1 (right)).

Aggregation operations can also be defined on each dimension of the cube model. For example, sessions can be aggregated to clusters of different levels through clustering operations. Page values can be aggregated to categories using a classification scheme.

The Component dimension presents an important characteristic of the cube model. In this dimension, the visit order of the pages in a session is maintained. Because it uses component positions as variables instead of page ids as taken by others [19], it provides a regular and flexible matrix representation of page sequences which can be easily analyzed by existing data mining algorithms such as clustering and sequential association analysis.

The Attribute dimension allows the components of sessions to hold more information. For example, we can easily include time spent in each page in cluster analysis. From the these attributes, traditional Web log summary statistics such as the top pages by hits and spending time can be easily obtained.

3   The K-Modes Algorithm for Clustering Categorical Sessions

If we slice from the cube model only the Page variable in the Attribute dimension, we obtain a matrix which contains sessions described in categorical values. We can use the k-modes algorithm to cluster these categorical sessions. In this section we brief the k-modes algorithm. The experimental results of using k-modes to cluster categorical sessions extracted from two real Web log files will be given in Section 5. Furthermore, if we can also slice more variables such as Page ID and Time and form a session matrix of mixture data types. In this case, we can employ the k-prototypes algorithm [11] that is designed for mixture data types. However, in this paper, we focus on categorical sessions while the results of clustering sessions in mixture data types will be discussed elsewhere.

The k-modes algorithm is a variant of the k-means algorithm for clustering categorical data. It has made the following modifications to the k-means algorithm: (i) using a simple matching dissimilarity measure for categorical objects, (ii) replacing the means of clusters with the modes, and (iii) using a frequency based method to find the modes to minimize the following objective function

$$J_c(W, Z) = \sum_{l=1}^{k} \sum_{i=1}^{n} w_{li} d_c(Z_l, X_i) \tag{1}$$

subject to $\sum_{l=1}^{k} w_{li} = 1$, for $1 \leq i \leq n$ and $w_{li} \in \{0, 1\}$, for $1 \leq l \leq k$, where $k(\leq n)$ is a known number of clusters, $W = [w_{li}]$ is a k-by-n real matrix, $Z = [Z_1, Z_2, \ldots, Z_k] \in \mathcal{R}^{mk}$, and $d_c(Z_l, X_i)(\geq 0)$ is the simple matching dissimilarity measure between Z_l and X_i defined as

$$d_c(Z_l, X_i) \equiv \sum_{j=1}^{m} \delta(z_{lj}, x_{ij},) \quad \text{where } \delta(z_{lj}, x_{ij}) = \begin{cases} 0, & x_{ij} = z_{lj} \\ 1, & x_{ij} \neq z_{lj} \end{cases} \tag{2}$$

Here, Z represents a set of k modes for k clusters[1]. It is easy to verify that the function d_c defines a metric space on the set of categorical objects.

---

[1] The mode for a set of categorical objects $\{X_1, X_2, \ldots, X_n\}$ is defined as an object Z that minimizes $\sum_{i=1}^{n} d_c(X_i, Z)$ [11].

Function (1) can be optimized with the k-means type algorithm.

The k-means type algorithm
1. Choose an initial point $Z^{(1)} \in \mathcal{R}^{mk}$.
   Determine $W^{(1)}$ such that $J(W, Z^{(1)})$ is minimized. Set $t = 1$.
2. Determine $Z^{(t+1)}$ such that $J(W^{(t)}, Z^{(t+1)})$ is minimized.
   If $J(W^{(t)}, Z^{(t+1)}) = J(W^{(t)}, Z^{(t)})$, then stop; otherwise goto step 3.
3. Determine $W^{(t+1)}$ such that $J(W^{(t+1)}, Z^{(t+1)})$ is minimized.
   If $J(W^{(t+1)}, Z^{(t+1)}) = J(W^{(t)}, Z^{(t+1)})$, then stop;
   otherwise set $t = t + 1$ and goto Step 2.

The $W^{(t)}$ is updated using Function (2) in each iteration. After each iteration, $Z^{(t)}$ is updated using the method as shown in Theorem 1. This guarantees the convergence of the algorithm.

Theorem 1. *Let $\mathcal{X}$ be a set of categorical objects described by categorical attributes $A_1, A_2, ..., A_m$ and $DOM(A_j) = \{a_j^{(1)}, a_j^{(2)}, ..., a_j^{(n_j)}\}$, where n_j is the number of categories of attribute A_j for $1 \leq j \leq m$. Let the cluster centres Z_l be represented by $[z_{l,1}, z_{l,2}, \cdots, z_{l,m}]$ for $1 \leq l \leq k$. Then the quantity $\sum_{l=1}^{k} \sum_{i=1}^{n} w_{li} d_c(Z_l, X_i)$ is minimized iff $z_{l,j} = a_j^{(r)} \in DOM(A_j)$ where*

$$\left| \{ w_{li} | x_{i,j} = a_j^{(r)}, w_{lj} = 1 \} \right| \geq \left| \{ w_{li} | x_{i,j} = a_j^{(t)}, w_{li} = 1 \} \right|, \quad 1 \leq t \leq n_j, \quad (3)$$

for $1 \leq j \leq m$. Here $|\mathcal{X}|$ denotes the number of elements in the set $\mathcal{X}$.

A proof of the theorem is given in [12]. According to (3), the category of attribute A_j of the cluster mode Z_l is determined by the mode of categories of attribute A_j in the set of objects belonging to cluster l.

4   Clustering Methods Based on Transition Frequency and Probability Matrices

In this section, we use the transition frequency (or probability) matrix to cluster sessions. The rationale of using this technique is explained below.

Assume that a sequence of pages visited in a user session was generated by a "Markov process" of a finite number of states, (see [24]). The next page (state) to visit depends on the current page (state) only. Let n be the number of different pages. The user is said to be in the state $i(i = 1, 2, ..., n)$ if his current page is $P_i(i = 1, 2, ..., n)$. Let Q_{ij} be the probability of visiting page P_j, when the current page is P_i, i.e., the one-step transition probability. Q_{ij} and the transition frequency can be estimated by using the information of the sequence.

Suppose the transition probability matrix Q is known for a given user and X_m is the probability row vector of the user's state at his mth visit. We have

$$X_{m+1} = X_m Q \quad \text{and} \quad X_{m+1} = X_0 Q^m. \quad (4)$$

The distribution of the transition frequency of the pages in the sequence (assuming the length of the sequence is much longer than the number of states n)

Table 1. Distances between sequences based on transition frequency.

$$||N^{(1)}(A_1) - N^{(1)}(A_2)||_F = \sqrt{2} = 1.414$$
$$||N^{(1)}(A_1) - N^{(1)}(A_3)||_F = \sqrt{8} = 2.828$$
$$||N^{(1)}(A_2) - N^{(1)}(A_3)||_F = \sqrt{10} = 3.162$$

should be consistent with the steady state probability distribution X in theory. This provides a method for verifying our assumptions. This Markovian approach can be illustrated by the following examples.

Consider the two sequences with three ($n = 3$) possible pages to visit:

$$A_1 = \underbrace{P_1 P_2 P_3}_{I} \underbrace{P_2 P_2 P_3}_{II} \underbrace{P_3 P_2 P_3}_{III} \underbrace{P_1 P_2 P_3}_{IV} \quad A_2 = \underbrace{P_2 P_2 P_3}_{II} \underbrace{P_1 P_2 P_3}_{I} \underbrace{P_1 P_2 P_3}_{IV} \underbrace{P_3 P_2 P_3}_{III}.$$

The sequence A_2 is obtained by interchanging the subsequences I and II and also the subsequences III and IV in the sequence A_1. Let $N^{(1)}(A_k)$ be the 3×3 one-step transition frequency matrix with the ijth entry $[N^{(1)}(A_k)]_{ij}$ being the number of transitions from page P_i to page P_j in the sequence A_k. Therefore we have

$$N^{(1)}(A_1) = \begin{pmatrix} 0 & 2 & 0 \\ 0 & 1 & 4 \\ 1 & 2 & 1 \end{pmatrix} \quad \text{and} \quad N^{(1)}(A_2) = \begin{pmatrix} 0 & 2 & 0 \\ 0 & 1 & 4 \\ 2 & 1 & 1 \end{pmatrix}.$$

One possible way to compare (distance) these two sequences is to consider the Frobenius norm of the difference of their transition frequency matrices, i.e. $||N^{(1)}(A_1) - N^{(1)}(A_2)||_F$, where $||B||_F = \sqrt{\sum_{i=1}^{n} \sum_{j=1}^{n} [B_{ij}]^2}$. Clearly this method works for two sequences of similar length. If we have a much shorter sequence $A_3 = P_1 P_2 P_3 P_2 P_2 P_3$ which is the first half of the sequence A_1 then we have

$$N^{(1)}(A_3) = \begin{pmatrix} 0 & 1 & 0 \\ 0 & 1 & 2 \\ 0 & 1 & 0 \end{pmatrix}.$$

Table 1 shows the distances among the sequences. We note that although A_3 is part of A_1, $||N^{(1)}(A_1) - N^{(1)}(A_3)||_F$ is quite large. For two sequences of very different length, one may consider the one-step transition probability matrix instead of the transition frequency matrix. The one-step transition probability matrix can be obtained from the transition frequency matrix by dividing the entries of each row by its corresponding row sum. Denote the transition probability matrix of $N^{(1)}(A_k)$ by $Q^{(1)}(A_k)$, we have

$$Q^{(1)}(A_1) = \begin{pmatrix} 0 & 1 & 0 \\ 0 & \frac{1}{5} & \frac{4}{5} \\ \frac{1}{4} & \frac{1}{2} & \frac{1}{4} \end{pmatrix}, \quad Q^{(1)}(A_2) = \begin{pmatrix} 0 & 1 & 0 \\ 0 & \frac{1}{5} & \frac{4}{5} \\ \frac{1}{2} & \frac{1}{4} & \frac{1}{4} \end{pmatrix} \quad \text{and} \quad Q^{(1)}(A_3) = \begin{pmatrix} 0 & 1 & 0 \\ 0 & \frac{1}{3} & \frac{2}{3} \\ 0 & 1 & 0 \end{pmatrix}.$$

The new distances under the one-step transition probability matrix approach are given in Table 2. In the next section, we apply the transition frequency and probability matrix to cluster the real data sets.

Table 2. Distances between sequences based on transition probability.

$$||Q^{(1)}(A_1) - Q^{(1)}(A_2)||_F = \sqrt{\frac{1}{8}} = 0.354$$
$$||Q^{(1)}(A_1) - Q^{(1)}(A_3)||_F = \sqrt{\frac{1478}{3600}} = 0.632$$
$$||Q^{(1)}(A_2) - Q^{(1)}(A_3)||_F = \sqrt{\frac{3278}{3600}} = 0.954$$

Table 3. Distribution of sessions in the NASA Web log data.

Data set	NASA6-9	NASA10-15	NASA16-20
Session length	between 6 and 9	between 10 and 15	between 16 and 20
Number of sessions	13475	6492	4510

Table 4. Distribution of sessions in the EPA Web log data.

Data set	EPA6-9	EPA10-15	EPA16-20
Session length	between 6 and 9	between 10 and 15	between 16 and 20
Number of sessions	364	314	433

5 Experiments

Experiments were conducted on two real Web log files taken from the Internet. We first implemented a data preprocessing program to extract sessions from the log files and convert them into the cube model. We then extracted sessions with only Page ID values and used the k-modes algorithm to cluster these sessions. We used the transition probability matrix to analyze the validity of some identified clusters. Some of our analysis results are presented in this section.

5.1 Web Log Files and Preprocessing

We downloaded two Web log files from the Internet. The first data set was a Web log file from the NASA Kennedy Space Center WWW server in Florida. The log contained 1569898 transactions generated in the period of August 4-31, 1995. The second data set was a Web log file from the EPA WWW server located at Research Triangle Park, NC. This log contained 47748 transactions generated in 24 hours from 23:53:25 EDT, August 29, to 23:53:07, August 30, 1995.

In preprocessing, we removed all the invalid requests and the requests for images. We used Host id to identify visitors and a 30 minutes time threshold to identify sessions. 120406 sessions were identified from the NASA log file and 2682 sessions were identified from the EPA log file. To simplify the cluster analysis, we filtered out the sessions with less than 6 pages and more than 20 pages. From the rest sessions of the two log files, we generated six data sets with session lengths between 6 and 9, between 10 and 15, and between 16 and 20. The distributions of sessions from the log files are shown in Tables 3 and 4.

5.2 The k-Modes Cluster Analysis

The k-modes algorithm is a variant of the popular k-means algorithm with a capability of clustering categorical data. To use the algorithm to cluster a data set, the first task is to specify a k, the number of clusters to create. However, k is generally unknown for real data. A heuristic approach is often based on the assumption that a few clusters (say $k \leq 10$) exist in the data set. Although this approach works in many cases in practice, it has problems in clustering categorical session data. By exploring the session data from the two Web log files, we have observed that a cluster with a large number of similar sessions rarely exist. This is because in a complex Web site with variety of pages, and many paths and links, one should not expect that in a given time period, a large number of visitors follow only a few paths. If this was true, it would mean that the structure and content of the Web site had a serious problem because only a few pages and paths were interested by the visitors. In fact, most Web site designers expect that the majority of their pages, if not every one, are visited and paths followed (equally) frequently. In reality, some paths were followed more frequently than others in certain time period. Therefore, the session data should contain a fairly large number of small clusters.

Having the above observations, we tested to specify k as 5%, 10% and 15% of the total sessions in a data set. Even though we analyzed all six data sets, we only present the results of NASA6-9 here. The corresponding clusters for this data set are 674, 1010 and 1348, respectively. Although k was big in these specifications, k-modes can still process large data sets efficiently (the running time took a few seconds), which makes it a good candidate for this kind of mining tasks.

After generating the clusters, we need to identify which clusters are likely to present interesting session patterns. Because the large number of clusters, individual investigation of every cluster became difficult. We selected the average distance of objects to the cluster center, i.e., the mode of the cluster, as a measure for potential interesting clusters because the average distance implies the compactness of a cluster which is one of the important factors in cluster validation [13]. The distance was calculated using Equation (3) in Section 3. We expect that interesting patterns exist in compact clusters which have small average distances. Figure 2 shows the distributions of the number of clusters against the average distance of objects to cluster centers. From these figures, we can see that more clusters were created, more clusters with smaller average distances.

Next, we looked at the size of clusters, i.e., the number of sessions in a cluster. As we mentioned before, the chance of obtaining a large and compact cluster is very small. However, a reasonable size of clusters can represent the significance of interesting cluster patterns. In doing so, we plotted all clusters against their average distance and number of objects in each cluster. Figures 3 and 4 show the plots for the six data sets listed in tables 1 and 2. From these plots, we were able to identify the clusters with potential interesting patterns, given two thresholds of minimum size and maximum average distance. Tables 5 and 6 show potential interesting clusters identified from two data sets using this approach. For example, 34 clusters satisfy the conditions of (Average-Distance ≤ 2) and (Number-of-Sessions > 10). These clusters are located in the upper left part of Figure 3(a). Because the average distances of these clusters are small,

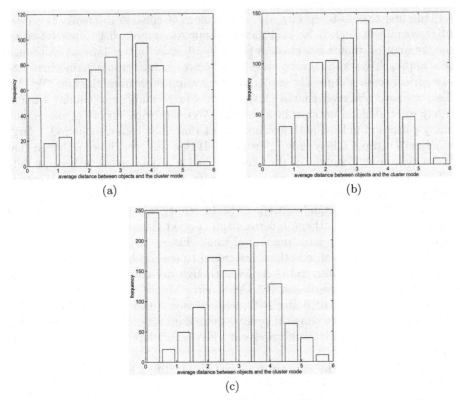

Fig. 2. Distribution of average distances within clusters (a) when there are 674 clusters, (b) when there are 1010 clusters, and (c) when there are 1348 clusters for the data set NASA6-9.

all of them present a clear pattern of Web site paths. Table 7 shows the pattern of the cluster that is marked as ⊗ in Figure 3(a). The mode of this cluster is {59,47,60,45,76,1,0,0,0}.

These strong patterned clusters only cover 2.52% of the total clusters generated from the data set. To identify more potential clusters, we can ease the threshold of the average distance. For example, in the area of (2 < Average-Distance ≤ 4), 186 clusters were identified from the data set NASA6-9. One of the interesting clusters with strong patterns is listed in Table 5. However, this was a grey area where not every cluster had a strong pattern. To select potential interesting clusters from the grey area, we used another condition that limited the clusters in which at least 50% of sessions had distances to the cluster center smaller than 2. Under this condition, 77 clusters were identified. Easing this condition could further identify more potential clusters from the grey area, for instance, see the last row in Table 5.

When the sessions became long, less potential interesting clusters could be identified. This was because the diversity of the sessions increased and similarity

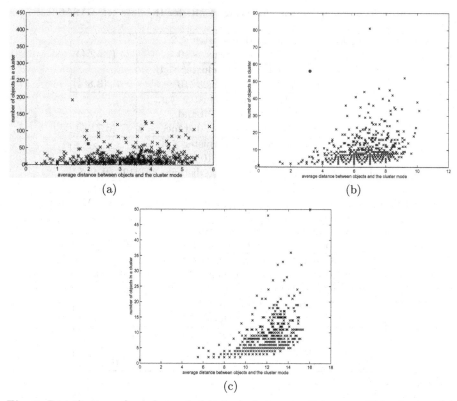

Fig. 3. Distribution of numbers of objects and average distances within clusters (a) when there are 1348 clusters for the data set NASA6-9, (b) when there are 974 clusters for the data set NASA10-15, and (c) when there are 677 clusters for the data set NASA16-20.

decreased. This trend can be observed from Figures 3(b) and 3(c) as well as Table 6. However, interesting clusters with strong patterns could still be found. The cluster $\otimes$ in Figure 3(b) was clearly singled out from other clusters. Its pattern is shown in Table 7. The mode of this cluster is {59, 45, 47, 60, 76, 59, 45, 47, 60, 76, 0, 0, 0, 0, 0 }. We see that this mode constructs from two repeated pattern {59, 45, 47, 60, 76}. This patterns refers to { 7367 /images/ ; 12128 /icons/menu.xbm ; 12047 /icons/blank.xbm ; 10300 /icons/image.xbm ; 4782 /icons/unknown.xbm }. These visitors might be interested in finding some images from the NASA Kennedy Space Center WWW sever. Moreover, from the table, one can see a clear similarity among these sessions. Another interesting observation was that if there were not enough sessions in the data set, interesting clusters may not only show up in the short sessions. One can see this phenomenon in Figure 4. This was still caused by the diversity of long sessions. This exercise may tell us that a large number of sessions may be a precondition to mine interesting session patterns. If so, the efficiency of the clustering algorithm would become crucial in session data mining.

Table 5. Summary of the clustering results for the data set NASA6-9.

average distance within cluster ≤ 2 and the number of sessions > 10	34 (2.52%)
$2 <$ average distance within cluster ≤ 4 and the number of sessions > 10	186 (13.8%)
$2 <$ average distance within cluster ≤ 4, the number of sessions > 10 and at least 50% of these sessions have distance ≤ 2	77 (5.71%)
$2 <$ average distance within cluster ≤ 4, the number of sessions > 10 and at least 50% of these sessions have distance ≤ 3	127 (9.42%)

Table 6. Summary of the clustering results for the data set NASA10-15.

average distance within cluster ≤ 2 and the number of sessions > 10	0 (0.00%)
$2 <$ average distance within cluster ≤ 6 and the number of sessions > 10	29 (2.98%)
$2 <$ average distance within cluster ≤ 6, the number of sessions > 10 and at least 50% of these sessions have distance ≤ 2	3 (0.31%)
$2 <$ average distance within cluster ≤ 4, the number of sessions > 10 and at least 50% of these sessions have distance ≤ 3	7 (0.72%)

5.3   Cluster Analysis Using Transition Frequency Matrices

In Section 4, we have proposed to use transition frequency matrix to cluster sessions because of the order of variables. For the cluster listed in Table 7, we computed the Frobenius norm of the differences between the objects in Table 7 and their mode. The results are listed in Figure 5. The Frobenius norm of the differences between the objects and their mode are between 0 and 3. The average difference is about 1.8. It is obvious that the cluster is valid.

In the data set NASA10-15, we found that there is a cluster containing the following session:

$$s = \{1, 59, 45, 47, 60, 76, 59, 47, 45, 60, 76, 1, 0, 0, 0\}.$$

This cluster contains 45 sessions. Their patterns are quite different and therefore the average difference within this cluster is about 8.2444. It is clear that this cluster is not valid.

However, the highlighted session looks quite similar to the mode of the cluster:

$$m = \{59, 45, 47, 60, 76, 59, 45, 47, 60, 76, 0, 0, 0, 0, 0\}$$

listed in Table 7 (right). We note that their categorical distance measure $d_c(s, m)$ is equal to 11. Because of the large distance measure, we put the session s into a

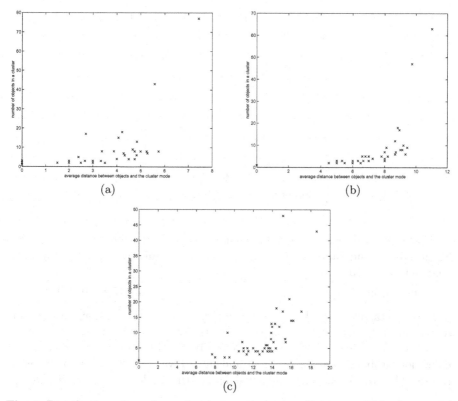

Fig. 4. Distribution of numbers of objects and average distances within clusters (a) when there are 55 clusters for the data set EPA6-9, (b) when there are 47 clusters for the data set EPA10-15, and (c) when there are 65 clusters for the data set EPA16-20.

different cluster. Because of the order of variables in the session and the mode, we can consider the transition frequency matrix to measure the distance between s and m. According to the discussion in Section 4, the transition frequency matrices of the sessions s and m are given by

	1	45	47	59	60	76
1	0	0	0	1	0	0
45	0	0	1	0	1	0
47	0	1	0	0	1	0
59	0	1	1	0	0	0
60	0	0	0	0	0	2
76	1	0	0	1	0	0

	1	45	47	59	60	76
1	0	0	0	0	0	0
45	0	0	1	0	1	0
47	0	1	0	0	1	0
59	0	1	1	0	0	0
60	0	0	0	0	0	2
76	0	0	0	1	0	0

respectively. The Frobenius norm of the difference of these two transition frequency matrices is $\sqrt{2}$ which is less than 1.8. It is obvious that the session s should be in this cluster listed in Table 7 (right).

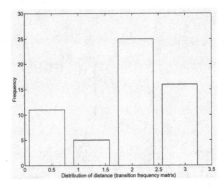

Fig. 5. Distribution of distances within clusters listed in Table 6.

Using the transition probability matrix, we can analyze the clusters of different lengths and validate clustering results more effectively. For instance, we pick a cluster mode

$$m' = \{59, 45, 47, 60, 76, 59, 45, 47, 60, 76, 1, 76, 59, 45, 47, 60, 0, 0, 0, 0\}$$

from the data set NASA16-20. Because the length of the sessions in this data set is longer than 15, the clustering results for the data set NASA16-20 are not mixed with those in the data set NASA10-15. However, we can analyze the transition probability matrices of m and m', so we can validate two clustering results. The transition probability matrices of the mode m' and m are given by

$$
\begin{array}{c|cccccc}
 & 1 & 45 & 47 & 59 & 60 & 76 \\
\hline
1 & 0 & 0 & 0 & 0 & 0 & 1 \\
45 & 0 & 0 & 1 & 0 & 0 & 0 \\
47 & 0 & 0 & 0 & 0 & 1 & 0 \\
59 & 0 & 1 & 0 & 0 & 0 & 0 \\
60 & 0 & 0 & 0 & 0 & 0 & 1 \\
76 & \frac{1}{3} & 0 & 0 & \frac{2}{3} & 0 & 0 \\
\end{array}
\qquad
\begin{array}{c|cccccc}
 & 1 & 45 & 47 & 59 & 60 & 76 \\
\hline
1 & 0 & 0 & 0 & 0 & 0 & 0 \\
45 & 0 & 0 & 0.5 & 0 & 0.5 & 0 \\
47 & 0 & 0.5 & 0 & 0 & 0.5 & 0 \\
59 & 0 & 0.5 & 0.5 & 0 & 0 & 0 \\
60 & 0 & 0 & 0 & 0 & 0 & 1 \\
76 & 0 & 0 & 0 & 1 & 0 & 0 \\
\end{array}
$$

respectively. The Frobenius norm of the difference of these two transition probability matrices is 1.64 which is not large. We can interpret that both clusters should contain some common interesting patterns.

Next we present the clustering results for the data set EPA16-20 using the transition matrix approach. We tested to specify the number of clusters $k = 30, 35, 40, 45, 50, 55, 65, 70, 75, 80, 85, 90$. After generating the clusters, we need to identify which clusters are likely to present interesting session patterns. We plotted in Figure 6 all clusters against their average distance of objects to the cluster center (the mean transition frequency matrix of the cluster) and the number of objects in each cluster. The cluster $\otimes$ in Figure 6 was analyzed. We find that there is a clear similarity among these sessions in the cluster. Figure 7 (left) shows the mean transition probability matrix of this cluster. There are 107 pages involved in this cluster. We find that the transition probability matrix is

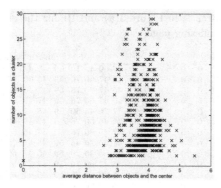

Fig. 6. Distribution of numbers of objects and average distances within clusters for the data set EPA16-20.

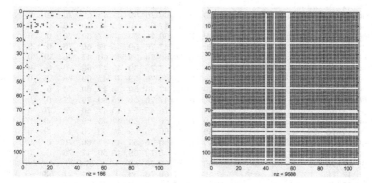

Fig. 7. Left: The mean transition probability matrix and Right: The mean transition probability matrix after 4 steps.

very sparse and there are only 186 nonzero entries. For the transition probability matrix of this cluster, we find that a set of pages

$$\mathcal{C} = \{22, 37, 54, 70, 71, 77, 83, 84, 86, 87, 96, 104, 106\}$$

is closed, i.e., no page outside this set $\mathcal{C}$ can be reached from any page in $\mathcal{C}$. If in this transition probability matrix all rows and all columns corresponding to pages outside this closed set $\mathcal{C}$ are deleted, there remains transition probability matrix Q for which the corresponding Markov chain is irreducible (i.e., there exists no closed set other than the set of all pages or every page can be reached from every other pages). The higher-order transition probability matrix is shown as in Figure 7 (right). We see that the matrix is dense and all the entries are nonzero except the probabilities related to the closed set $\mathcal{C}$. Using the transition probability matrix Q, a stationary (or invariant) probability distribution of pages can be computed. We show these probability distribution in Figure 8. We find that the probabilities of visiting the other 94 pages (not the pages in $\mathcal{C}$) in the cluster are about the same.

Table 7. Left: the cluster ⊗ in Figure 3(a) and Right: the cluster ⊗ in Figure 3(b), where 0 represents the missing page.

Object Attributes (Left)

59	47	60	45	76	1	0	0	0
59	47	60	45	76	1	0	0	0
59	47	60	45	76	1	0	0	0
59	47	60	45	76	1	0	0	0
59	47	60	45	76	1	0	0	0
59	47	60	45	76	1	0	0	0
59	47	60	45	76	1	0	0	0
59	47	60	45	76	1	0	0	0
59	47	60	45	76	1	0	0	0
59	47	60	45	76	59	0	0	0
59	47	60	45	76	59	0	0	0
59	47	60	45	76	59	0	0	0
59	47	60	45	76	23	0	0	0
59	47	60	45	76	59	0	0	0
59	47	60	45	76	59	0	0	0
59	47	60	45	76	1	161	0	0
59	47	60	45	76	1	25	0	0
59	47	60	45	76	1	79	0	0
59	47	60	45	76	13	0	0	0
59	47	60	45	76	23	0	0	0
59	47	60	76	45	1	0	0	0
59	47	60	76	45	1	0	0	0
59	47	60	76	45	1	0	0	0
59	47	60	45	76	1	86	179	0
59	47	60	76	45	1	0	0	0
269	47	60	45	266	1	0	0	0
59	47	60	45	76	28	1	0	0
59	47	60	45	76	3	131	0	0
59	45	60	47	76	1	0	0	0
59	45	60	47	76	1	0	0	0
59	45	60	47	76	1	0	0	0
59	45	60	47	76	1	0	0	0
59	45	60	47	76	1	0	0	0
59	47	60	45	1	76	0	0	0
59	47	60	45	59	76	0	0	0
59	47	60	45	59	76	0	0	0
59	47	76	45	60	161	0	0	0
59	47	76	45	60	45	0	0	0
59	47	76	45	60	59	0	0	0
59	60	47	45	76	59	0	0	0
59	60	47	45	76	59	0	0	0
59	60	76	45	47	1	0	0	0
59	60	76	45	47	1	0	0	0
59	60	76	45	47	1	0	0	0
59	76	60	45	47	99	0	0	0
59	47	60	45	76	28	25	213	0
59	47	60	45	76	28	6	19	0
59	47	60	45	76	3	17	232	0
59	47	60	45	76	3	6	843	0
59	47	60	45	76	59	47	45	0
59	47	60	45	76	99	46	101	0
269	47	60	45	46	48	0	0	0
275	47	60	45	46	30	0	0	0
59	45	60	47	76	1	206	0	0
59	45	60	47	76	1	48	0	0
59	45	60	47	76	1	59	0	0
59	47	60	45	59	60	47	45	0
60	76	47	45	59	1	0	0	0
59	60	47	45	76	99	46	0	0
59	47	60	45	76	99	46	101	46

Object Attributes (Right)

59	47	60	45	76	59	45	47	60	76	1	0	0	0	0
59	45	47	60	76	59	45	60	47	76	0	0	0	0	0
59	45	47	60	76	59	47	45	60	76	0	0	0	0	0
59	45	47	60	76	59	47	45	60	76	0	0	0	0	0
59	47	76	45	60	59	45	47	60	76	0	0	0	0	0
59	47	45	60	76	59	47	45	60	76	0	0	0	0	0
59	47	45	60	76	59	45	47	60	76	0	0	0	0	0
59	47	60	76	45	59	45	47	76	60	0	0	0	0	0
59	47	60	45	76	59	45	47	60	76	0	0	0	0	0
59	45	47	60	76	59	47	23	92	74	30	33	224	0	0
59	45	47	60	76	59	45	47	60	76	59	0	0	0	0
59	45	47	60	76	59	45	47	60	76	45	60	79	157	79
59	45	47	60	76	59	1	17	23	86	0	0	0	0	0
59	45	47	76	60	59	45	47	60	76	0	0	0	0	0
59	45	47	60	76	59	45	47	60	76	770	59	45	47	60
59	47	45	60	76	59	47	45	60	76	36	0	0	0	0
59	45	47	60	76	59	47	45	60	76	59	47	45	60	76
59	76	45	47	60	59	45	47	60	76	0	0	0	0	0
59	45	47	60	76	59	45	47	60	76	0	0	0	0	0
59	45	60	47	76	59	45	47	60	76	0	0	0	0	0
45	47	59	60	76	59	45	60	47	76	59	0	0	0	0
59	45	60	47	76	59	45	47	60	76	0	0	0	0	0
59	45	47	60	76	59	45	47	60	76	59	0	0	0	0
59	45	60	47	76	59	45	47	60	76	0	0	0	0	0
59	45	60	47	76	59	45	60	76	47	0	0	0	0	0
59	47	60	76	45	59	45	47	60	76	770	0	0	0	0
59	47	45	60	76	59	47	45	60	76	59	47	45	60	76
59	45	47	60	76	59	47	60	76	45	59	0	0	0	0
59	45	47	60	76	59	45	47	60	76	0	0	0	0	0
59	60	47	45	76	59	45	60	47	76	0	0	0	0	0
59	45	47	60	76	59	1	3	374	294	46	345	80	0	0
59	45	47	60	76	59	1	9	11	21	53	49	142	0	0
59	45	47	60	76	59	45	47	60	76	1	0	0	0	0
59	45	47	60	76	59	45	47	60	76	1	25	0	0	0
266	45	47	1	48	266	45	47	1	266	269	46	60	0	0
59	45	47	60	76	59	45	47	60	76	63	17	0	0	0
59	45	47	60	76	59	45	47	60	76	60	0	0	0	0
59	45	47	60	76	59	45	47	60	76	0	0	0	0	0
59	45	47	60	76	59	45	47	60	76	0	0	0	0	0
59	45	47	60	76	59	45	47	60	76	0	0	0	0	0
59	45	47	60	76	59	45	47	60	76	0	0	0	0	0
59	45	47	60	76	59	45	47	60	76	0	0	0	0	0
59	47	45	60	76	59	45	47	60	76	0	0	0	0	0
59	47	45	60	76	59	45	47	60	76	0	0	0	0	0
59	47	45	60	76	59	45	47	60	76	0	0	0	0	0
59	60	45	76	47	59	45	47	60	76	59	0	0	0	0
59	47	45	60	76	59	45	47	60	76	0	0	0	0	0
59	45	47	60	76	59	47	60	45	76	99	46	0	0	0
59	47	45	60	76	59	47	45	60	76	0	0	0	0	0
59	45	47	60	76	59	45	47	60	76	0	0	0	0	0
59	47	45	60	76	59	47	45	60	76	0	0	0	0	0
59	60	45	76	1	59	45	47	60	76	1	50	0	0	0
59	45	47	76	59	60	59	47	60	76	45	0	0	0	0
59	45	47	60	76	59	45	47	60	76	9	0	0	0	0

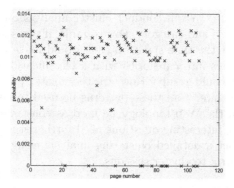

Fig. 8. Stationary probability distribution for each page.

6 Conclusions

In this paper, we have presented the cube model to represent Web access sessions. This model is different from other cube approaches [16] [27] in that it explicitly identifies the Web access sessions, maintains the order of session's components (or Web pages) and uses multiple attributes to describe the Web pages visited in sessions. The three dimensional cube structure simplifies the representation of sequential session data and allows different data analyses to be easily conducted, such as summary statistical analysis, clustering and sequential association analysis.

We have experimented the use of the k-modes algorithm to cluster categorical sessions extracted from two Web log files. Our preliminary cluster analysis has resulted in the following interesting observations:

1. Clusters with strong path patterns usually do not contain a large number of sessions due to the complexity of the Web structures and diversity of visitor's interests.
2. To effectively mine interesting path patterns using clustering techniques, the number of sessions in the data set should be sufficiently large. This requires that the clustering algorithm have to be efficient.
3. Because it is required to create a fair large number of clusters in each run of the clustering algorithm over a given data set, effective cluster evaluation methods are needed to identify potential interesting clusters with strong path patterns.

We have tested using the average distance of sessions to the cluster center and the size of clusters as two criteria to select potential interesting clusters from the set of clusters generated by the k-modes algorithm. Our results have shown that those criteria were effective. We were able to identify clusters with strong path patterns. Furthermore, we have proposed and tested the transition frequency (or probability) matrix approach to cluster sessions. Our initial results have shown that this approach is promising in cluster analysis of sequential data but more studies are needed.

In our future work we will conduct cluster analysis on sessions with more attributes such as time and category. For example, if two sessions have a similar set of pages, whether the time spent on each would make them different. If we consolidate Web pages into categories with a classification scheme, what kind of cluster patterns would result? How are the cluster patterns related to the topology of the Web site? Can these patterns be used to improve the Web site structure? How can the Web topology be used as constraints in the clustering algorithm? All these interesting questions need further studies to answer. Moreover, we will conduct a detailed clustering analysis using transition frequency (or probability) matrix to cluster sessions.

Acknowledgement

Research by Michael Ng is supported by by RGC Grant No. 7132/00P and HKU CRCG Grant Nos 10203501, 10203907 and 10203408. The authors would like to thank anonymous referees for their comments.

References

1. Banerjee, A. and Ghosh, J. (2001) Clickstream Clustering Using Weighted Longest Common Subsequences. Workshop on Web Mining, First SIAM International Conference on Data Mining, Chicago.
2. Berendt, B., Mobasher, B., Spiliopoulou, M. and Wiltshire, J. (2001) Measuring the Accuracy of Sessionizers for Web Usage Analysis. Workshop on Web Mining, First SIAM International Conference on Data Mining, Chicago.
3. Berkhin, P., Becher, J. and Randall, D. (2001) Interactive Path Analysis of Web Site Traffic. In Proceedings of the Seventh ACM SIGKDD International Conference on Knowledge Discovery and Data Mining, pp. 414-419, San Francisco, CA.
4. Cadez, I., Gaffney, S. and Smyth, P. (2000) A General Probabilistic Framework for Clustering Individuals and Objects. In Proceedings of the Sixth ACM SIGKDD International Conference on Knowledge Discovery and Data Mining, pp. 140-149, New York, NY.
5. Chen, M. S., Park, J. S. and Yu, P. S. (1998) Efficient data mining for path traversal patterns. IEEE Transactions on Knowledge and Data Engineering, Vol. 10, No. 2, pp. 209-221.
6. Cooley, R., Mobasher, B. and Srivastava, J. (1999) Data preparation for mining World Wide Web browsing patterns. Knowledge and Information Systems, Vol. 1, No. 1, pp. 1-27.
7. Etzioni, O. (1996) The World Wide Web: quagmire or gold mine? Communications of the ACM, Vol. 39, No. 11, pp. 65-68.
8. Fu, Y., Sandhu, K. and Shih, M. (1999) Clustering of Web users based on access patterns. WEBKDD99, Springer.
9. Han, J., Cai, Y. and Cercone, N. (1992) Knowledge discovery in databases: an attribute-oriented approach. In Proceeds of VLDB92, Canada.
10. Heer, J. and Chi, Ed H. (2001) Identification of Web user traffic composition using multi-modal clustering and information scent. Proceedings of the workshop on Web mining, SIAM conference on data mining, pp. 51-58.

11. Huang, Z. (1998) Extensions to the k-means algorithm for clustering large data sets with categorical values. Data Mining and Knowledge Discovery, Vol. 2, No. 3, pp. 283-304.

12. Huang, Z. and Ng, M. K. (1999) A Fuzzy k-modes algorithm for clustering categorical data. IEEE Transactions on Fuzzy Systems, Vol. 7, No. 4, pp.446-452.

13. Jain, A. K. and Dubes, R. C. (1988) Algorithms for Clustering Data. Prentice Hall.

14. Joshi, A. and Joshi K. (1999) On mining Web access logs. Technical Report, CSEE Department, UMBC, MD, USA. http://www.cs.ubmc.edu/ joshi/web-mine/publications.html

15. Kamdar, T. and Joshi, A. (2000) On creating adaptive Web servers using weblog mining. Technical report CS-TR-00-05, CSEE, UMBC, USA. http://www.cs.ubmc.edu/ joshi/web-mine/publications.html

16. Kimball, R. and Merx, R. (2000) The Data Webhouse Toolkit – Building Web-Enabled Data Warehouse. Wiley Computer Publishing.

17. Kosala, R. and Blockeel, H. (2000) Web mining research: a survey. SIDKDD Explorations, Vol. 2, No. 1, pp. 1-15.

18. Magid, J., Matthews, R. D. and Jones, P. (1995) The Web Server Book – Tools & Techniques for Building Your Own Internet Information Site. Ventana Press.

19. Nasraoui, O., Frigui, H., Joshi, A. and Krishnapuram, R. (1999) Mining Web access logs using relational competitive fuzzy clustering. Proceedings of the Eight International Fuzzy Systems Association Congress -IFSA99.

20. Ng, R. and Han, J. (1994) Efficient and effective clustering methods for spatial data mining. In Proceedings of VLDB, 1994.

21. Shahabi, C., Faisal, A., Kashani, F. B. and Faruque, J. (2000) INSITE: A tool for real-time knowledge discovery from users Web navigation. Proceedings of VLDB2000, Cairo, Egypt.

22. Spiliopoulou, M. and Faulstich, L. C. (1998) WUM: A Web utilization miner. In EDBT Workshop WebDB98, Valencia, Spain, Springer.

23. Srivastava, J., Cooley, R., Deshpande, M. and Tan, P. (2000) Web usage mining: discovery and applications of usage patterns from Web data. SIGKDD Explorations, Vol. 1, No. 2, pp. 12-23.

24. Taha, T. (1991) Operations Research, 3rd Edition, Collier Macmillan, N.Y., U.S.A.

25. www.w3.org/Daemon/User/Config/Logging.thml

26. W3C (1999) Web Characterization Terminology & Definitions Sheet. W3C Working Draft 24-May, 1999. http://www.w3.org/1999/05/WCA-terms/.

27. Zaiane, O. R., Xin, M. and Han, J. (1998) Discovering Web access patterns and trends by applying OLAP and data mining technology on Web logs. Proceedings of Advances in Digital Libraries Conference (ADL'98), Santa Barbara, CA, April 1998, pp.19-29.

28. Zhang, T. and Ramakrishnan, R. (1997) BIRCH: A new data clustering algorithm and its applications. Data Mining and Knowledge Discovery, Vol. 1, No. 2, pp. 141-182.

Exploiting Web Log Mining
for Web Cache Enhancement

Alexandros Nanopoulos, Dimitrios Katsaros, and Yannis Manolopoulos

Department of Informatics, Aristotle University
Thessaloniki 54006, Greece
{alex,dimitris,manolopo}@delab.csd.auth.gr

Abstract. Improving the performance of the Web is a crucial requirement, since its popularity resulted in a large increase in the user perceived latency. In this paper, we describe a Web caching scheme that capitalizes on prefetching. Prefetching refers to the mechanism of deducing forthcoming page accesses of a client, based on access log information. Web log mining methods are exploited to provide effective prediction of Web-user accesses. The proposed scheme achieves a coordination between the two techniques (i.e., caching and prefetching). The prefetched documents are accommodated in a dedicated part of the cache, to avoid the drawback of incorrect replacement of requested documents. The requirements of the Web are taken into account, compared to the existing schemes for buffer management in database and operating systems. Experimental results indicate the superiority of the proposed method compared to the previous ones, in terms of improvement in cache performance.

Keywords: Prediction, Web Log Mining, Web Caching, Prefetching, Association rules.

1 Introduction

The problem of modelling and predicting a user's accesses on a Web-site has attracted a lot of research interest. It has been used [20] to improve the Web performance through caching [2,12] and prefetching [34,22,35,29,39,40], recommend related pages [19,38], improve search engines [11] and personalize browsing in a Web site [39].

Nowadays, the improvement of Web performance is a very significant requirement. Since the Web's popularity resulted in heavy traffic in the Internet, the net effect of this growth was a significant increase in the user perceived latency. Potential sources of latency are the Web servers' heavy load, network congestion, low bandwidth, bandwidth underutilization and propagation delay.

The caching of Web documents at various points in the network (client, proxy, server [2,12]) has been developed to reduce latency. Caching capitalizes on the temporal locality. Effective client and proxy caches reduce the client perceived latency, the server load and the number of travelling packets, thus increase the available bandwidth. Several caching policies have been proposed during the

R. Kohavi et al. (Eds.): WEBKDD 2001, LNAI 2356, pp. 68–87, 2002.
© Springer-Verlag Berlin Heidelberg 2002

previous years, especially for proxy servers [2,12]. Nevertheless, there exist cases where the benefits reaped due to caching can be limited [28], e.g., when Web resources tend to change very frequently, resources cannot be cached (dynamically generated Web documents), they contain cookies (this issue matters only caching proxies), or when request streams do not exhibit high temporal locality. The negative effects of the first problem can be partially alleviated by employing some, costly though, cache consistency mechanism. The second problem could be addressed by enhancing the cache with some of the respective server's query processing capabilities, so as to perform the necessary processing on data [13]. The third and fourth problems seem that cannot be tackled by caching at all.

Web prefetching is the process of deducing client's future requests for Web documents and getting that documents into the cache, in the background, before an explicit request is made for them. Prefetching capitalizes on the spatial locality present in request streams, that is, correlated references for different documents, and exploits the client's idle time, i.e., the time between successive requests. The main advantages of employing prefetching is that it prevents bandwidth underutilization and hides part of the latency. However, an over-aggressive scheme may cause excessive network traffic. Additionally, without a carefully designed prefetching scheme, several transferred documents may not be used by the client at all, thus they waste bandwidth. We focus on predictive prefetching [18], since other categories, like informed prefetching [36], seem inapplicable due to the client-server paradigm of computing the Web implements and its hypertextual nature (i.e., a user in most cases does not know in advance his/her future document requests).

Web prefetching acts complementary to caching, it can significantly improve cache performance and reduce the user-perceived latency [34]. However, there are cases where a non-effective prefetching algorithm, presenting the aforementioned drawbacks, can impact cache performance [25]. For instance, if the accuracy of the prefetching algorithm is low, then several useful documents in the cache may be evicted by prefetched documents that are not going to be referenced. Therefore, there exists a requirement for both

- accurate prefetching algorithms, and
- caching schemes that will coordinate with prefetching.

In this paper we describe a scheme for: (a) Effective prefetching, which exploits Web log mining, it is not affected by factors like noise (i.e., random document requests) and high-order dependencies among document requests and thus, can significantly improve cache performance. (b) Coordination of caching and prefetching, by storing in the cache the prefetched documents separately from those which have been explicitly requested. The latter approach is based on the one of [25], which dedicates part of the cache to separately accommodate prefetched documents. However the scheme in [25] was designed for database disk buffer management. Therefore, it does not address the significantly different requirements encountered in the case of Web caching. Experimental results indicate that the proposed scheme outperforms existing ones in terms of improvement in cache performance.

The rest of the paper is organized as follows. Section 2 reviews related work. Section 3 describes the prefetching algorithm, whereas in Section 4 the caching scheme is presented. Section 5 provides the experimental results and finally, Section 6 contains the conclusions.

2   Related Work

Research on predictive Web prefetching has involved the significant issue of log file processing and the determination of user transactions (sessions) from it [17,14]. However, the most important factor in Web prefetching is the prediction algorithm. For the purpose of prediction, most of the Web prefetching schemes rely on existing algorithms from the context of file systems. This approach neglects issues that arise in the case of Web, and stem from both the contents of Web documents in a site (which induce dependencies to their references) and the site's structure, i.e., the links among documents (which affect user's navigation).

The scheme described in [34] uses a prefetching algorithm proposed in the context of file systems. It constructs a data structure, called the *Dependency Graph* (*DG*), which maintains the pattern of access to different documents stored at the server. As described above, the choice of forthcoming pages can depend, in general, on a number of previously visited pages [20]. *DG* considers only first order dependencies. Thus, if several previous visits have to be considered (i.e., high-order dependencies), *DG* does not take them into account. The work described in [9] uses essentially the approach of dependency graph, but it makes predictions by computing the transitive closure of this graph. This method was tested and did not show significantly better results compared to the simple dependency graph.

The scheme described in [35,22] also uses a prefetching algorithm from the context of file systems [18]. It is based on the notion of an m-order *Prediction-by-Partial-Match* (*PPM*) predictor. An m-order PPM predictor maintains Markov predictors of order j, for all $1 \leq j \leq m$. This scheme is also called *All-m^{th}-Order Markov model* [20]. For a complete description of the scheme see [18,35,22]. During a session, although a user may navigate according to a pattern, s/he may also randomly navigate to pages that do not belong to any pattern (and can be modelled as noise). Hence, a session can both contain documents belonging to patterns and others that do not, and these documents are interleaved. However, PPM considers only subsequences of consecutive documents inside sessions, thus it is affected by the existence of noise[1]. Moreover, PPM uses a constant maximum value for the order. However, no method for the determination of this value is provided in [35,22]. A choice of a small maximum may have a similar disadvantage as in the case of *DG*, whereas a choice of a large maximum may lead to unnecessary computational cost, due to maintenance of a large number of rules.

---

[1] The use of thresholds for statistical significance, e.g., support values [3], does not address the intervening of random accesses within the patterns.

Recently, several algorithms have been proposed for mining patterns from Web logs [14,8,17,37,32]. The Web prefetching strategy proposed in [29] develops a specialized association rule mining algorithm to discover the prefetched documents. It discovers dependencies between pairs of documents (association rules with one item in the head and one item in the body). However, the scheme in [29], similar to DG, considers only first order dependencies and, similar to PPM, it considers only consecutive subsequences within sessions. Therefore, it presents the deficiencies of both approaches, as they are described above. The improvement of the efficiency of PPM is examined in [20], based on three pruning criteria. These criteria are used in a post-processing step, on the set of discovered rules, and can be applied to any prefetching scheme, thus they are orthogonal issues to the subject examined in this paper. Finally, two variations of the PPM prefetcher are described in [39,40]. The first one is a subset of the PPM whereas in the second one the selection of prefetching rules to activate is determined by "weights" assigned on them.

Web caching has received significant attention and several new algorithms were proposed, ranging from extensions to traditional policies (like LRU, LFU, etc.) to *key-based policies* [1] and more sophisticated *function-based* policies, such as GD-$Size$ [12], PSS [2]. Moreover, significant results regarding optimal on-line and off-line caching policies for the Web were presented in [24].

Regarding the coordination of caching and prefetching, Jeon and Noh [25] presented the W^2R algorithm. Motivated by the $2Q$ algorithm [26], W^2R divides the available cache space into two partitions, called *Weighing Room* and *Waiting Room*. Prefetched documents initially enter the Waiting Room, before becoming "normal" cached documents in the Weighing Room. However, W^2R was designed for database disk buffer management. It uses the *One Block Lookahead* (*OBL*) prefetching algorithm, which prefetches only one page each time. Moreover, all pages are of the same size. Web caching presents significantly different requirements, since different prefetching algorithms than the simple *OBL* are used (several documents are allowed to be prefetched each time and thus we must prioritize among them), and documents of different sizes have to be accommodated in the cache.

3   Prefetching Algorithm

As described in Section 2, none of the existing prefetching algorithms addresses at the same time both the factors of noise and high-order dependencies, that may exist within transactions (i.e., user sessions). In this section we describe an algorithm that addresses all the aforementioned factors. It uses the history of user accesses, maintained in the Web server's log file, to derive rules. Since the rules, which are appropriate for the prefetching, should be based on the navigation behaviour of the client[2] (expressed as the process of visiting links) we describe a pruning criterion that is based on the site structure. This pruning

---

[2] These rules are not appropriate for the identification of other types of usage patterns (see also Section 3.2).

can significantly reduce the computational overhead. On the other hand, it is not adequate for other types of applications, such as recommendation systems.

3.1   Prefetching Based on Rules

Association rules [3] consider several orders of dependencies among items, and the maximum order is derived from the data, i.e., it does not have to be an arbitrary constant value as in PPM. For the support counting procedure, a transaction T supports sequences that do not necessarily contain consecutive documents in T. Thus, this procedure can effectively bypass random document visits (i.e., noise) that may exist within transactions. However, the ordering of documents inside a transaction is important for the purpose of prefetching but it is ignored by association rules mining algorithms [3].

Therefore, a different definition of the candidate generation procedure and the *containment* criterion, for the support counting procedure, are required. At the k-th phase, the candidates are derived from the self-join $L_{k-1} \bowtie L_{k-1}$ [3]. To take the ordering of documents into account, the joining is done as follows. Let two access sequences be $S_1 = \langle p_1, \ldots, p_{k-1} \rangle$ and $S_2 = \langle q_1, \ldots, q_{k-1} \rangle$, both in L_{k-1}. If $p_1 = q_1, \ldots, p_{k-2} = q_{k-2}$, then they are combined to form two candidate sequences, which are: $c_1 = \langle p_1, \ldots, p_{k-2}, p_{k-1}, q_{k-1} \rangle$ and $c_2 = \langle p_1, \ldots, p_{k-2}, q_{k-1}, p_{k-1} \rangle$ (i.e., c_1 and c_2 are not considered as identical, as in [3]). For instance, sequences $\langle A, B, C \rangle$ and $\langle A, B, D \rangle$ are joined to produce $\langle A, B, C, D \rangle$ and $\langle A, B, D, C \rangle$. The *containment* criterion is defined as follows:

Definition 1 *If $T = \langle p_1, \ldots, p_n \rangle$ is a transaction, an access sequence $S = \langle p'_1, \ldots, p'_m \rangle$ is contained by T iff:*

- *there exist integers $1 \leq i_1 < \ldots < i_m \leq n$ such that $p'_k = p_{i_k}$, for all k, where $1 \leq k \leq m$.* □

A sequence, S, of documents contained in a transaction, T, with respect to Definition 1 is called a *subsequence* of T and the containment is denoted as $S \preceq T$.

Based on a set of rules discovered with the approach described above (along with the corresponding confidence values), prefetching is performed with the procedure depicted in Figure 1. In this algorithm, R denotes the current request stream formed by the user and M is the maximum number of prefetched documents (user parameter). Also, we use an upper limit, called *maxSize*, in the size of each prefetched document, since it is not desired to transfer very large documents to avoid waste of bandwidth in case of an incorrect prediction.

Evidently, the fact that the ordering of documents within transactions is preserved during the discovery of rules, impacts the complexity of candidate generation and support counting procedures. For this reason, we present in the following section a pruning criterion according to the site structure, that reduces the overhead.

Finally, it has to be mentioned that, differently from [3], the approach in [14] takes into account the ordering within access sequences. However, similar to

Procedure Prefetch(**Array** R, **int** M, **float** maxSize)
//h, b are sequences of document ids
begin
1. $prefetchSeq = \emptyset$
2. **foreach** rule $h \Rightarrow b$ such that $h \preceq R$
3.   **foreach** $d \in b$ such that d.size $<$ maxSize
4. $prefetchSeq = prefetchSeq \bigcup d$
5.   **endfor**
6. **endfor**
7. sort documents in $prefetchSeq$ in decreasing order of the confidence
    of the corresponding rule and keep the first M ones.
8. **return** $prefetchSeq$
end

Fig. 1. Prefetching algorithm.

PPM algorithm [35], it considers only subsequences with consecutive accesses within transactions. The work described in [4,30] examines the problem of mining sequential patterns which consider ordering, as well. However, the algorithms in [4,30] do not take into account that user navigation is performed in a site which has a structure determined by its linkage. Therefore, they do not address the problem of dramatic increase in the number of candidates. Moreover, the work in [30] seeks patterns in a single large sequence of events using a sliding window over this sequence and thus it does not consider user sessions as is our case. The scheme proposed in [23] uses a scheme that is called mining of path fragments. It is based on discovering patterns containing regular expressions with the $*$ wild-card between accesses of a sequence. Although the use of wild-cards presents differences in a semantic level (it may distinguishes the sequences that explicitly do not contain consecutive accesses), for the purpose of Web-prefetching, the use of Definition 1 assures the addressing of noise within transactions without the need for wild-cards. Moreover, in the case of path fragments, the candidate-trie [3] should store, additionally to ordinary candidates, the ones containing wild-cards. Consequently, a significant space and time overhead (since the wild-cards may appear in a number of combinations that grows rapidly with the size of candidates). However, [23] does not present any method for the support counting phase to address the above issues, and no experimental results are provided to examine its performance.

3.2 Pruning Criterion

For the purposes of prefetching, we focus on the paradigm of *traversal patterns* [14], which will be used for prediction, not on *usage patterns*. Based on the assumption that navigation is performed by following the hypertext links, the traversal patterns have to reflect the way navigation is performed guided by the site structure. Thus, we can apply pruning according to the structure of the site. This is based on the approach in [32,33]. The work in [23] also mentions the possibility of taking into account the links between site documents but, differently from [32,33], it focuses only on the second phase of the algorithm. The pruning based on the structure of the site results in a significant reduction in the number of candidates. Without pruning, due to the consideration of ordering a large number of candidates would have been generated.

For instance, let three documents A, B and C for which the following linkage exists: $A \rightarrow B$ and $A \rightarrow C$. Assume a user-traversal $T = \langle A, B, A, C \rangle$, and that the second request for A is due to the 'back-button', which will be probably serviced by the client-cache. Thus, the server encounters the traversal $T' = \langle A, B, C \rangle$. T' may constitute a useful pattern for the description of site-usage, since it indicates a correlation between the usage of documents A, B and C. However, the objective of prefetching is to predict the forthcoming visits within the user's traversal. Based on the assumption of navigation through the hypertext links, let the corresponding traversal patterns will $\langle A, B \rangle$ and $\langle A, C \rangle$. Having visited document A, the prefetching of B and C can take place based on these patterns. Thus, along the lines of [14][3], we do not focus on usage patterns that indicate general correlation between document usage, as the correlation between the usage of A, B and C. In contrast, we are interested in the identifying the traversal patterns, like $\langle A, B \rangle$ and $\langle A, C \rangle$, in order to predict the forthcoming visits that will be done at A by following the corresponding links. Evidently, from the aspect of traversal patterns, the correlation between B and C exists only due to their linkage with A, differently than the usage pattern of T' that is based on the paradigm of association rules among basket data [3]. Thus, at A only the two aforementioned patterns will be required in order to prefetch B and C.

According to the proposed pruning criterion, an access sequence, and thus a candidate, has to correspond to a path in this graph. The candidate generation procedure and the apriori-pruning criterion [3] have to be modified appropriately, and the corresponding procedure is depicted in Figure 2 (for the generation of candidates at phase $k + 1$). L_k denotes the set of large sequences (i.e., frequent) at phase k and G the graph, which corresponds to the site structure.

Example 1 Let a site with the structure depicted in Figure 3a and a collection of transactions depicted in Figure 3b. Candidate $\langle B, E, C \rangle$ corresponds to a path in the graph. On the other hand, candidate $\langle B, C, E \rangle$ does not, thus it can be pruned. The reason of pruning the later candidate is that no user transaction will contain $\langle B, C, E \rangle$, since there are no links to produce such an access sequence that will contain (according to Definition 1) this candidate and increase its support. For instance, candidate $\langle B, E, C \rangle$ will have support equal to two (contained in first and fourth transaction), whereas candidate $\langle B, C, E \rangle$ is not supported by any transaction. The same applies for candidates of length equal to two. Among candidates $\langle A, B \rangle$ and $\langle B, A \rangle$, the former can be pruned. Evidently, $\langle B, A \rangle$ is contained in three transactions, whereas $\langle A, B \rangle$ in none. Containment is tested

---

[3] Please also notice that similar to [14] we consider maximum forward traversals, which discard backward movements.

Procedure GenCandidates(L_k, G)
begin
1. $candidate\text{-}trie = \emptyset$
2. **foreach** $L = \langle \ell_1, \dots, \ell_k \rangle$, $L \in L_k$
3. $N^+(\ell_k) = \{v | \exists \text{ arc } \ell_k \to v \in G\}$
4.   **foreach** $v \in N^+(\ell_k)$
5.   /* apply the modified apriori-pruning */
6.   **if** $v \notin L$ **and** $L' = \langle \ell_2, \dots, \ell_k, v \rangle \in L_k$
7. $C = \langle \ell_1, \dots, \ell_k, v \rangle$
8.   **if** $(\forall S \preceq C \Rightarrow S \in L_k, \text{ where } |S| = k \text{ and } S \neq L')$
9.   insert C in the $candidate\text{-}trie$
10.   **endif**
11.   **endif**
12.   **endfor**
13. **endfor**
14. **return** $candidate\text{-}trie$
end

Fig. 2. Candidate generation algorithm.

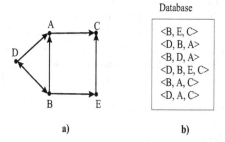

Fig. 3. *a:* An example of site structure. *b:* A database of access sequences.

with respect to Definition 1. Thus, candidate $\langle B, A \rangle$ is contained in the third transaction, i.e., $\langle B, D, A \rangle$, although documents B and A are not consecutive in the transaction.   ⊣

With the procedure described in Figure 2, candidate generation is performed by extending candidates according to their outgoing edges in the graph. Consequently, the ordering is preserved and only paths in the graph are considered. Additionally, the apriori-pruning criterion of [3] is modified, since, for a given candidate, only its subsequences have to be tested and not any arbitrary subset of documents (step 8), as in [3]. Candidates are stored in a trie structure. Each transaction that is read from the database is decomposed into the paths it contains and each one of them is examined against the trie, thus updating the support of the corresponding candidates. Procedure GenCandidates aims at improving the efficiency of candidate generation. For this reason, step 3 determines the set N^+ of nodes that are linked by the last element of the candidate.

This way, in step 6 the trie is probed only by the corresponding L' sequences. In contrast, if N^+ is not determined (because one may consider that the arc $l_k \to v$ will be examined during the probing of the trie for the L' sequences that are members of L_k), the formation of L' sequences would first require the consideration of any possible element to be appended at the end of L and then the probing of the trie for all possible L' (since no combination can be discarded without having first to look-up in the trie). Evidently, the cost for the separate determination of N^+ pays off in the former case due to the much smaller number of trie look-ups.

Although several heuristics have been proposed for the reduction of the number of candidates for the Apriori algorithm, they involve basket data. The pruning with respect to the site structure is required for the particular problem, due to the large increase in the number of candidates that is the result of preserving ordering. The pruning criterion does not have the objective of addressing the noise that may occur within user transactions. This is addressed by the containment criterion given in Definition 1. In contrast, it opts for a reduction in the number of candidates, since the latter significantly affects the overall execution time required for the candidate generation and support counting procedures [3]. Hence their efficiency is improved by this pruning criterion. The effectiveness of pruning is verified by experimental results in Section 5. More details can be found in [32,33], whereas a further examination of the generalization of the described prefetching algorithm compared to existing ones, can be found in [31]. Finally, it worths mentioning that the proposed pruning criterion is used in combination with the support-pruning criterion. However, the modified-apriori criterion is applied (steps 6–9 of the GenCandidates procedure), which examines only the subpaths of a sequence and not any arbitrary subsequence.

4 Caching Policy

Based on the idea in [25], we describe a caching scheme *PECache*, which divides the cache into a *Weighing Room* (with *LRU* as the replacement policy) and a *Waiting Room* (using the *FIFO* policy). This partitioning of the cache space aims at isolating the effect of document mispredictions or the effect of aggressive prefetching. It achieves this by dedicating part of the cache space to exploit the temporal locality of the request stream (on-demand requests) and the rest of the cache space is dedicated to exploit the spatial locality (prefetch requests). The relative size of the partitions should reflect the "amount" and type of the locality of the request stream.

The caching procedure *PECache* (Prefetch Enhanced Cache), given in Figure 4, has as input the requested document (d) and the current request stream of the user (R).

The *PECache* procedure uses the prefetching algorithm (step 3) that may return several documents, whereas W^{2}R uses the *OBL* prefetching algorithm, which always prefetches one document. Therefore, differently from the W^{2}R algorithm, the set of prefetched documents are inserted in the *FIFO* structure

---

Procedure *PECache*(**Array** *R*, **Document** *d*)
begin
1. $R = R \bigcup d$
2.   **if not** (*d* in Weighing Room **or** *d* in Waiting Room)
2.   put *d* at head of the *LRU* list of the Weighing Room
3.   *prefetchSeq* = Prefetch(*R*, *M*, *maxSize*)
4.   **foreach** *p* in *prefetchSeq*
5.   append *p* at the end of Waiting Room queue
6.   **endfor**
7.   **else if** *d* in Waiting Room
8.   remove *d* from Waiting Room
9.   put *d* at head of the *LRU* list of the Weighing Room
10. **else if** *d* in Weighing Room
11.   put *d* at head of the *LRU* list of the Weighing Room
12. **endif**
end

Fig. 4. The caching procedure.

of the Waiting Room according to the corresponding confidence values (this is performed at step 5 of the *PECache* procedure). It is assumed that at steps 4–5 of the *PECache* procedure the prefetched documents enter the *FIFO* structure in the exact order they were requested, i.e., the caching mechanism resolves the issues of identifying the documents that belong to the same *prefetchSeq* and sorting them according to the requested order. Moreover, differently from W^{2}R, the *PECache* procedure does not perform prefetching in the case the requested document *d*, is contained in the Waiting Room (step 7). Otherwise, this would result in excessive network traffic and bandwidth consumption (notice that W^{2}R is designed for buffer management in a DBMS).

It should be mentioned that the replacement policy used in the Weighing Room can be selected independently. For instance, the *2Q* algorithm can be used, as described in [25] or some other policy more appropriate for the Web, as in [6]. For simplicity and based on [25], we assume in the following that the *LRU* policy is used. *FIFO* seems the most appropriate policy for the Waiting Room, since it gives

4.1   The Cooperative Caching and Prefetching Mechanism

The caching scheme is applied at the client-side. Prefetching can be either client or server initiated. However, Web servers are in better position in making predictions about future references, since they log a significant[4] part of requests by all Internet clients for the resources they own. Moreover, the pruning criterion described in Section 3.2 can be easily applied in this case, since the site structure is available to the Web server.

---

[4] They only miss the requests satisfied by browser or proxy caches.

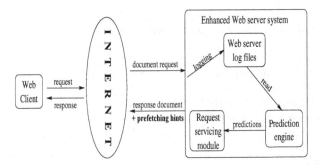

Fig. 5. Proposed architecture of a prediction-enabled Web server.

The prediction engine can be implemented by exchange of messages between the server and clients, having the server piggybacking information about the predicted resources onto regular response messages, avoiding establishment of any new TCP connections [16]. Such a mechanism has been implemented in [16,21] and seems the most appropriate, since it requires relatively few enhancements to the current request-response protocol and no changes to HTTP 1.1 protocol.

Therefore, we assume that there is a system implementing a server-based predictive prefetcher, which applies the Prefetch procedure of Section 3.1. The server piggybacks its predictions to the clients only as hints (in this case, the *prefetchSeq* in Prefetch procedure comprises these hints, i.e., *ID* numbers of the documents "to be prefetched"). The client receives these hints and discards all those which correspond to documents found in its cache. Then, in a second stage, prefetching takes place requesting the predicted documents. The caching of the requested documents (on-demand and prefetched) is performed with the *PECache* procedure.

Figure 5 illustrates how such an enhanced Web server could cooperate with a prefetch engine to disseminate hints every time a client requests a document of the server.

5   Performance Results

This section presents the experimental results. The cache performance is examined against the factors of high-order dependencies, amount of noise and cache size. The performance measure is the hit ratio achieved by the cache. We examine the performance of the proposed caching policy, presented in Section 4, in coordination with the prefetching algorithm, presented in Section 3. The proposed method is denoted as *PEC* (Prefetch Enhanced Cache). For the purposes of comparison, we also examine the cache performance in the case of using the *DG*, *PPM*, and LBOT[5] prefetching algorithms in coordination with the caching policy of Section 4, so as to clearly identify the advantages of the proposed prefetching algorithm.

---

[5] In the experiments, the algorithm proposed in [29] will be referenced as LBOT.

Additionally, we examine the performance of the plain *LRU* caching policy (i.e., when no prefetching is performed and only one cache partition is used), so as to identify the advantages of the proposed caching policy. In the case where one cache partition is used, its size is equal to the sum of sizes of the two partitions (i.e., Weighing and Waiting rooms) of the proposed caching policy. We separately examine the impact of the proposed pruning criterion (Section 3.2) on the reduction of the number of candidates during the generation of prefetching rules for the *PEC* method.

5.1   Generation of Synthetic Workloads

In order to evaluate the performance of the algorithms over a large range of data characteristics, we generated synthetic workloads. Each workload is a set of transactions. Our data generator implements a model for the documents and the linkage of the Web site, as well as a model for user transactions.

We choose so that all site documents have links to other documents, that is, they correspond to HTML documents. The fanout of each node, that is, the number of its outgoing links to other nodes of the same site, is a random variable uniformly distributed in the interval $[1..NFanout]$, where *NFanout* is a parameter for the model. The target nodes of these links are uniformly selected from the site nodes. If some nodes have no incoming links after the termination of the procedure, then they are linked to the node with the greatest fanout. With respect to document sizes, following the model proposed in [7], we set the maximum size equal to 133KB and assign sizes drawn from a lognormal distribution[6] with mean value equal to 9.357KB and variance equal to 1.318KB.

In simulating user transactions, we generated a pool of P paths ("pattern paths", in the sequel). Each path is a sequence of linked in the site and pairwise distinct Web server documents, and will be used as "seeds" for generating the transactions. Each of these paths is comprised of 4 nodes (documents), simulating the minimum length of a transaction (clearly, for very small transactions i.e., of length two or three, the effect of prefetching is not significant, since user's interaction in this case does not allow for effective prediction of forthcoming requests). The paths are created in groups. Each group comprises a tree. The paths are actually the full length paths found in these trees. The fanout of the internal tree nodes is controlled by the parameter bf. Varying this parameter we are able to control the 'interweaving' of the paths. The nodes of these trees are selected using either the 80-20 fractal law or from the nodes that were used in the trees created so far. The percentage of these nodes is controlled by the parameter *order*, which determines the percentage of node dependencies that are non-first order dependencies. For example, 60% order means that 60% of the dependencies are non-first order dependencies. Thus, varying this parameter, we can control the order of the dependencies between the nodes in the path. The use of the fractal law results in some nodes to be selected more frequently than

---

[6] Without loss of generality, we assume that HTML files are small files. Thus, according to [7] their sizes follow a lognormal distribution.

Table 1. The parameters for the generator.

N	Number of site nodes
$NFanout$	Max num of nodes' links
T	Number of transactions
P	Number of pattern paths
bf	Branching factor of the trees
$order$	Order of the dependencies
$noiseMean$	Mean value of the noise
$noiseVar$	Variance of the noise
$corProb$	Prob. excluding a node

others. This fact reflects the different popularity of the site documents, creating the so-called "hot" documents.

In order to create the transactions, we first associate a weight with each path in the pool. This weight corresponds to the probability that this path will be picked as the "seed" for a transaction. This weight is picked from an exponential distribution with unit mean, and is then normalized so that the sum of the weights for all the paths equals 1. A transaction is created as follows. First, we pick a path, say $\langle A, B, C, x \rangle$, tossing a P-sided weighted coin, where the weight for a side is the probability of picking the associated path. Then, starting from node A we try to find a path leading to node B or with probability $corProb$ to node C, whose length is determined by a random variable, following a lognormal distribution, whose mean and variance are parameters of the model. This procedure is repeated for every node of the initial path except from those that, with probability $corProb$, were excluded from the path. The mean and variance of the lognormal distribution determine the "noise" inserted in each transaction. Low values for mean and variance leave the transaction practically unchanged with respect to its pattern path, whereas larger values increase its length with respect to the pattern path. Table 1 summarizes the parameters of the generator.

5.2   Results on Cache Performance

In order to carry out the experiments we generated a number of workloads. Each workload consisted of T=100,000 transactions. From these, 30,000 transactions were used to train the algorithms and the rest to evaluate their performance. The number of documents of the site for all workloads was fixed to N=1000 and the maximum fanout to $NFanout$=100, so as to simulate a dense site. The branching factor was set to bf=4 to simulate relatively low correlation between the paths. The number of paths of the pool for all workloads was fixed to P=1000. With several experiments, not shown in this report, it was found that varying the values of the parameters P and N does not affect the relative performance of the considered algorithms. For all the experiments presented here, the *order* of the *PPM* algorithm was set equal to 5, so as to capture both low and higher order dependencies. The default value for the mean transaction size was set to 10. Throughout the experiments, the range of cache size was selected to be in the range of few hundred KB, to simulate the fact that not all, but only a small part of the Web client's cache is "dedicated" to the documents of a particular Web server.

The confidence threshold was tuned separately for each algorithm, so as to derive the same network traffic overhead, which is defined to be the number of documents that the client gets when prefetching is used divided by the one when prefetching is not used. The examined network traffic was 150%. This is also the value of the average network byte overhead. This means that for each byte the user requested, the prefetchers fetched another 0.5 byte that the user never requested. This is a relatively conservative approach considering that existing techniques and implementations incur a much larger overhead (250% overhead by [27], 412% by [15]).

First, we evaluated the impact of varying order on the hit ratio (Notice that the order of dependencies varies with the type of the site [10]). The mean noise value was set to 1.0. The total cache size was set to 150 KB and 50 KB of this total size were dedicated to the Waiting Room (this does not apply for the case of plain LRU). The results of this set of experiments are reported in Figure 6a. As illustrated, PEC is not affected by increasing order. This is in accordance to what expected from the discussion in Section 3. PEC clearly outperforms all other methods, achieving the highest hit ratio in all cases. PPM, as expected, is not heavily affected by increasing order and presents the second best performance. Focusing on DG, the impact of order in this case is noticeable. The hit ratio when DG is used as the prefetching algorithm, is reduced significantly with increasing order. This verifies the discussion on DG given in Section 2. In the case of LBOT, the hit ratio is also reduced with increasing order, however the reduction is much smaller than that of DG. Nevertheless, DG outperforms LBOT for smaller order values, whereas they present comparable performance for larger ones. Finally, the plain LRU caching policy presents the worst performance, in all cases. This verifies the advantages of exploiting prefetching and using the cooperative caching mechanism presented in Section 4.

Next, we assessed the impact of noise on the hit ratio. The order value was set to 0.5. The results of this set of experiments are reported in Figure 6b. As shown, the performance of all methods reduces with increasing noise, since noise alters transactions and reduces the number of discovered patterns. However, PEC clearly is much less affected by increasing noise, and it achieves the highest hit ratio in all cases. This verifies the discussion in Section 3. In contrast, PPM is significantly affected by noise. As depicted, its performance downgrades with increasing noise, and although it outperforms DG and LBOT for low mean noise values, it performs much worse for larger ones. This is in accordance with what expected from the description of Section 2. As in the previous experiment, LRU presents the worst performance in all cases.

We measured the impact of cache size. We kept the Waiting Room size equal to 50 KB and varied the total cache size (which includes the size of the Waiting

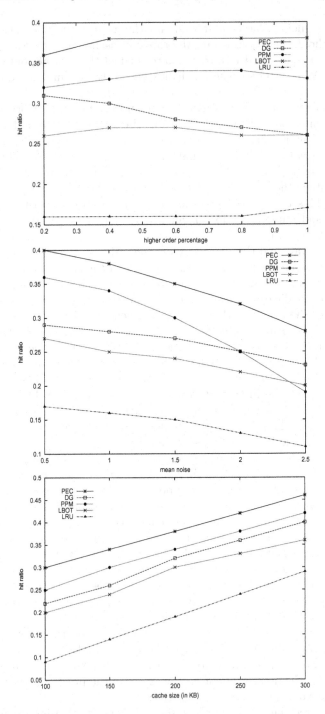

Fig. 6. Results on hit ratio w.r.t.: (a) order, (b) noise, and (c) cache size (from top to bottom, respectively).

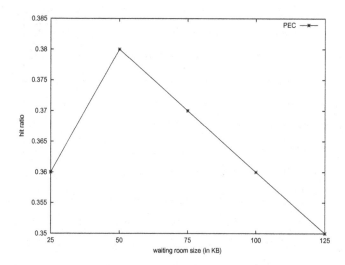

Fig. 7. Hit ratio w.r.t. Waiting Room size.

Room, besides the case of plain *LRU* caching policy). The mean noise value was set to 1.5 and the order was set to 0.5. Figure 6c illustrates the results for all methods. As depicted, the hit ratio increases linearly with increasing cache size. *PEC* presents the best performance in all cases, whereas *PPM* the second best. As in the previous cases, plain *LRU* presents the worst hit ratio among all methods.

To examine the impact of the size of the Waiting Room, we conducted a separate experiment. The total cache size was set to 200 KB and we varied the Waiting Room size. The results for the hit ratio of the *PEC* method are given in Figure 7 (We focus on *PEC* since this experiment concerns the tuning of the Waiting Room size and the performance of the remaining methods is analogous). For very small and large Waiting Room sizes, the hit ratio has lower values, compared to the case where it takes the maximum value (at the examined case, this value was 50 KB). This can be explained with the help of the notion of temporal and spatial locality [5]. When the size of the Waiting Room is very small, then only a relatively small percentage of the prefetched documents remain enough time in the cache, so as to get referenced and contribute to the hit ratio. Thus, the benefits of prefetching –even in the case of very accurate prefetching – are very limited. On the other hand, when the size of the Waiting Room is relatively large (compared to the total cache size), then the Waiting Room "steals" useful space from the Weighing Room and the cache is not capable of exploiting the temporal locality of the request stream. The tradeoff associated with the relative sizes of the Weighing and Waiting Rooms is obvious. For every request stream, depending on the "amount" of temporal and spatial locality (and of course, on the document sizes), there is an optimal value for the relative sizes of the two partitions. In our case, this value equals 50 KB.

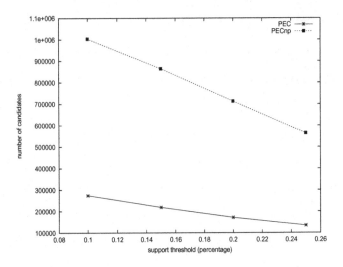

Fig. 8. Number of candidates w.r.t. support threshold.

5.3   Evaluation of Pruning Criterion

Finally, we examined the effectiveness of the proposed pruning criterion. We used a synthetic dataset with the same characteristics as the ones used in the experiments of Section 5.2. This experiment compares the PEC algorithm with a version that does not use pruning with respect to the site structure and is denoted as PEC_{np} (no pruning). It has to be noticed that the SP algorithm [4] generates candidates without taking into account the site structure. Moreover, SP also considers the ordering between items (for instance, in the second phase of SP, which is the bottleneck due to the very large number of candidates, let two large items A and B for which only the link $A \to B$ exists; however, SP generates both $\langle A, B \rangle$ and $\langle B, A \rangle$ as candidates whereas the latter can be pruned). Thus, for the same support threshold, the number of candidates produced by PEC_{np} corresponds to the one produced by SP.

Figure 8 illustrates the number of candidates for these methods with respect to the support threshold (given as a percentage). As it is depicted, PEC with pruning criterion significantly outperforms PEC_{np}, both for low and high support thresholds.

The number of candidates significantly impacts the performance of this type of algorithms. This is in accordance with related work on association rule mining [3]. Therefore, the efficiency of PEC is improved by the proposed pruning. Detailed experimental results on execution time for the case of pruning according to the graph structure can be found in [33].

6   Conclusions

We considered the problem of enhancing Web caching with the technique of predictive Web prefetching, that is, of deriving users' future requests for Web documents based on their previous requests. We also examined the problem of the coordination between Web caching and prefetching.

We proposed a new algorithm called *PEC*, which focuses both on attaining accurate prefetching and using cooperative caching so as to effectively accommodate the prefetched documents with the normal cached ones (i.e., the ones cached after an explicit user request). For the former factor, we described a prefetching algorithm, which exploits Web log mining techniques. To address the problem of large computational overhead for the rule generation phase, we described a pruning criterion that is based on the site structure. For the latter factor, based on the approach of [25], we presented an algorithm which uses a small part of the cache so as to separately store the prefetched documents. We addressed the new requirements due to the particularities of the Web, compared to the case of DBMS buffer management, as examined in [25].

Experimental results illustrated the superiority of *PEC*. In contrast to existing methods, *PEC* is not affected by factors like high-order dependencies among document references, or the existence of noise within user transactions. Also, experimental results showed the effectiveness of the pruning criterion.

Future work includes:

- The examination of other caching policies within the framework of *PEC*.
- The development of dynamic methods for the tuning of the Waiting Room size.

References

1. M. Abrams, C.R. Standridge, G. Abdulla, E.A. Fox, and S. Williams. Removal policies in network caches for World-Wide Web documents. In *Proceedings of the ACM Conference on Applications, Technologies, Architectures and Protocols for Computer Communication (ACM SIGCOMM'96)*, pages 293–305, 1996.
2. C. Aggarwal, J. Wolf, and P.S. Yu. Caching on the World Wide Web. *IEEE Transactions on Knowledge and Data Engineering*, 11(1):95–107, 1999.
3. R. Agrawal and R. Srikant. Fast algorithms for mining association rules. In *Proceedings of the 20th Conference on Very Large Data Bases (VLDB'94)*, pages 487–499, 1994.
4. R. Agrawal and R. Srikant. Mining sequential patterns. In *Proceedings of the IEEE Conference on Data Engineering (ICDE'95)*, pages 3–14, 1995.
5. V. Almeida, A. Bestavros, M. Crovella, and A. de Oliveira. Characterizing reference locality in the WWW. In *Proceedings of the IEEE Conference on Parallel and Distributed Information Systems (IEEE PDIS'96)*, pages 92–103, 1996.
6. M. Arlitt, L. Cherkasova, J. Dilley, R. Friedrich, and T. Jin. Evaluating content management techniques for Web proxy caches. *ACM SIGMETRICS Performance Evaluation Review*, 27(4):3–11, 2000.
7. P. Barford and M. Crovella. Generating representative Web workloads for network and server performance evaluation. In *Proceedings of the ACM Conference on Measurement and Modeling of Computer Systems, (ACM SIGMETRICS'98)*, pages 151–160, 1998.

8. B. Berendt and M. Spiliopoulou. Analysis of navigation behavior in Web sites integrating multiple information systems. *The VLDB Journal*, 9(1):56–75, 2000.

9. A. Bestavros. Speculative data dissemination and service to reduce server load, network traffic and service time. In *Proceedings of the IEEE Conference on Data Engineering (ICDE'96)*, pages 180–189, 1996.

10. J. Borges and M. Levene. Data mining of user navigation patterns. In *Proceedings of the Workshop on Web Usage Analysis and User Profiling (WEBKDD'99)*, pages 92–111, 1999.

11. S. Brin and L. Page. The anatomy of large-scale hypertextual Web search engine. In *Proceedings of the World Wide Web Conference (WWW'98)*, pages 107–117, 1998.

12. P. Cao and S. Irani. Cost-aware WWW proxy caching algorithms. In *Proceedings USENIX Symposium on Internet Technology and Systems (USITS'97)*, pages 193–206, 1997.

13. P. Cao, J. Zhang, and K. Beach. Active Cache: Caching dynamic contents on the Web. In *Proceedings of the IFIP Conference on Distributed Systems Platforms and Open Distributed Processing (Middleware'98)*, pages 373–388, 1998.

14. M.S. Chen, J.S. Park, and P.S. Yu. Efficient data mining for path traversal patterns. *IEEE Transactions on Knowledge and Data Engineering*, 10(2):209–221, 1998.

15. K. Chinen and S. Yamaguchi. An interactive prefetching proxy server for improvement of WWW latency. In *Proceedings of the INET Conference*, 1997.

16. E. Cohen, B. Krishnamurthy, and J. Rexford. Improving end-to-end performance of the Web using server volumes and proxy filters. In *Proceedings of the ACM Conference on Applications, Technologies, Architectures and Protocols for Computer Communication (ACM SIGCOMM'98)*, pages 241–253, 1998.

17. R. Cooley, B. Mobasher, and J. Srivastava. Data preparation for mining World Wide Web browsing patterns. *Knowledge and Information Systems*, 1(1):5–32, 1999.

18. K.M. Curewitz, P. Krishnan, and J.S. Vitter. Practical prefetching via data compression. In *Proceedings of the ACM Conference on Management of Data (ACM SIGMOD'93)*, pages 257–266, 1993.

19. J. Dean and M. Henzinger. Finding related pages in the World Wide Web. In *Proceedings of the World Wide Web Conference (WWW'99)*, pages 1467–1479, 1999.

20. M. Deshpande and G. Karypis. Selective Markov models for predicting Web page accesses. In *Proceedings of the SIAM Conference on Data Mining (SDM'01)*, 2001.

21. D. Duchamp. Prefetching hyperlinks. In *Proceedings of the USENIX Symposium on Internet Technologies and Systems (USITS'99)*, 1999.

22. L. Fan, P. Cao, W. Lin, and Q. Jacobson. Web prefetching between low-bandwidth clients and proxies: Potential and performance. In *Proceedings of the ACM Conference on Measurement and Modeling of Computer Systems (ACM SIGMETRICS'99)*, pages 178–187, 1999.

23. W. Gaul and L. Schmidt-Thieme. Mining Web navigation path fragments. In *Proceedings of the Workshop on Web Usage Analysis and User Profiling (WEBKDD'00)*, 2000.

24. S. Hosseini-Khayat. On optimal replacement of nonuniform cache objects. *IEEE Transactions on Computers*, 49(8):769–778, 2000.

25. H.S. Jeon and S.H. Noh. A database disk buffer management algorithm based on prefetching. In *Proceedings of the ACM Conference in Information and Knowledge Management (ACM CIKM'98)*, pages 167–174, 1998.

26. T. Johnson and D. Shasha. 2Q: A low overhead high performance buffer manage-
    ment replacement algorithm. In *Proceedings of the 20th Conference on Very Large
    Data Bases (VLDB'94)*, pages 439–450, 1994.
27. R. Klemm. WebCompanion: A friendly client-side Web prefetching agent. *IEEE
    Transactions on Knowledge and Data Engineering*, 11(4):577–594, 1999.
28. T. Kroeger, D.E. Long, and J. Mogul. Exploring the bounds of Web latency
    reduction from caching and prefetching. In *Proceedings of the USENIX Symposium
    on Internet Technologies and Systems (USITS'97)*, pages 13–22, 1997.
29. B. Lan, S. Bressan, B.S. Ooi, and Y. Tay. Making Web servers pushier. In *Proceed-
    ings of the Workshop on Web Usage Analysis and User Profiling (WEBKDD'99)*,
    1999.
30. H. Mannila, H. Toivonen, and A.I. Verkamo. Discovery of frequent episodes in
    event sequences. *Data Mining and Knowledge Discovery*, 1(3):259–289, 1997.
31. A. Nanopoulos, D. Katsaros, and Y. Manolopoulos. A data mining algorithm for
    generalized Web prefetching. *IEEE Transactions on Knowledge and Data Engi-
    neering*, 2002. to appear.
32. A. Nanopoulos and Y. Manolopoulos. Finding generalized path patterns for Web
    log data mining. In *Proceedings of the East-European Conference on Advances in
    Databases and Information Systems (ADBIS-DASFA'00)*, pages 215–228, 2000.
33. A. Nanopoulos and Y. Manolopoulos. Mining patterns from graph traversals. *Data
    and Knowledge Engineering (DKE)*, 37(3):243–266, 2001.
34. V. Padmanabhan and J. Mogul. Using predictive prefetching to improve World
    Wide Web latency. *ACM SIGCOMM Computer Communications Review*, 26(3),
    1996.
35. T. Palpanas and A. Mendelzon. Web prefetching using partial match prediction.
    In *Proceedings of the 4th Web Caching Workshop*, 1999.
36. H. Patterson, G. Gibson, E. Ginting, D. Stodolsky, and J. Zelenka. Informed
    prefetching and caching. In *Proceedings of the ACM Symposium on Operating
    Systems Principles (ACM SOSP'95)*, pages 79–95, 1995.
37. J. Pei, J. Han, B. Mortazavi-Asl, and H. Zhu. Mining access patterns efficiently
    from Web logs. In *Proceedings of the Pacific-Asia Conference on Knowledge Dis-
    covery and Data Mining (PAKDD'00)*, 2000.
38. P. Pirolli, H. Pitkow, and R. Rao. Silk from a sow's ear: Extracting usable struc-
    tures from the Web. In *Proceedings of the ACM Conference on Human Factors
    and Computing Systems (ACM CHI '96)*, pages 118–125, 1996.
39. J. Pitkow and P. Pirolli. Mining longest repeating subsequences to predict World
    Wide Web surfing. In *Proceedings of the USENIX Symposium on Internet Tech-
    nologies and Systems (USITS'99)*, 1999.
40. R. Sarukkai. Link prediction and path analysis using Markov chains. *Computer
    Networks*, 33(1–6):377–386, 2000.

LOGML: Log Markup Language
for Web Usage Mining

John R. Punin, Mukkai S. Krishnamoorthy, and Mohammed J. Zaki

Computer Science Department,
Rensselaer Polytechnic Institute, Troy NY 12180
{puninj,moorthy,zaki}@cs.rpi.edu

Abstract. Web Usage Mining refers to the discovery of interesting information from user navigational behavior as stored in web access logs. While extracting simple information from web logs is easy, mining complex structural information is very challenging. Data cleaning and preparation constitute a very significant effort before mining can even be applied. We propose two new XML applications, XGMML and LOGML to help us in this task. XGMML is a graph description language and LOGML is a web-log report description language. We generate a web graph in XGMML format for a web site using the web robot of the WWWPal system. We generate web-log reports in LOGML format for a web site from web log files and the web graph. We further illustrate the usefulness of LOGML in web usage mining; we show the simplicity with which mining algorithms (for extracting increasingly complex frequent patterns) can be specified and implemented efficiently using LOGML.

1 Introduction

Recently XML has gained wider acceptance in both commercial and research establishments. In this paper, we suggest two XML languages and a web data mining application which utilizes them to extract complex structural information. Extensible Graph Markup and Modeling Language (XGMML) is an XML 1.0 application based on Graph Modeling Language (GML; see *http://www.infosun.-fmi.uni-passau.de/Graphlet/GML/*) which is used for graph description. XGMML uses tags to describe nodes and edges of a graph. The purpose of XGMML is to make possible the exchange of graphs between different authoring and browsing tools for graphs. The conversion of graphs written in GML to XGMML is straight forward. Using Extensible Stylesheet Language (XSL) with XGMML allows the translation of graphs to different formats. In Section 2, we present details of XGMML.

Log Markup Language (LOGML) is an XML 1.0 application designed to describe log reports of web servers. Web data mining is one of the current hot topics in computer science. Mining data that has been collected from web server logfiles, is not only useful for studying customer choices, but also helps to better organize web pages. This is accomplished by knowing which web pages are most frequently accessed by the web surfers. In section 2, we explain how the structure

R. Kohavi et al. (Eds.): WEBKDD 2001, LNAI 2356, pp. 88–112, 2002.

of a web site can be represented as a web graph using XGMML. When mining the data from the log statistics, we use the web graph for annotating the log information. Further we produce summary reports, comprising of information such as client sites, types of browsers and the usage time statistics. We also gather the client activity in a web site as a subgraph of the web site graph. This subgraph can be used to get better understanding of general user activity in the web site. In LOGML, we create a new XML vocabulary to structurally express the contents of the logfile information. In section 3, we discuss LOGML in detail. Section 4 describes LOGML generator as an additional module for the WWWPal system [1].

Recently web data mining has been gaining a lot of attention because of its potential commercial benefits. For example, consider a web log database at a popular site, where an object is a web user and an attribute is a web page. The mined patterns could be the sets or sequences of most frequently accessed pages at that site. This kind of information can be used to restructure the web-site, or to dynamically insert relevant links in web pages based on user access patterns. Furthermore, click-stream mining can help E-commerce vendors to target potential online customers in a more effective way, at the same time enabling personalized service to the customers. Web mining is an umbrella term that refers to mainly two distinct tasks. One is web content mining [2], which deals with problems of automatic information filtering and categorization, intelligent search agents, and personalize web agents. Web usage mining [2] on the other hand relies on the structure of the site, and concerns itself with discovering interesting information from user navigational behavior as stored in web access logs. The focus of this paper is on web usage mining. While extracting simple information from web logs is easy, mining complex structural information is very challenging. Data cleaning and preparation constitute a very significant effort before mining can even be applied. The relevant data challenges include: elimination of irrelevant information such as image files and cgi scripts, user identification, user session formation, and incorporating temporal windows in the user modeling. After all this pre-processing, one is ready to mine the resulting database.

The proposed LOGML and XGMML languages have been designed to facilitate this web mining process in addition to storing additional summary information extracted from web logs. Using the LOGML generated documents the pre-processing steps of mining are considerably simplified. We also propose a new mining paradigm, called Frequent Structure Mining, to extract increasingly informative patterns from the LOGML database. Our approach and its application to real log databases are discussed further in Section 5. We provide an example to demonstrate the ease with which information about a web site can be generated using LOGML with style sheets (XSLT). Additional information about web characterization can also be extracted from the mined data.

The overall architecture of our system is shown in Figure 1. The two inputs to our web mining system are 1) web site to be analyzed, and 2) raw log files spanning many days, months, or extended periods of time. The web site is used to populate a XGMML web graph with the help of a web crawler. The

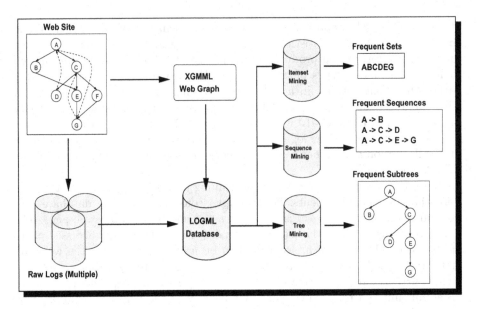

Fig. 1. Web Usage Mining Architecture

raw logs are processed by the LOGML generator and turned into a LOGML database. This processed database contains log information that can be used to mine various kinds of frequent pattern information such as itemsets, sequences and subtrees. The LOGML database and web graph information can also be used for web characterization, providing detailed statistics on top k pages, addresses, browsers, and so on.

It should be noted that association and sequence mining have also been applied to web usage mining in the past. Chen et al. [3] introduced the notion of a maximal forward chain of web pages and gave an algorithm to mine them. The WUM system [4] applies sequence mining to analyze the navigational behavior of users in a web site. WUM also supports an integrated environment for log preparation, querying and visualization. Cooley et al. [5] describe various data preparation schemes for facilitating web mining. Recent advances and more detailed survey on various aspects of web mining spanning content, structure and usage discovery can be found in [6,7]. Our work differs in that our system uses new XML based languages to streamline the whole web mining process and allows multiple kinds of mining and characterization tasks to be performed with relative ease.

2 XGMML: Extensible Graph Markup & Modeling Language

A graph, G= (V,E), is a set of nodes V and a set of edges E. Each edge is either an ordered (directed graph) or unordered (undirected) pair of nodes. Graphs can be described as data objects whose elements are nodes and edges (which are themselves data objects). XML is an ideal way to represent graphs. Structure of the World Wide Web is a typical example of a graph where the web pages are "nodes," and the hyperlinks are "edges." One of the best ways to describe a web site structure is using a graph structure and hence XGMML documents are a good choice for containing the structural information of a web site. XGMML was created for use within the WWWPal System [1] to visualize web sites as a graph. The web robot of W3C (webbot), a component of the WWWPal System, navigates through web sites and saves the graph information as an XGMML file. XGMML, as any other XML application, can be mixed with other markup languages to describe additional graph, node and/or edge information.

Structure of XGMML Documents: An XGMML document describes a graph structure. The root element is the `graph` element and it can contain `node`, `edge` and `att` elements. The `node` element describes a node of a graph and the `edge` element describes an edge of a graph. Additional information for graphs, nodes and edges can be attached using the `att` element. A `graph` element can be contained in an `att` element and this graph will be considered as subgraph of the main graph. The `graphics` element can be included in a `node` or `edge` element, and it describes the graphic representation either of a node or an edge. The following example is a graph with just one node.

```
<?xml version="1.0"?>
<!DOCTYPE graph PUBLIC "-//DTD graph description//EN"
          "http://www.cs.rpi.edu/~puninj/XGMML/xgmml.dtd">
<graph directed="1" id="2">
<node id="1" label="Node 1"/>
</graph>
```

XGMML well formed documents can be part of other XML documents using namespaces. The following example is a graph inside of an XHTML document:

```
<?xml version="1.0" encoding="UTF-8"?>
<html xmlns="http://www.w3.org/1999/xhtml"
      xmlns:xsi="http://www.w3.org/2000/10/XMLSchema-instance"
      xmlns:xgmml="http://www.cs.rpi.edu/XGMML"
      xsi:schemaLocation="http://www.w3.org/1999/Style/Transform
              http://www.w3.org/1999/Style/Transform/xslt.xsd
              http://www.w3.org/1999/xhtml
              http://www.w3.org/1999/xhtml/xhtml.xsd
              http://www.cs.rpi.edu/XGMML
              http://www.cs.rpi.edu/~puninj/XGMML/xgmml.xsd"
      xml:lang="en">
<head>
<title>Graph Information</title>
</head>
<body>
<!-- XHTML Document here -->
      <xgmml:graph directed="1" graphic="1" Layout="points">
```

```
        <xgmml:node id="1" label="1" weight="0">
          <xgmml:graphics type="circle" x="250" y="90" />
        </xgmml:node>
        <xgmml:node id="2" label="2" weight="0">
          <xgmml:graphics type="circle" x="190" y="150" />
        </xgmml:node>
        <xgmml:edge source="1" target="2" weight="0" />
      </xgmml:graph>
  <!-- XHTML Document here -->
  </body>
  </html>
```

Resource Description Framework (RDF) is one way to describe metadata about resources. XGMML includes metadata information for a graph, node and/or edge using the att tag. Example 3 is part of a graph describing a web site. The nodes represent web pages and the edges represent hyperlinks. The metadata of the web pages is included as attributes of a node. RDF and Dublin Core (DC) vocabularies have been used to describe the metadata of the nodes.

```
<?xml version="1.0"?>
<graph xmlns = "http://www.cs.rpi.edu/XGMML"
    xmlns:xsi="http://www.w3.org/2000/10/XMLSchema-instance"
    xsi:schemaLocation="http://www.cs.rpi.edu/XGMML
    http://www.cs.rpi.edu/~puninj/XGMML/xgmml.xsd"
    directed="1" >
<node id="3" label="www.cs.rpi.edu/courses/" weight="5427">
<att>
<rdf:RDF
  xmlns:rdf="http://www.w3.org/1999/02/22-rdf-syntax-ns#"
  xmlns:dc="http://purl.org/dc/elements/1.0/">
  <rdf:Description about="http://www.cs.rpi.edu/courses/"
    dc:title="Courses at Rensselaer Computer Science
    Department"
    dc:subject="www@cs.rpi.edu; M.S. requirements; CSCI-1190
    Beginning C Programming for Engineers; Courses; People;
    Graduate Program; CSCI-4020 Computer  Algorithms; CSCI-
    2220-01  Programming in Java; Research; Course Selection
    Guide; CSCI-4961-01,  CSCI-6961-01 Advanced Robotics;
    Programming in Java; CSCI-2400 Models  of Computation"
    dc:date="2000-01-31"
    dc:type="Text"
    >
  <dc:format>
    <rdf:Bag
      rdf:_1="text/html"
      rdf:_2="5427 bytes"
    />
```

```
   </dc:format>
  </rdf:Description>
 </rdf:RDF>
</att>
</node>
....
<edge src="1" target="3" weight="0" label="SRC IMG X.jpg" />
<edge src="7" target="3" weight="0" label="SRC IMG ../X.jpg" />
</graph>
```

Valid XGMML Documents: A valid XGMML document must be an well-formed XML document. A valid XGMML document additionally can be validated against an XGMML DTD or XGMML Schema. The XGMML Schema is based on the XML Schema Working Draft 22 September 2000. A valid XML document can have multiple schemas. The namespace for XGMML is: *www.cs.rpi.-edu/XGMML* and the suffix for the XGMML elements is *xgmml:*. The examples above show two valid XML documents that can be validated using several XML schemas including XGMML Schema.

XGMML Elements and Attributes: The main elements of XGMML are: graph, node, edge, att and graphics. The graph element is the root element of an XGMML valid document. The graph element may not be unique in the XGMML document. Other graphs can be included as subgraphs of the main graph. All XGMML elements have global attributes that are id, name and label. The id attribute is an unique number to identify the XGMML element. The name is a string to identify the elements and the label is a string used as a text representation of the elements. The graph element has the directed attribute that is a boolean value to express whether the graph is directed or not.

Nodes and edges can reference XGMML documents. For example, a node may represent a graph that can be shown when the user points inside the node. This behavior is similar to hyperlinks in HTML documents. XGMML uses XLink framework to create hyperlinks either in nodes or edges. The XLink attributes: type, role, title, show, actuate and href, are added as attributes of the node and edge elements. All these attributes are taken directly from the XLink Working Draft.

The node element describes the properties of a node object. The node can be rendered as a graphic object and also can have additional meta information to be used for the application program. The only elements allowed inside the node are graphics and att. The graphic representation of the node is reported on the graphics element. For example, a graphical representation of a node can be a rectangle, a circle or a bitmap. The additional meta information is reported on the att element. For example, if a node is a representation of a web page, useful metadata is the title, date of creation and size of the web page.

The edge element describes the properties of an edge object. For each edge element two node elements have to be included in the graph element. An edge is between a source node and a target node. The application program must verify if the source node and target node are included in the XGMML document.

The weight attribute is used to save the weight number for weighted graphs. The edge element as the node element can have a graphical representation and additional metadata information. The graphics element shows the graphical representation of an edge. For example, a graphical representation of an edge can be a line or an arc. An att element is used to attach additional meta information related to an edge. For example, if an edge is a representation of a hyperlink, useful metadata is the anchor string and the type of the hyperlink (Typed Links) [8].

An att element is used to hold meta information about the element that contains the att element. An att element can contain other att elements, say to represent structured metadata such as records, lists, etc. For example, the metadata of a person object A is name: John, ssn: 123456789 and e-mail: john@rpi.edu. To attach this metadata to a node of a graph using the att element, the following lines must be included in the node element:

```
<att type="list" name="person_description">
<att name="name" value="John"/>
<att name="ssn" value="123456789"/>
<att name="e-mail" value="john@rpi.edu"/>
</att>
```

The graphics element defines the graphical representation of a graph, a node or an edge. Line, center and att elements are the only elements that can be contained in a graphics element. Line element is defined between two point elements and it is used to represent edges. A center element is a special point element to represent the central point of the graphical representation of a node. The att element permits to add information to the graphical representation. All these elements are inherited from GML.

3   LOGML (Log Markup Language)

Log reports are the compressed version of logfiles. Web masters in general save web server logs in several files. Usually each logfile contains a single day of information. Due to disk space limitation, old log data gets deleted to make room for new log information. Generally, web masters generate HTML reports of the logfiles and do not have problems keeping them for a long period of time as the HTML reports are an insignificant size. If a web master likes to generate reports for a large period of time, he has to combine several HTML reports to produce a final report. LOGML is conceived to make this task easier. Web masters can generate LOGML reports of logfiles and combine them on a regular basis without much effort. LOGML files can be combined with XSLT to produce HTML reports. LOGML offers the flexibility to combine them with other XML applications, to produce graphics of the statistics of the reports. LOGML can also be combined with RDF to provide some metadata information about the web server that is being analyzed. LOGML is based on XGMML. LOGML document can be seen as a snapshot of the web site as the user visits web pages and traverses hyperlinks. It also provides a succinct way to save the user sessions. In the W3C Working Draft "Web Characterization Terminology & Definitions Sheet", the user session is defined as "a delimited set of user clicks across one or more Web servers".

Structure of LOGML Documents: A typical LOGML document has three sections under the root element logml element. The first section is a graph that describes the log graph of the visits of the users to web pages and hyperlinks. This section uses XGMML to describe the graph and its root element is the graph element. The second section is the additional information of log reports such as top visiting hosts, top user agents, and top keywords. The third section is the report of the user sessions. Each user session is a subgraph of the log graph. The subgraphs are reported as a list of edges that refer to the nodes of the log graph. Each edge of the user sessions also has a timestamp for when the edge was traversed. This timestamp helps to compute the total time of the user session. LOGML files are large files; example below shows part of a LOGML file.

```
<?xml version="1.0"?>
<logml xmlns="http://www.cs.rpi.edu/LOGML"
       xmlns:xsi="http://www.w3.org/2000/10/XMLSchema-instance"
       xsi:schemaLocation="http://www.cs.rpi.edu/LOGML
       http://www.cs.rpi.edu/~puninj/LOGML/logml.xsd"
        start_date="12/Oct/2000:05:00:05"
        end_date="12/Oct/2000:16:00:01">
<graph xmlns="http://www.cs.rpi.edu/XGMML"
       xmlns:lml="http://www.cs.rpi.edu/LOGML"
       xsi:schemaLocation="http://www.cs.rpi.edu/XGMML
       http://www.cs.rpi.edu/~puninj/XGMML/xgmml.xsd
       http://www.cs.rpi.edu/LOGML
       http://www.cs.rpi.edu/~puninj/LOGML/logml.xsd"
       directed="1">
<node id="234" label="http://www.cs.rpi.edu/~puninj/JAVA/projects/lfarrw.gif"
 lml:hits="1" weight="1">
<att name="title" value="No title"/>
<att name="mime" value="image/gif"/>
<att name="size" value="1291"/>
<att name="date" value="Sun Jun 11 02:14:28 2000"/>
<att name="code" value="200"/>
</node>
....
<edge source="191" target="234" label="SRC IMG lfarrw.gif" lml:hits="1" weight="1">
<att value="image"/>
</edge>
....
<edge source="550" target="561" lml:hits="1" weight="1" lml:indp="1"/>
....
</graph>
<hosts count="35">
<host name="vamos.inria.fr" access_count="43" bytes="487397" html_pages="43"/>
<host name="kbl-ternzn1200.zeelandnet.nl" access_count="13" bytes="46354"
html_pages="1"/>
....
</hosts>
<domains count="9">
<domain name="unknown" access_count="25" bytes="388608" html_pages="16"/>
<domain name="com" access_count="21" bytes="229979" html_pages="19"/>
....
</domains>
<directories count="30">
<directory name="http://www.cs.rpi.edu/~puninj/XGMML" access_count="21"
total_count="49" bytes="1116521"/>
....
```

```
</directories>
<userAgents count="23">
<userAgent name="Mozilla/4.0 (compatible; MSIE 5.0; Windows 98; DigExt)"
access_count="27" bytes="670815" html_pages="9"/>
....
</userAgents>
<hostReferers count="14">
<hostReferer name="No Referer" access_count="66" bytes="945527"/>
<hostReferer name="http://www.cs.rpi.edu" access_count="41" bytes="701097"/>
....
</hostReferers>
<referers count="11">
<referer name="No referer" access_count="66" bytes="945527"/>
access_count="1" bytes="35272" target="8"/>
<referer name="http://informant.dartmouth.edu/" access_count="1" bytes="1112"
 target="2"/>
....
</referers>
<keywords count="10" search_count="9">
<keyword name="java" count="3"/>
<keyword name="xhtml" count="2"/>
....
</keywords>
<summary
 requests="132" sessions="6" bytes="1796173"
 html_pages="56" nhtml_pages="17" inline_objects="10" hyperlink_html="7"
 hyperlink_nhtml="16"
 html_entry_pages="55" nhtml_entry_pages="4" unique_sites="35" unique_host_referers="8"
 unique_se_referers="6"
 unique_external_url_referers="7" unique_internal_url_referers="4" unique_user_agents="23"
 requests_hour="12.00" requests_day="288.03" kbytes_day="159.48" kbytes_hour="3827.46"
 searches="9" unique_keywords="10">
<httpCode code="200" name="200 - OK " count="118" bytes="1793393" html_pages="83"/>
<httpCode code="404" name="404 - Not Found" count="5" bytes="1722" html_pages="5"/>
<httpMethod name="GET" count="131" bytes="1796173" html_pages="95"/>
<httpMethod name="HEAD" count="1" bytes="0" html_pages="1"/>
<httpCode name="HTTP/1.0" count="97" bytes="1399288" html_pages="83"/>
<httpCode name="HTTP/1.1" count="35" bytes="396885" html_pages="13"/>
<dateStat>
<monthStat month="10" hits="132" bytes="1796173" html_requests="96"/>
<dayStat day="12" hits="132" bytes="1796173" html_requests="96"/>
<hourStat hour="5" hits="12" bytes="15622" html_requests="12"/>
<hourStat hour="6" hits="15" bytes="103280" html_requests="14"/>
</dateStat>
</summary>
....
<userSessions count="2" max_edges="100" min_edges="2">
<userSession name="proxy.artech.com.uy" ureferer="No referer"
entry_page="http://www.cs.rpi.edu/~puninj/XGMML/" start_time="12/Oct/2000:12:50:11"
access_count="4">
<path count="3">
<uedge source="3" target="10" utime="12/Oct/2000:12:50:12"/>
<uedge source="3" target="21" utime="12/Oct/2000:12:51:41"/>
<uedge source="21" target="22" utime="12/Oct/2000:12:52:02"/>
</path>
</userSession>
<userSession name="207.234.33.12"
ureferer="http://search.excite.com/search.gw?search=XHTML"
entry_page="http://www.cs.rpi.edu/~puninj/TALK/head.html"
start_time="12/Oct/2000:14:05:10" access_count="3">
<path count="2">
<uedge source="2" target="7" utime="12/Oct/2000:14:05:24"/>
<uedge source="2" target="8" utime="12/Oct/2000:14:06:14"/>
</path>
</userSession>
</userSessions>
</logml>
```

LOGML Valid Documents: A LOGML valid document is a well-formed XML document that can be validated against a LOGML DTD or LOGML Schema. The namespace for LOGML is *http://www.cs.rpi.edu/LOGML* and the suffix for LOGML elements is *lml:*.

LOGML Elements and Attributes: The root element of a LOGML document is the `logml` element. The rest of the elements are classified with respect to the three sections of the LOGML document. The first section is the report of the log graph and we use the XGMML elements to describe this graph. The second section report the general statistics of the web server such as top pages, top referer URLs, top visiting user agents, etc. And, the last section reports the user sessions.

The following global attributes are used by most of the LOGML elements: `id` - unique number to identify the elements of LOGML document. `name` - string to identify the elements of LOGML document. `label` - text representation of the LOGML element `access_count` - number of times the web server has been accessed. For example, the number of times of a specific user agent accessed the web server. `total_count` - total number of times that an element is found in a logfile. For example, the total count of a keyword. `bytes` - number of bytes downloaded. `html_pages` - number of HTML pages requested from the web server. For example, the number of html pages requested by a specific site.

The XGMML elements that we use to describe the log graph are `graph`, `node`, `edge` and `att`. We add the `hits` attribute to the `node` and `edge` elements to report the number of visits to the node (web page) and the number of traversals of the edge (hyperlink). The `att` element is used to report metadata information of the web page such as mime type and size of the file. The elements of the second section are:

• `hosts, host` - This host list is composed by a container `hosts` element whose attribute is the `count` of the `host` element inside of the `hosts` element. The `host` element is an empty element and contains information about the visiting site such as hostname, IP and number of bytes transferred by the site.

• `domains, domain` - The `domains` element is a list of all domains visiting the web server. The domain is the suffix of the domain name of the sites. For example: *edu* is the domain of the site *www.cs.rpi.edu*.

• `directories, directory` - The directories list contains the top directories of the web site that have most requested web pages. The directory is the prefix of the URI of the web page. For example: The directory of the web page: *http://www.rpi.edu/dept/urp/find.html* is *http://www.rpi.edu/dept/urp*

• `userAgents, userAgent` - The list of user agents contains all user agents (browsers and/or spiders) that have made requests to the web server. The LOGML reader can refine this list to compute the top platforms and top web browsers since the User Agent name contains information about the platform and name of web browser.

• `referers, referer` - The `referers` list contains two lists: The list of the top external referers and the list of the top internal referers. The external referers are the referers whose host are different than the web server. The host of the internal referers are the same as the web server.

- `hostReferers, hostReferer` - The host referers list contains the top host referers of the web pages of the web server. This list combines the number of accesses of the referers with the same host.
- `keywords, keyword` - Keywords are the searching words found in the URI referers of the search engines. Several `keywords` lists can be reported. Each `keywords` list is associated with a particular search engine.
- `summary` - The `summary` element contains a brief overview of the essential information of the web server. This information is very important for web masters to know the efficiency of the web server. The `summary` attributes are: `requests` - the total number of requests. `sessions` - the total number of user sessions. `bytes` - the total number of bytes transferred. `html_pages` - the total number of unique html pages. `nhtml_pages` - the total number of unique non html pages. `inline_objects` - the total number of unique inline objects. Inline objects are the objects inside of a html page such as images `hyperlinks_html` - the total number of unique hyperlinks to html pages. `hyperlinks_nhtml` - the total number of unique hyperlinks to non html pages. `html_entry_pages` - the total number of unique html pages that are entry pages to the web site of the web server. `nhtml_entry_pages` - the total number of unique non html pages that are entry pages to the web site of the web server. `unique_sites` - the total number of unique visiting sites. `unique_host_referers` - the total number of the unique host. referers to the web pages of the web server. `unique_se_referers` - the total number of the unique search engines that access the web server. `unique_external_url_referers` - the total number of unique external URI referers to the web pages of the web server. `unique_internal_url_referers` - the total number of unique internal URI referers to the web pages of the web server. `unique_user_agents` - the total number of the unique user agents that access the web pages of the web server. `requests_hour` - the number of requests per hour. `requests_day` - the number of requests per day. `kbytes_hour` - the number of kilobytes transferred per hour. `kbytes_day` - the number of kilobytes transferred per day. `searches` - the total number of searching requests. `uniquekeywords` - the total number of unique keywords in the searching requests.
- `httpCode` - The `httpCode` element gives the summary of the HTTP status code of the requests.
- `httpMethod` - The `httpMethod` element gives the summary of the HTTP methods used by the web clients to communicate with the web server.
- `httpVersion` - The `httpVersion` element gives the summary of the HTTP version used by the web clients to communicate with the web server.
- `dateStat, monthStat, dayStat` and `hourStat.` - The date elements give the summary of the statistics by date of the requests.

The third section of the LOGML document reports the user sessions and the LOGML elements are: • `userSessions, userSession` - The `userSessions` element is the container element for the set of the user sessions. Each user session is described using the `userSession`, `path` and `uedge` elements where a `path` is the collection of hyperlinks that the user has traversed during the session.

- **path** - The **path** element contains all hyperlinks that the user has traversed during the user session.
- **uedge** - The **uedge** element reports a hyperlink that has been traversed during the user session. The **source** and the **target** attributes are reference to nodes of the Log Graph in the first section and the **utime** attribute is the timestamp where the user traversed this hyperlink. Example below is the report of one user session in a LOGML document:

```
<userSession name="proxy.artech.com.uy" ureferer="No referer"
entry_page="http://www.cs.rpi.edu/~puninj/XGMML/"
        start_time="12/Oct/2000:12:50:11" access_count="4">
<path count="3">
<uedge source="3" target="10" utime="12/Oct/2000:12:50:12"/>
<uedge source="3" target="21" utime="12/Oct/2000:12:51:41"/>
<uedge source="21" target="22" utime="12/Oct/2000:12:52:02"/>
</path>
</userSession>
```

4 LOGML Generator

We have written a simple LOGML Generator as part of our WWWPal System. The LOGML Generator reads a common or extended log file and generates a LOGML file. The LOGML Generator also can read the webgraph (XGMML file) of the web site being analyzed and combine the information of the web pages and hyperlinks with the log information.

The information that we extract from the common log files include host name or IP, date of the request, relative URI of the requested page, HTTP version, HTTP status code, HTTP method and the number of bytes transferred to the web client. The extended log files additionally contain the absolute URI of the referer web page and a string that describes the User Agent (web browser or web crawler) that has made the request. This information is saved in a data structure to generate the corresponding LOGML document. The LOGML Generator also can output HTML reports making this module a powerful tool for web administrators.

Several algorithms have been developed to find the user sessions in the log files [5,9,10]. A simple algorithm uses the IP or host name of the web client to identify a user. SpeedTracer System [10] also checks the User Agent and date of the request to find the user session. Straight ways to find user session requires "cookies" or remote user identification [5]. The LOGML Generator algorithm, to find user sessions, is very similar to the algorithm used by SpeedTracer System.

The LOGML Generator has a module called the User Manager. The User Manager is invoked for each web log line that is processed. It received the following information: current date, URL of the requested page, URL of the referer, IP of the user and user agent. The User Manager has access to the container of the user sessions and the web graph of the web site of the web logs so the

User Manager can add user sessions and get metadata information from the web graph such as title, size and mime type of the web page.

These are the following steps that the User Manager takes to create and finish user sessions:

• Check if any of the current user sessions has finished. A user session is considered finished when the lapse time between the last request time of the user session and the current request time is greater than a time window. This time window is a parameter of the LOGML generator and from experience we set the value to be 30 minutes. The User Manager marks the finished user sessions so they can be reported in the LOGML document.

• Check if the user agent is a spider. A Spider is being recognized by the name of the user agent or by the excessive number of requests to the web site. Spider sessions are not considered user sessions so the User Manager skips the requests of the spiders.

• Check if the current requested page is an inline object. User sessions are reported as a set of hyperlinks between HTML pages so inline object are not reported in the user session. We can expand the user sessions' inline objects using the log graph of the first section of the LOGML document. The User Manager skips the inline object requests.

• Search for a user session in the table of user sessions. A user session is identified by IP or domain name, and the name of the user agent. If a user session is not found, a new user session is created and stored in the table of user sessions.

• Verify if the referer of the requested page is an external or internal URL of the web site being analyzed. If the referer is external, it means that the requested page is an entry page and a new possible user session has started. The User Manager checks if the current user session has more than two requests and it considers the user session. If the current user session has just one request, the user session is discarded.

• Add the new hyperlink (edge) to the graph of the user session. Each edge is saved with the date (timestamp) where the user has traversed this hyperlink. This timestamp is used for Web usage mining purposes.

Once that the LOGML generator reads all the web log lines, only those finished user sessions are reported in the LOGML document. This is the general algorithm that the User Manager uses to create, add and finish the user sessions.

```
int user_session_manager(WebStat ws, Date d, URL page,
        URL referer, IP ip, UserAgent ua, WebGraph g)
{
    User u;
    check_finished_users(ws,d);
    if(is_spider(ua)) return IS_SPIDER;
    if(is_inline_object(g,page)) return IS_INLINE_OBJECT;
    u = find_user(ws,ip,ua); // find user in the users table
    if(!u) // if user was not found, create a new user session
        u = new_user_session(ws,d,ip,ua);
    if(is_external(referer)) {
        finish_user_session(ws,u);
```

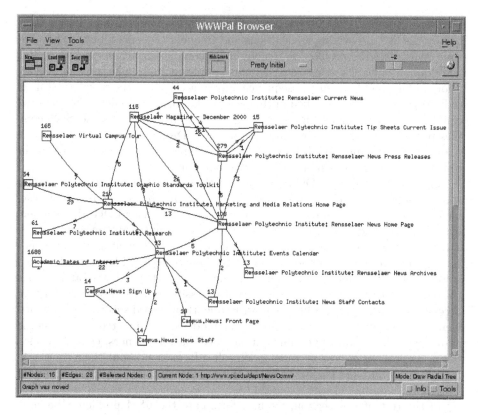

Fig. 2. Log graph of RPI News Website

```
    u = new_user_session(ws,d,ip,ua);
}
add_hyperlink(u,page,referer,d);
return 0;
}
```

We use the Graph Visualizer of WWWPal System to display the log graph of the LOGML document or any of the user sessions that has been identified in the log files. Figure 2 shows part of the log graph of the Rensselaer News web site (*http://www.rpi.edu/web/News/*). The numbers on the edges are the times that a user has traversed that edge (hyperlink). The number in the nodes are the times that a user has requested the corresponding web page. For visualization purposes just the main nodes of the log graph have been displayed.

5   LOGML for Web Data Mining

In this section, we propose solving a wide class of mining problems that arise in web data mining, using a novel, generic framework, which we term Frequent

Structure Mining (FSM). FSM not only encompasses important data mining techniques like discovering associations and frequent sequences, but at the same time generalizes the problem to include more complex patterns like tree mining and graph mining. These patterns arise in complex domains like the web. Association mining, and frequent subsequence mining are some of the specific instances of FSM that have been studied in the past [11,12,13,14]. In general, however, we can discover increasingly complex structures from the same database. Such complex patterns include frequent subtrees, frequent DAGs and frequent directed or undirected subgraphs. As one increases the complexity of the structures to be discovered, one extracts more informative patterns.

The same underlying LOGML document that stores the web graph, as well as the user sessions, which are subgraphs of the web graph, can be used to extract increasingly complex and more informative patterns. Given a LOGML document extracted from the database of web access logs at a popular site, one can perform several mining tasks. The simplest is to ignore all link information from the user sessions, and to mine only the frequent sets of pages accessed by users. The next step can be to form for each user the sequence of links they followed, and to mine the most frequent user access paths. It is also possible to look at only the forward accesses of a user, and to mine the most frequently accessed subtrees at that site. Generalizing even further, a web site can be modeled as a directed graph, since in addition to the forward hyperlinks, it can have back references, creating cycles. Given a database of user accesses (with full information about their traversals, including forward and backward links) one can discover the frequently occurring subgraphs.

In the rest of this section, we first formulate the FSM problem. We show how LOGML facilitates the creation of a database suitable for web mining. We illustrate this with actual examples from RPI logs (from one day). Using the same example we also describe several increasingly complex mining tasks that can be performed.

5.1   Frequent Structure Mining

FSM is a novel, generic framework for mining various kinds of frequent patterns. Consider a database $\mathcal{D}$ of a collection of structures, built out of a set of primitive *items* $\mathcal{I}$. A structure represents some relationship among items or sets of items. For a given structure G, let $S \preceq G$ denote the fact that S is a substructure of G. If $S \preceq G$ we also say that G *contains* S. The collection of all possible structures composed of the set of items $\mathcal{I}$ forms a partially ordered set under the substructure relation $\preceq$. A structure formed from k items is called a *k-structure*. A structure is called *maximal* if it is not a substructure of any other in a collection of structures. We define the *support* of a structure G in a database $\mathcal{D}$ to be the number of structures in $\mathcal{D}$ that contain G. Alternately, if there is only one very large structure in the database, the support is the number of times G occurs as a substructure within it. We say that a structure is *frequent* if its support is more than a user-specified *minimum support (min_sup)* value. The set of frequent k-structures is denoted as $\mathcal{F}_k$.

A *structural rule* is an expression $X \Rightarrow Y$, where X and Y are structures. The *support* of the rule in the database of structures is the joint probability of X and Y, and the *confidence* is the conditional probability that a structure contains Y, given that it contains X. A rule is *strong* if its confidence is more than a user-specified *minimum confidence (min_conf)*.

The frequent structure mining task is to generate all structural rules in the database, which have a support greater than *min_sup* and have confidence greater than *min_conf*. This task can be broken into two main steps: 1) *Find all frequent structures having minimum support and other constraints*. This step is the most computational and I/O intensive step, since the search space for enumeration of all frequent substructures is exponential in the worst case. The minimum support criterion is very successful in reducing the search space. In addition other constraints can be induced, such as finding maximal, closed or correlated substructures. 2) *Generate all strong structural rules having minimum confidence*. Rule generation is also exponential in the size of the longest substructure. However, this time we do not have to access the database; we only need the set of frequent structures.

5.2   Database Creation from LOGML

We designed the LOGML language to facilitate web mining. The LOGML document created from web logs has all the information we need to perform various FSM tasks. For structure mining from web logs, we mainly make use of two sections of the LOGML document. As described above, the first section contains the web graph; i.e., the actual structure of the web site in consideration. We use the web graph to obtain the page URLs and their node identifiers. For example, the example below shows a snippet of the (node id, URL) pairs (out of a total of 56623 nodes) we extracted from the web graph of the RPI computer science department:

```
1 http://www.cs.rpi.edu/
4 http://www.cs.rpi.edu/guide/machines/
6 http://www.cs.rpi.edu/courses/
8 http://www.cs.rpi.edu/current-events/
10 http://www.cs.rpi.edu/grad/
12 http://www.cs.rpi.edu/People/
14 http://www.cs.rpi.edu/research/
16 http://www.cs.rpi.edu/undergrad/
31 http://www.cs.rpi.edu/guide/
. . .
```

For enabling web mining we make use of the third section of the LOGML document that stores the user sessions organized as subgraphs of the web graph. We have complete history of the user clicks including the time at which a page is requested. Each user session has a session id (the IP or host name), a path count (the number of source and destination node pairs) and the time when a link is traversed. We simply extract the relevant information depending on the mining task at hand. For example if our goal is to discover frequent sets of pages accessed, we ignore all link information and note down the unique source or destination nodes in a user session. For example, let a user session have the following information as part of a LOGML document:

```
<userSession name=''ppp0-69.ank2.isbank.net.tr'' ...>
<path count=''6''>
<uedge source=''5938'' target=''16470''
utime=''24/Oct/2000:07:53:46''/>
<uedge source=''16470'' target=''24754''
utime=''24/Oct/2000:07:56:13''/>
<uedge source=''16470'' target=''24755''
utime=''24/Oct/2000:07:56:36''/>
<uedge source=''24755'' target=''47387''
utime=''24/Oct/2000:07:57:14''/>
<uedge source=''24755'' target=''47397''
utime=''24/Oct/2000:07:57:28''/>
<uedge source=''16470'' target=''24756''
utime=''24/Oct/2000:07:58:30''/>
```

We can then extract the set of nodes accessed by this user:

```
#format: user name, number of nodes accessed, node list
ppp0-69.ank2.isbank.net.tr 7 5938 16470 24754 24755 47387
                           47397 24756
```

After extracting this information from all the user sessions we obtain a database that is ready to be used for frequent set mining, as we shall see below. On the other hand if our task is to perform sequence mining, we look for the longest forward links, and generate a new sequence each time a back edge is traversed. Using a simple stack-based implementation all maximal forward node sequences can be found. For the example user session above this would yield:

```
#format: user name, sequence id, node position, node accessed
ppp0-69.ank2.isbank.net.tr 1 1 5938
ppp0-69.ank2.isbank.net.tr 1 2 16470
ppp0-69.ank2.isbank.net.tr 1 3 24754
ppp0-69.ank2.isbank.net.tr 2 1 5938
ppp0-69.ank2.isbank.net.tr 2 2 16470
ppp0-69.ank2.isbank.net.tr 2 3 24755
ppp0-69.ank2.isbank.net.tr 2 4 47387
ppp0-69.ank2.isbank.net.tr 3 1 5938
ppp0-69.ank2.isbank.net.tr 3 2 16470
ppp0-69.ank2.isbank.net.tr 3 3 24755
ppp0-69.ank2.isbank.net.tr 3 4 47397
ppp0-69.ank2.isbank.net.tr 4 1 5938
ppp0-69.ank2.isbank.net.tr 4 2 16470
ppp0-69.ank2.isbank.net.tr 4 3 24756
```

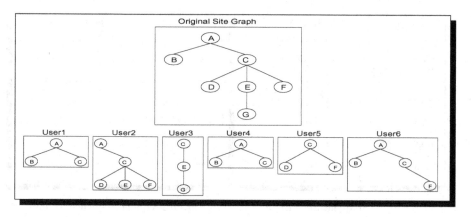

Fig. 3. LOGML Document: Web Site Graph and User Sessions

For frequent tree mining, we can easily extract the forward edges from the user session (avoiding cycles or multiple parents) to obtain the subtree corresponding to each user. For our example above this yields the following record (note: the tree is encoded as a string, using a depth-first traversal of the nodes; a -1 indicates a back edge).

```
#format: user name, number of nodes, node list in tree
ppp0-69.ank2.isbank.net.tr 7 5938 16470 24754 -1 24755 47387
            -1 47397 -1 -1 24756 -1 -1
```

For a more complex mining task like graph mining, once again the appropriate information can be directly produced from the LOGML user sessions.

We will illustrate various instances of the FSM paradigm in web mining using the example in Figure 3, which pictorially depicts the original web graph of a particular web site. There are 7 pages, forming the set of primitive items $\mathcal{I} = \{A, B, C, D, E, F, G\}$ connected with hyperlinks. Now the LOGML document already stores in a systematic manner the user sessions, each of them being a subgraph of the web graph. The figure shows the pages visited by 6 users. We will see below how this user browsing information can be used for mining different kinds of increasingly complex substructures, starting with the frequently accessed pages, to the frequently traversed paths, to the frequent subtrees, and so on.

5.3   Web Data Mining

Frequent Sets: This is the well known association rule mining problem[11,12]. Here the database $\mathcal{D}$ is a collection of *transactions*, which are simply subsets of primitive items $\mathcal{I}$. Each structure in the database is a transaction, and $\preceq$ denotes the subset relation. The mining task, then, is to discover all frequent subsets in $\mathcal{D}$. These subsets are called *itemsets* in association mining literature.

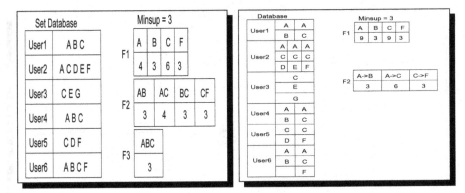

Fig. 4. Frequent Set Mining   **Fig. 5.** Frequent Sequence Mining

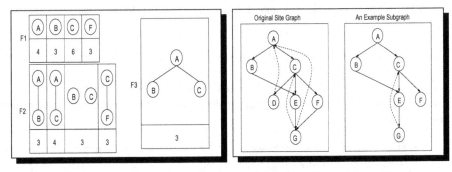

Fig. 6. Frequent Tree Mining   **Fig. 7.** A General User Graph

Consider the example web logs database shown in Figure 4. For each user (in Figure 3) we only record the pages accessed by them, ignoring the path information. The mining task is to find all frequently accessed sets of pages. Figure 4 shows all the frequent k-itemsets $\mathcal{F}_k$ that are contained in at least three user transactions; i.e., $min\_sup = 3$. *ABC*, *AF* and *CF*, are the maximal frequent itemsets.

We applied the Charm association mining algorithm [15] to a real LOGML document from the RPI web site (one day's logs). There were 200 user sessions with an average of 56 distinct nodes in each session. It took us 0.03s to do the mining with 10% minimum support. An example frequent set found is shown below:

```
Let Path=http://www.cs.rpi.edu/~sibel/poetry
FREQUENCY=22, NODE IDS = 25854 5938 25649 25650 25310 16511
          Path/poems/nazim_hikmet/turkce.html
          Path/sair_listesi.html
          Path/frames/nazim_hikmet_1.html
          Path/frames/nazim_hikmet_2.html
          Path/links.html
          Path/nazim_hikmet.html
```

Frequent Sequences: The problem of mining sequences [13,14] can be stated as follows: An *event* is simply an itemset made up of the items $\mathcal{I}$. A *sequence* is an ordered list of events. A sequence α is denoted as $(\alpha_1 \to \alpha_2 \to \cdots \to \alpha_q)$, where α_i is an event; the symbol $\to$ denotes a "happens-after" relationship. We say α is a *subsequence* (not necessarily consecutive) of another sequence β, denoted as $\alpha \preceq \beta$, if α is completely contained within β.

The structure database $\mathcal{D}$ consists of a collection of sequences, and $\preceq$ denotes the subsequence relation. The mining goal is to discover all frequent subsequences. For example, consider the sequence database shown in Figure 5, by storing all paths from the starting page to a leaf (note that there are other ways of constructing user access paths; this is just one example). With minimum support of 3 we find that $A \to B$, $A \to C$, $C \to F$ are the maximal frequent sequences.

We applied the SPADE sequence mining algorithm [14] to an actual LOGML document from the RPI web site. From the 200 user sessions, we obtain 8208 maximal forward sequences, with an average sequence size of 2.8. It took us 0.12s to do the mining with minimum support set to 0.1% (or a frequency of at least 8). An example frequent sequence found is shown below:

```
Let Path=http://www.cs.rpi.edu/~sibel/poetry
FREQUENCY = 21, NODE IDS =  37668 -> 5944 -> 25649 -> 31409
        Path/ ->
        Path/translation.html ->
        Path/frames/nazim_hikmet_1.html ->
        Path/poems/nazim_hikmet/english.html
```

Frequent Trees: We denote an ordered, labeled, and rooted tree as $T = (V_t, E_t)$, where V_t is the vertex set, and E_t are the edges or branches. We say that a tree $S = (V_s, E_s)$ is a subtree of T, denoted as $S \preceq T$, if and only if $V_s \subseteq V_t$, and for all edges $e = (v_1, v_2) \in E_s$, v_1 is an ancestor of v_2 in T. Note that this definition is different from the usual definition of a subtree. In our case, we require that for any branch that appears in S, the two vertices must be on the same path from a root to some leaf. For example, in Figure 3 the tree S, with $V = \{C, G\}$ and $E = \{CG\}$ is a subtree of the site graph.

Given a database $\mathcal{D}$ of trees (i.e., a forest) on the vertex set $\mathcal{I}$, the frequent tree mining problem [16] is to find all subtrees that appear in at least min_sup trees. For example, for the user access subtrees shown in Figure 3, we mine the frequent subtrees shown in Figure 6. There are two maximal frequent subtrees, $(V = \{C, F\}, E = \{CF\})$ and $(V = \{A, B, C\}, E = \{AB, AC\})$ for $min\_sup = 3$.

We applied the TreeMinerV algorithm [16] to the same RPI LOGML file used above. From the 200 user sessions, we obtain 1009 subtrees (a single user session can lead to multiple trees if there are multiple roots in the user graph), with an average record length of 84.3 (including the back edges, -1). It took us 0.37s to do the mining with minimum support set to 5% (or a frequency of at least 50). An example frequent subtree found is shown below:

```
Let Path=http://www.cs.rpi.edu/~sibel/poetry
Let Poet = Path/poems/orhan_veli
FREQUENCY = 65, NODE IDS = 16499 31397 37807 -1 37836 -1 -1 25309
                Path/orhan_veli.html
              /                    \
            /                        \
     Poet/turkce.html        Path/frames/orhan_veli_2.html
        /        \
      /            \
Poet/golgem.html   Poet/gunes.html
```

Other Generalizations: It is instructive to compare the patterns returned by the above three tasks from a common web logs database. We started by ignoring all link information to obtain frequent sets of pages. We then found the frequent paths, and finally the frequently traversed subtrees. These tasks were arranged according to increasing order of complexity (and thus increasing execution time), but at the same time in increasing order of information conveyed to the user. For example, in frequent set mining, we only know that the pages A, B, and C were frequently accessed. Sequence mining gives us partial sequence information about the order in which pages are traversed, e.g., $A \rightarrow B$. But in tree mining, we obtain full knowledge about the relationships between the three pages; e.g. A is the root with two children B and C. Not only can one mine such patterns, but it is relatively easy in our framework based on the LOGML document information to apply constraints on the patterns as well. For example, a web site analyst might want to know only those patterns that occur within a short time window, or those that occur after long gaps between accesses, etc. All this information can directly be extracted from the edge times in the user sessions.

There are many other generalizations that are possible. For example, we can generalize the tree mining problem to directed acyclic graphs, and more generally to directed and undirected graphs. Continuing the web mining example, a general web site can be modeled as a directed graph, since in addition to the forward hyperlinks, it can have back references, creating cycles. Figure 7 shows an example web graph. Given a database of user accesses (with full information about their traversal, including both forward and backward links) one might be able to discover the frequently occurring subgraphs, such as the one shown.

Experiments: We ran detailed experiments on logs files collected over 1 month at the RPI computer science department. Experiments were run on a 450Mhz Pentium II processor with 256MB memory, running Linux 6.0. The logs touched a total of 27343 web pages within our department's web site. After processing the LOGML database with 34838 user graphs, we had as many transactions for association mining, with 8.24 items per transaction on average. For the sequence database, from the same LOGML file, we generated 165276 sequences, where the average sequence (or page reference) length was 2.6. Finally for tree mining, we obtained 59691 trees (stored in string format) from the 34838 user graphs, with an average of 20.1 items per tree (including -1's). Note that we can have more trees than the number of user graphs, since a user can have multiple entry points

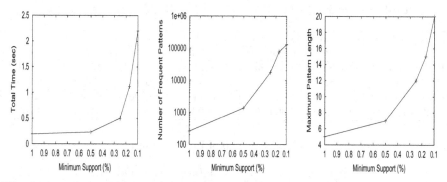

Fig. 8. Association Mining: a) Total Time, b) Num. Patterns, and c) Max. Pattern Length

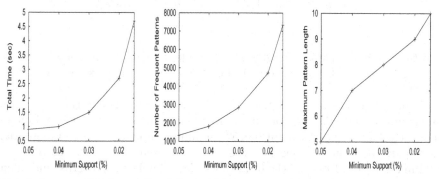

Fig. 9. Sequence Mining: a) Total Time, b) Num. Patterns, and c) Max. Pattern Length

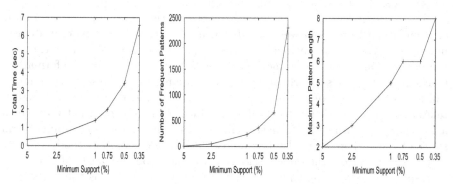

Fig. 10. Tree Mining: a) Total Time, b) Num. Patterns, and c) Max. Pattern Length

into a web site, and each such entry point (i.e., a page with no parent or with an external parent) serves as the root of a new subtree for the same user.

Figure 8 shows the total time taken for mining association rules for various minimum support values. It also shows the total number of frequent sets found

Table 1. Size of Raw Log Files versus LOGML Files (Size is in Bytes)

Source	Raw Logs		LOGML		#Requests	#Sessions
	Regular	Compressed	Regular	Compressed		
RPI1(14Jun01)	52,428,686	5,544,951	19,850,273	2,103,298	275726	5891
RPI2(15Jun01)	52,428,742	5,457,778	19,485,594	2,063,934	275061	5436
CS1 (28Jun01)	10,506,256	1,065,771	4,633,113	520,290	51950	2153
CS2 (29Jun01)	10,323,505	1,089,098	5,269,929	580,146	49378	2063

Table 2. Breakup of LOGML Files

Source	Webgraph	UserSessions	Other
RPI1(14Jun01)	88.3%	8.3%	3.4%
RPI2(15Jun01)	88.2%	8.4%	3.4%
CS1 (28Jun01)	74.6%	16.7%	8.7%
CS2 (29Jun01)	75.8%	16.6%	7.6%

and the maximum pattern length. For example, at 0.1% minimum support, we found more than 130,000 patterns in just 2.2 seconds; the maximum set length was 20!

Figure 9 shows the total time taken, total number of patterns found, and maximum sequence length, for mining frequent sequences for various minimum support values. For example, at 0.015% minimum support, we found more than 7,000 patterns in just 4.7 seconds; the maximum sequence length was 10.

Finally Figure 10 shows the total time taken, number of patterns, and maximum subtree length, for mining frequent subtrees for various minimum support values. For example, at 0.35% minimum support, we found about 2,300 trees in 6.5 seconds; the maximum subtree had 8 nodes.

These results lead to several interesting observations that support the mining of complex patterns from web logs. For example, if one performs only itemset mining, one discovers many long patterns. Sequence mining takes longer time but the patterns are likely to be more useful, since they contain path information. One has to lower the support compared to set mining, since the same set of nodes can lead to many maximal forward sequences. However, tree mining, though it takes more time than sequence mining, produces relatively fewer patterns which are even more informative. As in sequence mining, an itemset can contain several subtrees, since there is exactly one itemset per user session, but there could be several subtrees from the same session. Furthermore, one frequent subtree many correspond to several maximal forward sequences (as many as the number of leafs in the tree).

Size of LOGML Documents: Since raw log files can be large, there is a concern that the LOGML files will be large as well. Table 1 shows the observed size of raw log files compared to the LOGML documents (with and without compression), the number of requests and user sessions, and the breakdown of LOGML files for the CS department (*www.cs.rpi.edu*) and RPI web site (*www.rpi.edu*).

For example, for RPI1 (logs from 14th June, 2001) there were about 275,000 request for different nodes comprising 6,000 user sessions. The LOGML file is more than 2.5 times *smaller* than the raw log file. The same trends are observed for the other sources.

The potential benefits of LOGML for web usage mining become prominent when we consider the breakdown of the LOGML files in Table 2. For the RPI site we find that about 88% of the LOGML file is used to store the webgraph, while the user sessions occupy only 8% (the other elements to store statistics, etc. use up 3.4% space). For the CS department site, we find that the webgraph takes about 75% space, while the user sessions occupy 17%. In general, the webgraph is not likely to change much from one day to the next, and even if it does, one can always store a master webgraph spanning several days or months separately. Then on a per day basis we need only store the user sessions (and the other LOGML sections if desired). For example for the RPI site this would require us to store 174,573 bytes per day, while for the CS site is comes to 86,888 bytes per day for storing only the user sessions (with compression). Thus, not only does LOGML facilitate web usage mining, it also can drastically reduce the amount of daily information that needs to be stored at each site.

6   Conclusion

In this paper, we defined two new XML languages, XGMML and LOGML, and a web usage mining application. XGMML is a graph file description format, and an ideal candidate to describe the structure of web sites. Furthermore XGMML is a container for meta-data information. LOGML, on the other hand, is an extension of XGMML to collect web usage. LOGML is not only a preprocessor for our data mining applications, but also useful for web characterization and report generation.

Future work includes mining user graphs (structural information of web usages), as well as visualization of mined data using WWWPal system [1]. To perform web content mining, we need keyword information and content for each of the nodes. Obtaining this information will involve analyzing each of the web pages and collecting relevant keywords. Work is under way to accomplish this task.

We would also like to add that LOGML is being used to support other kinds of log files. For instance LOGML is one of the supported output formats for the Lire open source log reporting and analysis software by the Logreport Foundation (see http://www.logreport.com/), which supports email, DNS, web server, firewall and even printer logs. When combined with data mining techniques presented above, one can extract valuable information from such diverse kinds of logs in addition to web logs.

The LOGML 1.0 and XGMML 1.0 draft specifications, with their respective DTDs, Schemas and other details are available online at:
http://www.cs.rpi.edu/~puninj/LOGML/
http://www.cs.rpi.edu/~puninj/XGMML/

References

1. Punin, J., Krishnamoorthy, M.: WWWPal System - A System for Analysis and Synthesis of Web Pages. In: Proceedings of the WebNet 98 Conference, Orlando (1998)
2. R. Cooley, B. Mobasher, and J. Srivastava: Web Mining: Information and Pattern Discovery on the World Wide Web. In: 8th IEEE Intl. Conf. on Tools with AI. (1997)
3. Chen, M., Park, J., Yu, P.: Data mining for path traversal patterns in a web environment. In: International Conference on Distributed Computing Systems. (1996)
4. Spiliopoulou, M., Faulstich, L.: WUM: A Tool for Web Utilization Analysis. In: EDBT Workshop WebDB'98, LNCS 1590, Springer Verlag (1998)
5. Cooley, R., Mobasher, B., Srivastava, J.: Data preparation for mining world wide web browsing pattern. Knowledge and Information Systems 1 (1999)
6. Masand, B., Spiliopoulou, M., eds.: Advances in Web Usage Mining and User Profiling: Proceedings of the WEBKDD'99 Workshop. Number 1836 in LNAI. Springer Verlag (2000)
7. Kosala, R., Blockeel, H.: Web mining research: A survey. SIGKDD Explorations 2 (2000)
8. Thüring, M., Hannemann, J., Haake, J.: Hypermedia and cognition: Designing for comprehension. Communications of the ACM 38 (1995) 57–66
9. Pirolli, P., Pitkow, J., Rao, R.: Silk from a Sow's Ear: Extracting Usable Structure from the Web. In Tauber, M.J., Bellotti, V., Jeffries, R., Mackinlay, J.D., Nielsen, J., eds.: Proceedings of the Conference on Human Factors in Computing Systems: Commun Ground, New York, ACM Press (1996) 118–125
10. Wu, K., Yu, P., Ballman, A.: Speed Tracer: A Web usage mining and analysis tool. Internet Computing 37 (1997) 89
11. Agrawal, R., Mannila, H., Srikant, R., Toivonen, H., Verkamo, A.I.: Fast discovery of association rules. In Fayyad, U., et al, eds.: Advances in Knowledge Discovery and Data Mining, AAAI Press, Menlo Park, CA (1996) 307–328
12. Zaki, M.J.: Scalable algorithms for association mining. IEEE Transactions on Knowledge and Data Engineering 12(3):372–390 (2000)
13. Srikant, R., Agrawal, R.: Mining sequential patterns: Generalizations and performance improvements. In: 5th Intl. Conf. Extending Database Technology. (1996)
14. Zaki, M.J.: SPADE: An efficient algorithm for mining frequent sequences. Machine Learning Journal 42 (2001) 31–60
15. Zaki, M.J., Hsiao, C.J.: CHARM: An efficient algorithm for closed itemset mining. In: 2nd SIAM International Conference on Data Mining. (2002)
16. Zaki, M.J.: Efficiently mining trees in a forest. Technical Report 01-7, Computer Science Dept., Rensselaer Polytechnic Institute (2001)

A Framework for Efficient and Anonymous Web Usage Mining Based on Client-Side Tracking

Cyrus Shahabi and Farnoush Banaei-Kashani

Department of Computer Science, Integrated Media Systems Center,
University of Southern California, Los Angeles, CA 90089-2561, USA
{shahabi,banaeika}@usc.edu

Abstract. *Web Usage Mining (WUM)*, a natural application of data mining techniques to the data collected from user interactions with the web, has greatly concerned both academia and industry in recent years. Through WUM, we are able to gain a better understanding of both the web and web user access patterns; a knowledge that is crucial for realization of full economic potential of the web. In this chapter, we describe a framework for WUM that particularly satisfies the challenging requirements of the web personalization applications. For on-line and anonymous web personalization to be effective, WUM must be accomplished in real-time as accurately as possible. On the other hand, the analysis tier of the WUM system should allow compromise between scalability and accuracy to be applicable to real-life web-sites with numerous visitors. Within our WUM framework, we introduce a distributed user tracking approach for accurate, efficient, and scalable collection of the usage data. We also propose a new model, the Feature Matrices (FM) model, to capture and analyze users access patterns. With FM, various features of the usage data can be captured with flexible precision so that we can trade off accuracy for scalability based on the specific application requirements. Moreover, due to low update complexity of the model, FM can adapt to user behavior changes in real-time. Finally, we define a novel similarity measure based on FM that is specifically designed for accurate classification of partial navigation patterns in real-time. Our extensive experiments with both synthetic and real data verify correctness and efficacy of our WUM framework for efficient web personalization.

1 Introduction

In this chapter, we describe a complete framework for *Web Usage Mining (WUM)*, an emergent domain in Web Mining that has greatly concerned both academia and industry in recent years [45]. WUM is the process of discovering and interpreting patterns of user access to the web information systems by mining the data collected from user interactions with the system. Knowledge of user access patterns is useful in numerous applications: supporting web-site design decisions such as content and structure justifications [44,14], optimizing systems by enhancing caching schemes and load-balancing, making web-sites adaptive [34], supporting business intelligence and marketing decisions [8], testing user interfaces, monitoring for security purposes, and more importantly, in

R. Kohavi et al. (Eds.): WEBKDD 2001, LNAI 2356, pp. 113–144, 2002.
© Springer-Verlag Berlin Heidelberg 2002

web personalization applications such as recommendation systems [36] and target advertising. Commercial products such as *Personify*[TM] [50], *WebSideStory*[TM] [51], *BlueMartini*[TM] [52], and *WebTrends*[TM] [55], and acquired companies such as *Matchlogic*[TM], *Trivida*[TM], *Andromedia*[TM], and *DataSage*[TM] are all witnesses of commercial interests in WUM.

Within WUM-based web personalization applications, the user access patterns are utilized to identify needs and preferences of each individual user, and subsequently, customize the content and/or structure of the web information system based on user needs. This process often consists of two components. First, an off-line component learns a comprehensive users access model by mining typical access patterns from training datasets. Second, once the access model is identified, it is used by an on-line component to interpret navigational behavior of the active users and to identify the user needs in real-time. The system should treat each user as an anonymous individual and identify user needs per session, otherwise besides violating users privacy by tracking users across sessions, the system will be incapable of distinguishing between various user roles and/or different users using the same client[1].

Web personalization applications impose a set of challenging requirements that are partially in conflict with each other. With anonymous web personalization, the on-line component of the system should run in real-time, particularly it should be able to identify user needs in a fraction of the session period. In most cases, violation of this time constraint renders the result of the personalization totally useless; for example in a recommendation system, usually there is little use for the recommendations that are generated after user leaves the site. Thus, the time complexity for the process of applying the access model to interpret active sessions must be sufficiently low. Moreover, on the one hand the volume of navigation data generated per site is usually very large. For example, $Yahoo^{TM}$ has 166 million visitors every day, generating 48GB clickstream data per hour [54]. Even assuming the analysis model is built off-line, this data cannot be analyzed/classified in real-time unless some features of the data be dropped while interpreting the active sessions. On the other hand, since with anonymous web personalization the available information about a user is limited to the user interactions with the web during an active session period, necessarily we want to consider every single action of a user and to be as accurate as possible, otherwise the customization will be inefficacious. Therefore, for efficient customization, users access model learned in the personalization system should be flexible enough to allow an engineering compromise between scalability and accuracy based on the application specifications.

A typical WUM system consists of two tiers: 1) Tracking, in which user interactions are captured and acquired, and 2) Analysis, in which user access patterns are discovered and interpreted by applying typical data mining techniques to the acquired data. The WUM framework described in this chapter comprises an accurate, efficient, and scalable tracking tier, and a flexible and

---

[1] In case static profiling is unharmful/desirable, with a hybrid approach anonymous WUM can be employed for more flexible predictions.

adaptive analysis tier to support anonymous web personalization efficiently. Our tracking approach [39] is 1) *accurate* because it collects accurate data as close as possible to the real data, 2) *efficient* because it imposes minimum amount of overhead to the WUM system to allow real-time analysis, and 3) *scalable* because it scales to be applicable to large-scale applications where volume of the data to be acquired by the WUM system exceeds tens of GBs per day. Our analysis tier takes advantage of a novel model, the *Feature Matrices (FM)* model [40], to capture users navigation. FM is a model with flexible complexity to allow striking a compromise between accuracy and scalability, given the specific requirements of an application. The FM model benefits from two types of flexibility. First, FM is an open model; it can be tuned to capture various features of the web usage data and incorporated new features as required by any particular application domain. Second, by tuning *order* of the FM model, one can determine the accuracy of the data captured about various features of navigation; hence, trade-off between accuracy and scalability is easily accomplished. Besides, the FM model can be updated both off-line and, incrementally, online so that it can adapt to both short-term and long-term changes in user behaviors. Finally, we propose a novel similarity measure, *PPED*, to compare the FM models of partial paths with clusters of paths. With anonymous WUM, accurate classification of partial navigation paths of new users to the cluster representatives is crucial.

It is important to note that although we motivate and discuss this framework in the context of web personalization applications, it is as much applicable for other WUM applications. The remainder of this chapter is organized as follows. Section 2, summarizes the related work. We explain how to implement the tracking tier of the WUM framework in Section 3. In Section 4, we formally characterize the analysis tier of the WUM framework by defining our access pattern model, describing our similarity measures, and discussing our dynamic clustering technique. The results of our experiments are included in Section 5. Finally, Section 6 concludes the chapter and discusses our future directions.

2 Related Work

Web mining is broadly defined as the discovery and analysis of useful information from the World Wide Web. A detailed taxonomy of Web Mining domains is provided in [26]. Here, first we briefly characterize different domains that pertain to Web Mining. Thereafter we will focus on some of the current researches being performed on WUM.

Target data sets for data mining in the context of the web are classified into the following types:

- **Content data:** The data meant to be conveyed to the web user. Naturally, *Web Content Mining* is the process of extracting knowledge from the content of the web documents [12].
- **Structure data:** The meta data that defines the organization of the web information systems. *Web Structure Mining* is the process of inferring knowledge from the structure of data [21,18].

- **Usage data:** The data collected from user interactions with the web. As mentioned before, WUM is the process of discovering and interpreting patterns of user access to the web information system [5].

The idea of exploiting usage data to customize the web for individuals was suggested by researchers as early as 1995 [4,24,32]. A comprehensive survey of the existing efforts in WUM is provided by Srivastava et al. [45]. Some of the current approaches with the two tiers of WUM, tracking and analysis, are summarized in the following sections.

2.1   User Interaction Tracking

The usage data are usually obtained from either web server log, at the server side, or web browser, at the client side[2]. Server log is not reliable as a source of usage data for WUM because server log data are not accurate. There are various levels of caching embedded in the web, mainly to expedite users access to the frequently used pages. Those pages requested by hitting the "Back" button, which is heavily used by the web users nowadays [16], are all retrieved from the web browser cache. Also, proxy servers provide an intermediate level of caching in the enterprise level. Unfortunately, cache hits are missing from the server log, rendering it as an incomplete source of information to acquire spatial features of user interactions such as hit-count [13,35]. Moreover, even for those entries captured by the server log, the temporal aspects of user interactions are recorded inaccurately, whereas temporal features such as view-time of pages are considered highly informative in deducing user preferences [20]. The timestamps recorded for each server log entry includes the network transfer time. It is important to note that due to non-deterministic behavior of the network, the amount of this noise varies rapidly and there is no trivial way to filter it out from the server log data.

Furthermore, data acquisition via server log is inefficient because when server log is used as the data source, preprocessing of the data becomes the prerequisite of the WUM process. Preprocessing imposes many difficulties and results in a large amount of overhead to the actual process of WUM [13], so that practically it renders on-line mining of user behaviors impossible. Specifically, *user session identification* and *data cleansing* are the most difficult and time-consuming tasks performed during preprocessing of the server log. Due to stateless service model of the HTTP protocol, pages requested in a user session are logged independently in the server log. However, for meaningful WUM these requests must be re-identified and re-grouped into user sessions as semantic units of analysis. This process, the so called user session identification, is usually performed based on the IP address of the client machine recorded in the log entry for each HTTP request. However, since there is a many-to-many relationship between users and

---

[2] Proxy server log can also be considered as a source of web usage data; however, this source is often used only to characterize browsing behavior of a group of anonymous users sharing a common proxy server. As far as this chapter is concerned, proxy server logs have the same characteristics as web server logs.

IP addresses, this approach cannot provide reliable information. Due to proxy servers and/or IP masquerading, a single IP address can be used by multiple users. On the other hand, some ISPs assign a different IP address to HTTP requests of a user during a single session. Moreover, missing cache hits in the server log makes the user identification process even harder. Researchers have proposed various methods to resolve this problem, but none of these methods are without serious drawbacks. *Cookies*, which allow inter-session tracking of users, violate users privacy [17]; web-sites requiring *user registration* are often neglected by anonymous users; *dynamic URLs* embedding session ID restricts intermediate caching and does not correctly handle the exchange of URLs between people [35]; *cache-busting* defeats the speed up advantage gained by caching; the *hit-metering* scheme proposed by Mogul et al. [29] requires modification to the HTTP protocol; the *heuristics* proposed by Cooley et al. [13] only provide relative accuracy in the absence of additional information; and data acquisition at *application servers* [3] is only possible when actually users interact with the application services of a web-site (many user interactions are directly handled by the front-tier of the web-site; and many web-sites do not have a middle-tier, i.e. application server, at all). Another time-consuming preprocessing task is data cleansing. Often a page request results in recording several extra entries in the server log for the graphics and scripts besides the entry for the actual HTML file. These extra entries should not be included in the input to the analysis tier of the WUM system because they are not indicators of explicit user requests. During data cleansing these entries must be identified and eliminated from the server log.

In [37], we introduced a remote agent that acquires the user interactions from the browser at the client side. In this chapter, we describe a client-side web usage data acquisition system developed based on this remote agent[3]. When a user first enters a web-site enabled with the remote agent, the remote agent is uploaded into the browser at the client side. Thereafter, it captures all required features of user interactions with the web-site such as hits and view-times of web-pages, and transfers the acquired data to a data acquisition server, the *acquisitor*, where data are *directly* dumped into a database to be used by the analysis tier of the WUM system without any further preprocessing. This mechanism satisfies requirements of an accurate, efficient, and scalable data acquisition system. First, since with remote agent the data are collected at the client side, all cache hits are captured and variable network transfer time is excluded from recorded view-times for pages. Second, preprocessing tasks are totally eliminated with this approach. When the agent is uploaded to the browser, it receives a globally unique session ID from the acquisitor and labels all captured data sent to the server with that ID. Thus, the acquisitor can transparently store data captured by different agents as separate semantic units, i.e., user sessions, in the database without further requirement for user session re-identification. It is important to note that with this approach 1) unlike cookies, session IDs are only valid during a

---

[3] This system is currently operational and was demonstrated at VLDB 2000 Conference [38].

single active user session, so they do not violate users privacy, 2) unlike dynamic URLs and cache-busting, the caching mechanism is not affected/defeated, 3) unlike hit-metering, system works based on the current common protocols and technologies, 4) unlike heuristic algorithms for user session identification, user sessions can be identified with absolute reliability, and 5) unlike application servers, entire user interactions are observed and logged. Thus, this approach provides us with a safe method to superimpose state on the HTTP protocol and perform implicit user session identification with slight overhead on the clients. Moreover, since data to be captured are actively selected by the remote agent, as opposed to the server log that passively records any type of request, the required data cleansing is reduced. Finally, the acquisitor benefits for a scalable architecture to satisfy requirements of large-scale WUM systems. Of course, our approach has some drawbacks that are discussed in Section 3.1.

2.2   Access Pattern Analysis

As mentioned in Section 1, due to the large volume of usage data, they cannot be analyzed in real-time unless some features of the data be dropped while modeling access patterns. Page *hit-count*, which indicates frequency of the page visits during a session, has been traditionally considered as an informative indicator of the user preferences [47]. Also, *order* or *sequence* of page accesses is recently identified as an important piece of information [11]. Dependency models such as aggregate tree [43] and hidden Markov model [9] are used to capture this feature and to predict forward references. In addition to spatial features, temporal features such as page *view time* are also of significant concern, specially in the context of web personalization applications [20]. Although Yan et al. [47] and Levene et al. [23] show that view time has the Zipfian distribution and might be misleading in cases where long accesses obscure the importance of other accesses, we argue that using view time in combination with other features can alleviate this unwanted effect. The model described in this chapter is defined so that it can capture any number of these and/or any other feature that might seem informative. The features are captured per *segment*, which is the building block of a session (see Section 4.1). Variable number of the features and size of the segment allow to strike a compromise between accuracy and complexity of the model depending on the application requirements.

Researchers have investigated various models and data mining techniques to capture these features and to represent the user access patterns. Mobasher et al. [28] have applied the classical association rule Apriori algorithm [2] to find "frequent item sets" based on their patterns of co-occurrence across user sessions. They deploy association rules to find related item sets to be recommended to user based on the observed items in the user session. Mobasher et al. [27] show that clustering techniques provide a better overall performance as compared with association rules when applied in the context of web personalization.

Another set of models, which we denote as dependency models, are applied to predict forward references based on partial knowledge about the history of the session. These models learn and represent significant dependencies among page references. Zukerman et al. [49] and Cadez et al. [9] use Markov model for this purpose. Borges et al. [6] define a probabilistic regular grammar whose higher probability strings corresponds to user's preferred access pattern. Breese et al. [7] perform an empirical analysis of predictive algorithms such as Bayesian classification and Bayesian Network in the context of web personalization and demonstrate that performance of these algorithms is dependent on the nature of the application and completeness of the usage data. In Section 9, we compare our approach with the Markov model as a typical dependency model.

In this chapter, we use another classical data mining technique, *clustering*, to mine the usage data. This approach was first introduced by Yan et al. [47]. With this approach, usually user sessions are modeled as vectors. In the original form of the Vector model, each element of the vector represents the value of a feature, such as hit-count, for the corresponding web page. A clustering algorithm is applied to discover the user access patterns. Active user sessions are classified using a particular application-dependent similarity measure such as Euclidean distance. Recently, various clustering algorithms are investigated to analyze the clustering performance in the context of WUM. Fu et al. [15] employ *BIRCH* [48], an efficient hierarchical clustering algorithm; Nasraoui et al. [30] prefer a fuzzy relational clustering algorithm for WUM because they believe usage data is fuzzy in nature; Perkowitz et al. [33] introduce a new clustering algorithm, *cluster miner*, which is designed to satisfy specific web personalization requirements; Paliouras et al. [31] from Machine Learning community compare performance of the *cluster miner* with two other clustering methods widely used in Machine Learning research, namely *Autoclass* and *Self-Organizing Maps*, and show that *Autoclass* outperforms other methods. Mobasher et al. [27] observe that a user may demonstrate characteristics that are captured by different clusters while she/he is to be classified to a single cluster. Thus, they introduce the notion of *Usage Clustering*, a combination of clustering and association rules, to obtain clusters that potentially capture overlapping interests of different types of users. This goal is equivalently achievable by applying soft classification. The model described in this chapter is a generalization of the original Vector model introduced by Yan et al. [47], to be flexible in capturing users behavior anonymously and combining various features with tunable order of complexity. VanderMeer et al. [46] study anonymous WUM by considering dynamic profiles of users in combination with static profiles.

We analyze *Dynamic Clustering* as an approach to make the cluster model adaptive to short-term changes in users behavior. We also introduce an accurate similarity measure that avoids overestimation of distance between the partial user sessions and cluster representatives. Distance overestimation has been observed as a classification problem by Yan et al. [47] as well.

3   Tracking Tier

Our tracking system consists of two main components: 1) a remote agent, which is uploaded from the web server to the client machine as soon as client requests

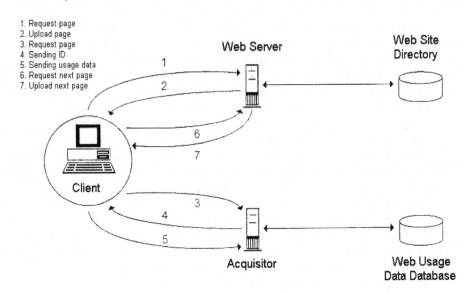

Fig. 1. Tracking Mechanism

the first page of the web-site[4], and 2) a central data acquisition server, termed *acquisitor*, which assigns globally unique IDs to the remote agents migrated to the active clients, and receives and stores the data collected by the remote agents in a database to be analyzed later by the analysis tier of the WUM system. To equip a web-site with this data acquisition system, the code that uploads the remote agent to the client machine should be embedded in the pages of the web-site. We have developed a simple utility that automates this process so that even for large web-sites with huge directories of pages the entire system installation process can be done in a short period.

The data acquisition mechanism in our system is illustrated in Figure 1. As an anonymous user enters an acquisition-enabled web-site by requesting the first page, the system components go through the following steps:

1. The client sends request for the first page to the web server;
2. Web server uploads the first page and the remote agent to the client machine;
3. The remote agent sends a request for an ID to the acquisitor;
4. The acquisitor assigns a globally unique ID to the agent and responds with the ID value;
5. The client's request for the next page causes the agent to send the collected usage data about previous page to the acquisitor before sending the request for the next page to the web server;
6. Request for the next page is sent to the web server;
7. The next page is uploaded to the client machine;

---

[4] This page can be any page of the web-site, not only the homepage. It is the entry point of the user to the web-site.

Steps 5 through 7 of this procedure are repeated as long as the user has not left the web-site, i.e. user session is not terminated. Since HTTP is a stateless protocol, web user does not explicitly indicate when she/he actually leaves a web-site. Therefore, termination of a user session can only probabilistically be determined considering a session timeout period. Catledge et al. [10] first measured a period of 25.5 minutes as the optimum timeout for a session; we use the same timeout value in our system. As a remote agent observes an idle period of at least 25.5 minutes during which user stops interaction with the web-site, it reports the session termination to the acquisitor so that it can inform the analysis tier of the WUM system.

It is important to note that browser uploads the remote agent to the client machine only *once*, as the user enters the web-site. Afterwards, the agent stays resident in the client machine for as long as the session is not terminated. Although our tracking mechanism may seem straightforward, its implementation imposes several challenges. In the following sections, we explain the detailed implementation of the remote agent and the acquisitor.

3.1   Remote Agent

The existence and activities of the remote acquisition agent should be transparent to users because users usually consider the tracking process as an overhead to their actual web browsing purpose. Specifically, the agent should be implemented as a light-weight piece of code[5] to minimize both the network transmission latency/overhread of uploading the agent to the client machine, and the CPU cycles spent by the client to execute the agent code. Agents implemented as browser plug-in's, such as Syskill and Webert [1], or those developed as separate heavy-weight processes that interact with the browser, such as Letizia [24], are not suitable for this purpose. Also, those agents require users to use special-purpose or modified browsers; therefore, it is difficult to convince users to use the new browser unless enough incentives are offered. Finally, user privacy is an important issue to be considered with any user tracking mechanism. Users are usually reluctant to be monitored; specially they do not want to be tracked from site to site and session to session over long period of time. For instance, the data acquisition system proposed by Lin et al. [25] assumes the environment where user privacy is not a concern; hence, it is not applicable to the web.

We have developed our remote agent as a light-weight Java applet that transparently runs at the client machine. As mentioned before, the agent is uploaded to the client machine only once as the user enters the web-site. Although JavaScript technology provides more facilities to acquire user-web interactions (or browsing events) [55], we prefer the Java applet technology because while it is well supported by all common browsers, it is designed to be secure and hence satisfies users' expectations of privacy [56]. Unlike cookies, which are stored at the client machine to allow keep tracking of user's history of interactions with the web-site from session to session, our agent tracks the user interactions

---

[5] Considering both size and execution time of the code.

only during a single session and does not store any information at the client machine. Therefore, not only user anonymity is maintained, but also different roles/behaviors of the user in different sessions is identifiable. This characteristic allows *anonymous* WUM.

The complete code for the remote agent is included in the appendix of this chapter. Each time the browser loads a web-page, it runs the applet. If it is the first time the applet is executed within the browser's JVM, i.e., when a user enters the web-site, the applet receives a unique ID from the acquisitor[6]. Besides, each time the applet is executed it records the load-time for the current page as it starts execution. Then, when the browser tries to load the next page, before the current page is unloaded, the applet records the unload-time for the page, computes its total view-time, connects to the acquisitor, and transfers a clean set of parameters including the unique agent ID to the acquisitor. Note that since view-time of a page is a time interval relative to the same client's clock (and not an absolute time value), clock synchronization between clients and acquisitor is not an issue. Here, for simplicity we are only capturing the view-time of the page, which provides the WUM system with view-time and hit-count features of user navigation. However, the same procedure is applicable in acquiring other navigational features.

There are some drawbacks with this approach. First, running the remote agent at the client side requires users cooperation in enabling Java at their browsers. This is the general problem with all client-side acquisition methods. However, considering the popularity of Java applets, Java is enabled by default in all common browsers such as Netscape™ and Internet Explorer™. Second, if a firewall blocks the TCP or UDP port used by the remote agent to communicate with the acquisitor, the captured usage data cannot be collected. This problem can be alleviated using the Remote Scripting technology developed by Microsoft™ [57]. Remote Scripting allows applets to use the HTTP port (port number 80) to communicate with the server. Since usually HTTP port is not blocked by firewalls, this will allow our remote agent to reach the server. Unfortunately, this technology is not supported by all web servers, e.g., Apache™. We are currently studying other technologies that can be used to eliminate this problem. Third, the delay of uploading the agent applet when the user first enters the web-site is undesirable, although with a light-weight agent the delay is typically tolerable. Finally, data traffic between the remote agent and the acquisitor is to be considered as the overhead of data collection for WUM. Since the payload of the packets exchanged between the agent and the acquisitor is light, using light-weight UDP packets for communication can alleviate this problem.

3.2   Acquisitor (Data Acquisition Server)

To be scalable, the data acquisition server should be able to handle requests from large number of active remote agents simultaneously. Our acquisitor is implemented as a multi-threaded daemon process with a standard single-dispatcher/

---

[6] Each window of the browser receives a separate ID, which allows distinguishing between various user roles.

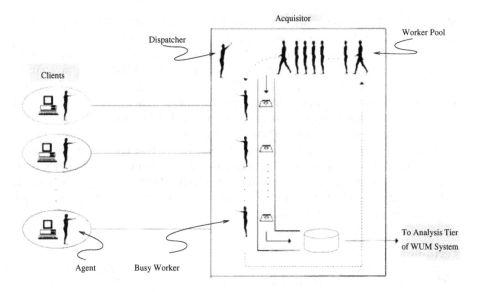

Fig. 2. Architecture of the acquisitor (data acquisition server)

multiple-worker architecture. This structure is similarly employed in common large-scale servers, e.g. web servers. Figure 2 illustrates the architecture of the acquisitor. All connection requests from the remote agents are received by a single dispatcher thread. The dispatcher simply assigns an idle worker thread from the worker pool to handle the received connection and returns to listen for the next connection request. The worker processes the agent request, i.e., either ID request or request for storing the captured usage data, and returns to the worker pool as soon as the process is finished. The ID is generated using a large global integer variable that is increased each time a new ID is assigned to an agent. The variable is large enough so that by the time it wraps around the old session IDs are analyzed and removed from the database. The usage data are directly dumped into the database as received from the agent.

It is important to note that the acquisitor is independent of the web server. Therefore, it can be executed at a separate machine, if required. Separating the data acquisition server from the web server not only results in a more scalable system, but also allows centralized acquisition of usage data for distributed applications such as distributed web-hosting (e.g., through Akamai [58]). This greatly facilitates usage data collection in such systems.

4   Analysis Tier

4.1   The Feature Matrices Model

Here, we present a novel model to represent both sessions and clusters in the context of WUM. We denote this model as the *Feature Matrices (FM)* model.

With FM, features are indicators of the information embedded in sessions. In order to quantify the features, we consider universal set of segments in a concept space as basis for the session space. Thus, features of a session are modeled and captured in terms of features of its building segments. This conceptualization is analogous to the definition of basis for a vector space, i.e. "a set of linearly independent vectors that construct the vector space". Therefore, the FM model allows analyzing sessions by analyzing features of their corresponding segments.

For the remainder of this section, we explain and analyze the FM model. First, we define our terminology. Next, basics of the FM model are explained: the features captured from user interactions, and the main data structure used to present these features. Subsequently, we discuss how to extract the session FM model and the cluster FM model, separately. Finally, we analyze complexity and completeness of the model.

Terminology

Web-site A web-site can be modeled as a set of static and/or dynamic web pages.

Concept Space (Concept) Each web-site, depending on its application, provides information about one or more concepts. For example, *amazon.com* includes concepts such as *Books, Music, Video*, etc. The web pages within a web-site can be categorized based on the concept(s) to which they belong. A *concept space* or simply *concept* in a web-site is defined as the set of web pages that contain information about a certain concept. Note that contents of a web page may address more than one concept, therefore concept spaces of a web-site are not necessarily disjoint sets[7].

Path A *path* P in a web-site is a finite or infinite sequence of pages:

$$x_1 \rightarrow x_2 \rightarrow ... \rightarrow x_i \rightarrow ... \rightarrow x_s$$

where x_i is a page belonging to the web-site. Pages visited in a path are not necessarily distinct.

Path Feature (Feature) Any spatial or temporal attribute of a path is termed a *path feature* or *feature*. Number of times a page has been accessed, time spent on viewing a page, and spatial position of a page in the path are examples of features.

Session The path traversed by a user while navigating a concept space is considered a *session*. Whenever a navigation leaves a concept space (by entering a page that is not a member of the current concept), the session is considered to

---

[7] Determination of the concept spaces for a Web-site can be done manually, automatically, or in a hybrid automatic/manual fashion. For example, a possible hybrid approach is to use an automatic content analysis technique, such as methods commonly employed by search engines, to categorize and classify the pages into different concepts based on their contents. Then, if required, categorization can be fine-tuned based on the application specifications.

be terminated. Since each page may belong to more than one concept, several *sessions* from different concepts may be embedded in a single *path*. Also, several sessions from the same concept may happen along a path, while a user leaves and then re-enters the concept. For analysis, we compare sessions from the same concept space with each other. Distinction between the "session" and the "path" notions makes the comparison more efficacious. To identify the user behavior, we can analyze all the sessions embedded in his/her navigation path, or prioritize the concepts and perform the analysis on the sessions belonging to the higher priority concept(s). Moreover, among the sessions belonging to the same concept space, we can restrict our analysis to the longer session(s), to decrease complexity of the analysis based on the application specifications. In any case, the result of the analysis on different sessions of the same path can be integrated to provide the final result. For example, in a recommendation system, the recommendation can be generated based on various user preferences detected by analyzing different sessions of the user's navigation path. Thus, hereafter we assume all sessions belong to the same concept. Similar analysis can be applied to sessions in any concept space.

Session Space The set of all possible sessions in a concept space is termed *session space*.

Path Segment (Segment) A *path segment* or simply *segment* E is an n-tuple of pages: $(x_1, x_2, ..., x_i, ..., x_n)$. We denote the value n, as the *order* of the segment E ($n \geq 1$). Note that there is a one-to-one correspondence between tuples and sequences of pages; i.e. $(x_1, x_2, ..., x_i, ..., x_n) \equiv x_1 \to x_2 \to ... \to x_i \to ... \to x_n$. We use tuple representation because it simplifies our discussion. Any subsequence of pages in a path can be considered as a segment of the path. For example, the path $x_1 \to x_3 \to x_2 \to x_5 \to x_2$ contains several segments such as 1st order segment (x_1), 2nd order segment (x_3, x_2), and 4th order segment (x_3, x_2, x_5, x_2). We exploit the notion of segment as the building block of sessions in order to model their features.

Universal Set of Segments $\varepsilon_C^{(n)}$, universal set of order-n segments, is the set of all possible n-tuple segments in the concept space C. Hereafter, since we focus on analysis within a single concept, we drop the subscript C from the notation.

Cluster A *cluster* is defined as a set of similar sessions. The similarity is measured quantitatively based on an appropriate similarity measure (see Section 4.2).

Basics

Features We characterize sessions through the following features:

- *Hit (H):* Hit is a spatial feature that reflects which pages are visited during a session. The FM model captures H by recording the number of times each *segment* is encountered in a traversal of the session. The reader may consider H as a generalization of the conventional "hit-count" notion. Hit-count counts number of hits per *page*, which is a segment of order 1.

- *Sequence (S):* Sequence is an approximation for the relative location of pages traversed in a session. As compared to H, it is a spatial feature that reflects the location of visits instead of the frequency of visits. With the FM model, S is captured by recording relative location of each segment in the sequence of segments that construct the session. If a segment has been repeatedly visited in a session, S is approximated by aggregating the relative positions of all occurrences. Thus, S does not capture the exact sequence of segments. Exact sequences can be captured through higher orders of H.
- *View Time (T):* View time captures the time spent on each segment while traversing a session. As opposed to H and S, T is a temporal feature.

Features of each session are captured in terms of features of the segments within the session. We may apply various orders of universal sets as basis to capture different features. Throughout our discussion, we have used $\varepsilon^{(1)}$ for T, and $\varepsilon^{(2)}$ for H and S, unless otherwise stated. Therefore, we extract the feature T for single-page segments, x_i, and features H and S for ordered page-pair segments (x_i, x_j). In Section 9, we will explain how using higher order bases results in more complete characterization of the session by the FM model in expense of higher complexity.

The FM model is an open model. It is capable of capturing any other meaningful session features in addition to those mentioned above. The same data structure can be employed to capture the new features. This is another option with which completeness of the FM model can be enhanced. However, our experiments demonstrate that the combination of our proposed features is comprehensive enough to detect the similarities and dissimilarities among sessions appropriately.

Data Structure Suppose $\varepsilon^{(n)}$ is the basis to capture a feature F for session U, we deploy an n-dimensional *feature matrix*, $M_{r^n}^F$, to record the F feature values for all order-n segments of U. n-dimensional matrix M_{r^n} is a generalization of 2-dimensional square matrix M_{r*r}. Each dimension of M_{r^n} has r rows, where r is the cardinality of the concept space. For example, $M_{4\times4\times4}$ that is a cube with 4 rows in each of its 3 dimensions, is a feature matrix for a 4-page concept space with ε^3 as the basis. Dimensions of the matrix are assumed to be in a predefined order. The value of F for each order-n segment $(x_\alpha, x_\beta, ..., x_\omega)$ is recorded in element $a_{\alpha\beta...\omega}$ of $M_{r^n}^F$. To simplify the understanding of this structure, reader may assume that rows in all dimensions of the matrix are indexed by a unique order of the concept space pages; then the feature value for the order-n segment $(x_\alpha, x_\beta, ..., x_\omega)$ is located at the intersection of row x_α on the 1st dimension, row x_β on the 2nd dimension, ... , and row x_ω on the n-th dimension of the feature matrix. Note that M_{r^n} covers all order-n segment members of $\varepsilon^{(n)}$. for instance, in a 100-page concept space with $\varepsilon^{(2)}$ as the basis, M_{100^2} has 10000 elements. On the other hand, number of segments existing in a session usually is in the order of tens. Therefore, M_{r^n} is usually a sparse matrix. The elements for which there is no corresponding segment in the session are set to zero.

To map a session to its equivalent FM model, the appropriate feature matrices are extracted for features of the session. The entire set of feature matrices generated for a session constitutes its FM model:

$$U^{fm} = \left\{ M^{F_1}_{r^{n_1}}, M^{F_2}_{r^{n_2}}, ..., M^{F_m}_{r^{n_m}} \right\}$$

If $n = \max(n_1, n_2, ..., n_m)$ then U^{fm} is an order-n FM model.

In subsequent sections, we explain how values of different features are derived for each segment from the original session, and how they are aggregated to construct the cluster model.

Session Model

Here, we explain how values of different features are extracted from a session to form the feature matrices of its FM model. Recall that we record features of a session in terms of features of its segments. Thus, it suffices if we explain how to extract various features for a sample segment E:

- For Hit (H), we count the number of times E has occurred in the session $(H \geq 0)$. Segments may partially overlap. As far as there is at least one non-overlapping page in two segments, the segments are assumed to be distinct. For example, the session $x_1 \to x_2 \to x_2 \to x_2 \to x_1$, has a total of 4 order-2 segments, including 1 occurrence of (x_1, x_2), 2 occurrences of (x_2, x_2), and 1 occurrence of (x_2, x_1).
- For Sequence (S), we find the relative positions of every occurrence of E and record their arithmetic mean as the value of S for E $(S > 0)$. To find the relative positions of segments, we number them sequentially in order of appearance in the session. For example, in the session $x_1 \to^1 x_2 \to^2 x_2 \to^3 x_2 \to^4 x_1$, S value for the segments (x_1, x_2), (x_2, x_2), and (x_2, x_1) are 1, 2.5 $\left(= \frac{2+3}{2}\right)$, and 4, respectively.
- For View Time (T), we add up the time spent on each occurrence of E in the session $(T \geq 0)$.

Cluster Model

With *clustering*, user sessions are grouped into a set of clusters based on similarity of their features. To cluster sessions, since the FM model is a distance-based model, we need a similarity measure to quantify the similarity between sessions, and a clustering algorithm to construct the clusters. Moreover, we need a scalable model for the cluster. Nowadays, any popular web-site is visited by a huge number of users. In such a scale, we may employ any similarity measure and clustering algorithm to group the sessions into clusters, but mere grouping the sessions is not sufficient. If a cluster is naively modeled as a set of session models, any analysis on a cluster will be dependent on the number of sessions in the cluster which is not a scalable solution. Particularly, for real-time classification of sessions using pre-generated clusters, the cluster model must be a "condensed" model so that the time complexity of the classification is independent of the number of cluster members. In this section, we describe our cluster model. Subsequently, in Section 4.2, we introduce an accurate similarity measure for the purpose of clustering, and finally, in Section 4.3, we propose a variation to conventional clustering algorithms to make them real-time adaptable to varying behaviors.

With our approach of modeling a cluster, we aggregate feature values of all clustered sessions into corresponding feature values of a virtual session, called cluster centroid. The cluster centroid is considered as a representative of all the sessions in the cluster, or equally as the model of the cluster. Consequently, the complexity of any analysis on a cluster will become independent of the cluster cardinality.

Suppose we have mapped all the sessions belonging to a cluster into their equivalent session models. In order to aggregate the features of the sessions into the corresponding features of the cluster model, it is sufficient to aggregate features for each basis segment. Assume we denote the value of a feature F for any segment E in the basis by $F(E)$. We apply a simple aggregation function, namely *arithmetic averaging*, to $F(E)$ values in all sessions of a cluster to find the aggregated value of $F(E)$ for the cluster model. Thus, if M^F is the feature matrix for feature F of the cluster model, and M_i^F is the feature matrix for feature F of the i-th session in the cluster, each element of M^F is computed by aggregating corresponding elements of all M_i^F matrices. This procedure is repeated for every feature of the FM model. The final result of the aggregation is a set of aggregated feature matrices that constitute the FM model of the cluster:

$$C^{fm} = \left\{ M^{F_1}, M^{F_2}, ..., M^{F_n} \right\}$$

Therefore, the FM model can uniquely model both sessions and clusters.

As mentioned before, the aggregation function we use for all features is the simple arithmetic averaging function. In matrix notation, the aggregated feature matrix for every feature F of the cluster model C^{fm} is computed as follows:

$$M^F = \frac{1}{N} \sum_{i=1}^{N} M_i^F$$

where N is the cardinality of the cluster C. The same aggregation function can be applied incrementally, when cluster model has already been created and we want to update it as soon as a new session, U_j, joins the cluster:

$$M^F \leftarrow \frac{1}{N+1} \left(N \times M^F + M_j^F \right)$$

This property is termed *dynamic clustering*. In Section 4.3, we leverage on this property to modify the conventional clustering algorithms to become real-time and adaptive.

Table 1. Parameters

Parameter	Definition
F_i	i-th feature captured in FM
n_i	Order of the basis used to capture F_i
m	Number of features captured in FM
n	$\max(n_1, n_2, \ldots, n_m)$
r	Cardinality of the concept space
L	Average length of sessions
M	Average cardinality of clusters

Analysis of the Model

Cluster-based WUM involves three categories of tasks: constructing clusters of sessions (clustering), comparing sessions with clusters, and integrating sessions into clusters. Regardless of the model employed for analysis and the algorithm used for clustering, complexity of constructing the clusters is dependent on N, which is the number of sessions to be clustered. This is true simply because during clustering each session should be analyzed at least once to detect how it relates to other sessions. The FM cluster model is defined so that it reduces the time complexity of the other two tasks. If the complexity of comparing a session with a cluster and integrating it into the cluster is independent of the cluster cardinality, user classification and cluster updating can be fulfilled in real-time.

The price we have to pay to achieve lower space and time complexity is to sacrifice *completeness*[8]. If the cluster model is merely the set of member sessions stored in their complete form, although the model is *complete* in representing the member sessions, it does not scale. On the other hand, if we aggregate member sessions to construct the cluster model, the model will lose its capability to represent its members with perfect accuracy. The more extensive aggregation is applied, the less complete the cluster model. The FM model is flexible in balancing this trade-off based on the specific application requirements[9].

FM Complexity versus the Vector and Markov Models Let $FM^{(n)}$ be an FM model of the order n (see Table 1 for the definitions of terms), where $n = \max(n_1, n_2, \ldots, n_m)$. In the worst case, $FM^{(n)}$ comprises m n-dimensional matrices M_{r^n}, one for each of the model features. Thus, *space* cost of $FM^{(n)}$ is $O(mr^n)$. *Time* complexity for user classification is $O(mL)$ and for updating a cluster by assigning a new session to the cluster is $O(mr^n)$. Therefore, space and time complexity of $FM^{(n)}$ model are both independent of M.

From $O(mr^n)$, complexity increases exponentially with n, which is the order of the FM model. Based on Property 1, as the order n increases, the FM model becomes more complete in describing its corresponding session or cluster:

---

[8] A model is more complete if it is a better approximation for the real session/cluster.
[9] A formal proof for uniqueness of the FM model for a sesson/cluster is included in [42].

Property 1. If $p_1 > p_2$ then $FM^{(p_1)}$ is more complete than $FM^{(p_2)}$

Thus, added complexity is the price for a more accurate model. An appropriate order should be selected based on the accuracy requirements of the specific application. Formal proof for Property 1 is included in [42].

The other crucial parameter in $O\left(mr^n\right)$ is m, the number of features captured by the FM model. Features are attributes of the sessions, used as the basis for comparison. The relative importance of these attributes in comparing the sessions is absolutely application-dependent. The FM model is an open model in a sense that its structure allows incorporating new features as the need arises for different applications. Performing comparisons based on more features result in more accurate clustering, though again the complexity is increased.

Now let us compare the performance of FM with two other conventional models, namely the Vector model and the Markov model. The Vector model can be considered as one special case of the FM model. As used in [47], the Vector model is equivalent to an $FM^{(1)}$ model with H as the only captured feature. Thus, the Vector model scales as $O\left(r\right)$, but as discussed above, since it is an order-1 FM model, it performs poorly in capturing information about sessions. Our experiments illustrate that an $FM^{(2)}$ model with S and H as its features outperforms the Vector model in accuracy (see Section 5). The other model, typically employed in dependency-based approaches, is the "Markov" model. Although whether or not web navigation is a Markovian behavior has been the subject of much controversy [19], the Markov model has demonstrated acceptable performance in the context of WUM [9]. The transition matrix of an order-n Markov model is extractable from H feature matrix of an $FM^{(n+1)}$ model. Thus, the FM model at least captures the same amount of information as with an equivalent Markov model. They also benefit from the same time complexity of $O\left(L\right)$ for dynamic user classification. However, the Markov model cannot be updated in real-time because the complexity of updating a cluster is dependent on the cardinality of the cluster. Moreover, the Markov model is not an *open* model, as described for FM because it is defined to capture order and hit.

4.2   Similarity Measure

A *similarity measure* is a metric that quantifies the notion of "similarity". To capture behaviors of the web-site users, user sessions are to be grouped into clusters, such that each cluster is composed of "similar" sessions. Similarity is an application-dependent concept and in a distance-based model such as FM, a domain expert should encode a specific definition of similarity into a pseudo-distance metric that allows the evaluation of the similarity among the modeled objects. With the FM model, these distance metrics, termed *similarity measures*, are used to impose order of similarity upon user sessions. Sorting user sessions based on the similarity is the basis for clustering the users. Some similarity measures are defined to be indicator of dissimilarity instead of similarity. For the purpose of clustering, both approaches are applicable.

In [37], we introduce a similarity measure for session analysis that does not satisfy an important precondition: "the basis segments used to measure the similarity among sessions must be orthogonal". Here, we define a new similarity measure, $PPED$, particularly defined to alleviate the overestimation problem attributed to pure Euclidean distance measure in the context of WUM [47]. This measure satisfies the mentioned precondition. Before defining the function of this similarity measure, let us explain how the FM model is interpreted by a similarity measure.

With a similarity measure, each feature matrix of FM is considered as a uni-dimensional matrix. To illustrate, assume all rows of an n-dimensional feature matrix are concatenated in a predetermined order of dimensions and rows. The result will be a uni-dimensional ordered list of feature values. This ordered list is considered as a vector of feature values in $R^{(r^n)}$, where r is the cardinality of the concept space. Now suppose we want to measure the quantitative dissimilarity between the two sessions U_1^{fm} and U_2^{fm}, assuming that the certain similarity measure used is an indicator of dissimilarity (analogous procedure applies when the similarity measure expresses similarity instead of dissimilarity). Each session model comprises a series of feature vectors, one for each feature captured by the FM model. For each feature F_i, the similarity measure is applied on the two F_i feature vectors of U_1^{fm} and U_2^{fm} to compute their dissimilarity, D^{F_i}. Since the dissimilarity between U_1^{fm} and U_2^{fm} must be based on all the FM features, the total dissimilarity is computed as the weighted average of dissimilarities for all features:

$$D^F = \sum_{i=1}^{m} w_i \times D^{F_i} \qquad \left(\sum_{i=1}^{m} w_i = 1 \right) \tag{1}$$

where m is the number of features in the FM model. D^F can be applied in both hard and soft assignment of sessions to clusters. Weight factor w_i is application-dependent and is determined based on the relative importance and efficacy of features as similarity indicators. In Section 5, we report on the results of our experiments in finding the compromised set of weight factors for H and S features.

Here, we explain our new similarity measure. Throughout this discussion, assume $\vec{A}$ and $\vec{B}$ are feature vectors equivalent to n-dimensional feature matrices M_1^F and M_2^F, and a_i and b_i are their i-th elements, respectively. Vectors are assumed to have $N = r^n$ elements, where r is the cardinality of the concept space.

Projected Pure Euclidean Distance (PPED)

$PPED$ is a variant of Pure Euclidean Distance measure (PED) to alleviate the *overestimation* problem. To illustrate the overestimation problem with PED, suppose a user navigates the session U that belongs to cluster C. It is not necessarily the case that the user traverses every segment as captured by C^{fm}. In fact, in most cases user navigates a path similar to only a subset of the access pattern represented by C^{fm} and not the entire pattern. In evaluating the similarity between U^{fm} and C^{fm}, we should avoid comparing them on that part of the access pattern not covered by U or else their dissimilarity will be overestimated. Overestimation of dissimilarity occasionally results in failure to classify a session to the most appropriate cluster.

Assume $\vec{A}$ and $\vec{B}$ are two feature vectors of the same type belonging to a session and a cluster model, respectively. To estimate the dissimilarity between $\vec{A}$ and $\vec{B}$, $PPED$ computes pure Euclidean distance between $\vec{A}$ and the projection of $\vec{B}$ on those coordinate planes at which $\vec{A}$ has non-zero components:

$$PPED\left(\vec{A}, \vec{B}\right) = \left(\sum_{i=1, a_i \neq 0}^{N} (a_i - b_i)^2 \right)^{\frac{1}{2}} \tag{2}$$

where $PPED \in [0, \infty)$. Note that $PPED$ is not commutative.

Non-zero components of $\vec{A}$ belong to those segments that exist in the session. Zero values, on the other hand, are related to the remainder of the segments in the basis universal set. By contrasting $\vec{A}$ with the projected $\vec{B}$, we compare the session and the cluster based on just the segments that exist in the session and not on the entire basis. Thus, the part of the cluster not covered in the session is excluded from the comparison to avoid overestimation.

Since $PPED$ can compare sessions with different lengths, it is an attractive measure for real-time clustering where only a portion of a session is available at any given time (see Section 4.3). $PPED$ also helps in reducing the time complexity of the similarity measurement. According to Equation 2, the time complexity of $PPED$ is $O(mL)$ (refer to Table 1 for the definitions of the terms). In Section 5, we report on the superiority of $PPED$ performance as compared to two classical similarity measures, i.e. PED and cosine of the angle formed by the feature vectors (Vector Angle or VA).

4.3   Dynamic Clustering

As discussed in Section 9, since the FM model of a cluster is independent of the cluster cardinality, any cluster manipulation with FM has a reasonably low complexity. Leveraging on this property, we can apply the FM model in real-time applications.

One benefit of this property is that FM clusters can be updated dynamically and in real-time. Note that in most common cluster representations, complexity of adding a new session to a cluster is dependent on the cardinality of the cluster. Therefore, practically in large scale systems, they are not capable of updating the clusters dynamically. By exploiting *dynamic clustering*, the WUM system can adapt itself to changes in users' behaviors in real-time. New clusters can be generated dynamically and existing clusters adapt themselves to the changes in users' tendencies. Delay-sensitive environments such as stock market, are among those applications for which this property is most advantageous. Figure 3 depicts a simple procedure to perform dynamic clustering when a new session is captured.

---

1. Find the distance/similarity between the session and every cluster available in the current cluster set using any reasonable similarity measure;

    // All similarity measures discussed in this paper are applicable. These similarity
    // measures are defined based on the data structure of the FM model

2. If there is no cluster closer than TDC to the session
        create a new cluster and use the FM model of the new session as the cluster model;
    else
        update the closest cluster to the session by joining the session to that cluster;

    // TDC is a threshold value specific to Dynamic Clustering. If the distance between the
    // new session and every existing cluster is more than TDC, then it is reasonable to
    // create a new cluster because a new user ehavior has been discovered

---

Fig. 3. An algorithm for *dynamic clustering*

Periodical re-clustering is the typical approach in updating the clusters. This approach results in high accuracy, but it cannot be performed in real-time. According to our experiments to compare the accuracy of the dynamic clustering with that of a periodical re-clustering (see Section 5), dynamic clustering shows lower accuracy in updating the cluster set. In fact, with dynamic clustering, we are trading accuracy for adaptability. Thus, dynamic clustering should not be used instead of classical clustering algorithms, but a hybrid solution is required. That is, the cluster set should be updated in longer periods through periodical re-clustering to avoid divergence of the cluster set from the trends of the real user behaviors. Meanwhile, dynamic clustering can be applied in real-time to adapt the clusters and the cluster set to short-term behavioral changes.

5 Performance Evaluation

5.1 Tracking Tier

We conducted several experiments to verify the mechanisms employed in tracking tier, and compared reliability of the usage data collected by our tracking system versus server log data reliability. We show that since with our remote agent the usage data are collected at the client side, the inaccuracy attributed to the server log data is entirely eliminated. Specifically, our data acquisition system is able to exclude the network transfer time from the recorded view-times for pages and also capture all cache hits.

To estimate the error due to the inclusion of network transfer time in page view-times, as recorded in the server log, we included a series of 10 pages within a real-world web-site directory[10]. This web-site comprises of 70 web-pages and it runs Apache web server version 1.3.12. The 10 included pages circularly call one another so that every 2 seconds the browser automatically requests the web server to upload the next page. We collected the page access entries for these

---

[10] USC Annenberg School of Communications (http://www.ascusc.org/jcmc)

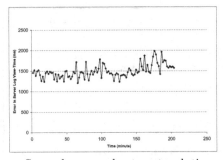 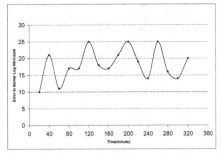

a. Server log error due to network time   b. Server log error due to cache hits

Fig. 4. Reliability of the server log usage data as compared to our system

pages as recorded both by our acquisitor and the server log for a period of 3.5 hours between 11:30am and 3:00pm during a working day of the week. The "NO-CACHE" option was used in the HTML pages to force the browser to retrieve the pages from the web server. Therefore, a server log entry is recorded for each page access and server log is not penalized for missing the cache hits. For each page access, we extracted the view-time of the page based on the corresponding server log entries and compared it with the exact view-time captured by our system to estimate the server log error. We computed the average error over successive time periods of 2 minutes each.

Results of this study are reported in Figure 4-a. In this figure, the X-axis is the time period of the experiment (in minutes) and the Y-axis is the average server log error (in milliseconds) in capturing the view-times of pages. As illustrated, the error can be as large as 2 seconds in each page view-time. Also, we extracted the average page view-time in this web-site from a server log containing real user access entries. The average page view-time for the web-site is 15 seconds; therefore, our system can improve the view-time accuracy up to 13%.

It is important to note that due to the large variance of network transfer time, as measured 1) at different times of the day and week and 2) at the same time but for different users dispersed in the Internet, we cannot simply eliminate the network transfer time by deducting a fixed value from all view-times captured by server log. Since our experiment is performed in a fairly short period of time, the variation of the network transfer time is not quite obvious in our results. However, as reported by Leighton et al. [22] variance of network transfer time can be as large as 7-10 seconds.

Finally, to measure the number of cache hits missing from the server log, we tracked real users access to the same web-site for a period of 5.5 hours. We counted number of page access entries existing in the acquisitor log but missing from the server log. These are the pages that are retrieved either from the browser cache or the proxy cache. In Figure 4-b, we demonstrate average number of cache hits missing from the server log (Y-axis) as a function of time (X-axis). The average is computed over successive time periods of 20 minutes each. The total average number of missing hits from the server log amounts to 0.9 pages per minute, whereas average number of total page accesses for this site is 2.23 pages per minute. Thus, our system can improve the hit-count accuracy up to 40%.

5.2   Analysis Tier

We conducted several experiments to: 1) compare the efficacy of the path features in characterizing user sessions, 2) study the accuracy of our similarity measures in detecting the similarity among user sessions, 3) compare the performance of the FM model with that of the traditional Vector model, 4) investigate the accuracy of the dynamic clustering, and 5) investigate performance of the FM model in capturing meaningful clusters in real data. Except for the last set of experiments, which verifies capabilities of our system in handling real data, we preferred to use synthetic data with our experiments so that we could have more control over our input characteristics. Here, we summarize the results of these experiments. The detailed description of the results, and also our experimental methodology is included in [42].

Efficacy of the Path Features A set of experiments was conducted to study the relative efficacy of the path features H and S in detecting similarities between user sessions. In Equation 1, the weight factor w_i indicates relative importance of the path feature F_i in computing the aggregated similarity measure. The higher weights are assigned to the features that are more effective in capturing the similarities. Our experiments were intended to find the compromised set of weight factors w_S (weight factor for S) and w_H that results in the optimum accuracy in capturing the similarities.

The experiment results show that regardless of the weight factors applied, the accuracy is always above 94%. Thus, both features (Hit and Sequence) are equally successful in identifying the spatial similarities. Depending on distinguishability of the dataset, the optimum accuracy is achieved by employing a compromised combination of the similarities detected in *Hit* and *Sequence*. In brief, when similarity among users of the same cluster decreases, it is more important to track which pages they visit (*Hit*) rather than where in the session they visit each page (*Sequence*).

Accuracy of the Similarity Measures In Section 4.2, we introduced $PPED$ as an accurate similarity measure. Here, we compare accuracy of $PPED$ with two classical similarity measures, i.e. PED and cosine (VA).

The experiment results demonstrate that for real data, which assumes low distinguishability, $PPED$ outperforms VA with a wide margin. The results also show that since $PPED$ can measure the similarity between a user and a cluster based on user characteristics rather than cluster characteristics, overestimation of the distance between the session and its intended cluster is avoided by disregarding unnecessary cluster characteristics in distance estimation. Therefore, $PPED$ can achieve up to 30% improvement in accuracy as compared to PED.

Performance of the FM Model We conducted some experiments to compare performances of a sample FM model, namely $FM^{(2)}$ with H and S as its features, with the traditional Vector model, which is considered equivalent to $FM^{(1)}$ with H as its only feature.

Results of this study demonstrate that accuracy of the Vector model decreases as the user sessions become less distinguishable, while the FM model can reasonably maintain its accuracy even with highly indistinguishable datasets. This superiority is because of: 1) incorporating *Sequence* into the model, and 2) capturing features based on order-2 segments.

Performance of the Dynamic Clustering In Section 4.3, we introduced *dynamic clustering* as an approach to update cluster models in real-time. However, we also mentioned that dynamic clustering trades accuracy for adaptability. We conducted several experiments to study the degradation of the accuracy due to applying the dynamic clustering. For this purpose, we compared dynamic clustering with K-Means.

The experiment results show that as expected accuracy of dynamic clustering is less than that of K-Means but the degradation of the accuracy is tolerable. Thus, the dynamic clustering can be applied to achieve adaptability but it should be complemented by long-term periodical re-clustering. The results also demonstrate that the performance of the dynamic clustering is much better in updating the existing clusters as compared to creating new clusters.

Performance of the FM Model with Real Data We conducted several experiments to study the performance of the FM model in handling the real data. Particularly, we investigated FM capabilities in capturing meaningful clusters in real data. To collect the real data, we tracked the web-site of a journal, Journal of Computer-Mediated Communication (JCMC) at University of Southern California[11], for a 15-day period in Summer 2001. We used our remote agent described in Section 3.1 for tracking. The JCMC web-site provides on-line access to 20 published issues of the journal. JCMC is a quarterly journal. Publications in each year is dedicated to a particular general topic and each quarterly issue of the journal is devoted to a special topic under the general annual topic (see Table 2 for the categorization of the journal issues).

During the tracking period, we collected a total of 502 sessions with the maximum length of 56. The entire web-site is dedicated to Computer-Mediated Communication issues; hence, we consider all 554 pages of the web-site in the same concept space. As mentioned in Section 3, when a remote agent observes an idle period of at least 25.5 minutes during which user stops interaction with the web-site, it reports the session termination. We used all three features, Hit, Sequence, and View Time ($w_H = w_S = w_T = \frac{1}{3}$, after normalization) with the FM of various orders, 1, 2, 3, and 4 (the same order used for all features) to model the captured sessions.

---

[11] http://www.ascusc.org/jcmc/

Table 2. Journal issues and their categorization based on topic

Category	Topic of the Issue	Associated Web-Page IDs*
(1-1)	Collaborative Universities	63-67 and 465-500
(1-2)	Play and Performance in CMC	69-104
(1-3)	Electronic Commerce	109-127
(1-4)	Symposium on the Net	128-145
(2-1)	Emerging Law on the Electronic Frontier, 1	148-170
(2-2)	Emerging Law on the Electronic Frontier, 2	171-192
(2-3)	Communication in Information Spaces	194-207
(2-4)	Network and Netplay	208-224
(3-1)	Studying the Net	226-237
(3-2)	Virtual Environments, 1	239-248
(3-3)	Virtual Environments, 2	249-260
(3-4)	Virtual Organizations	262-275
(4-1)	Online Journalism	276-290
(4-2)	CMC and Higher Education, 1	291-329
(4-3)	CMC and Higher Education, 2	330-359
(4-4)	Persistent Conversation	360-371
(5-1)	Searching for Cyberspace	372-382
(5-2)	Electronic Commerce and the Web	384-396
(5-3)	Computer-Mediated Markets	398-411
(5-4)	Visual CMC	414-437

* The page IDs are assigned to the web pages of the web-site using an off-line utility that crawls the web-site directory and labels the pages with unique IDs. The same IDs are used by the remote agents to refer to the pages when reporting the usage information.

Thereafter, corresponding to the number of topics of the journal issues, we used K-Means with $PPED$ to cluster the sessions into 20 clusters. To discover the relation between the generated clusters and the topics at the web-site, first we estimated the correspondence between a cluster and each topic by adding up the hit values of those segments (of all sessions included in the cluster) that are completely contained within the range of the pages associated to the topic (see Table 2). Second, using this measure, termed *correspondence*, we determined the topics most related to each cluster by filtering out unrelated (or less related) topics via a fixed threshold as the minimum acceptable correspondence value[12]. Finally, to identify the "meaningful" clusters, we manually reviewed the topics associated to each cluster. Assuming users of the web-site are often seeking information about a certain topic at each session (a logical assumption for a journal site), we consider a meaningful cluster as a cluster that its associated topics are related to each other (according to expert human view).

---

[12] We used *correspondence* = 15 as the threshold value, a threshold selected logically by observing the distribution of the correspondence value. It is important to note that since our analysis is comparative, the actual value of the threshold does not affect the results reported.

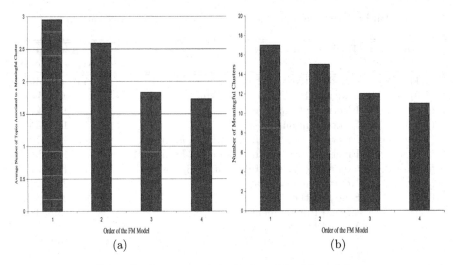

Fig. 5. Performance of the FM model with real data

Figure 5 depicts the results of our experiments with the real data. Figure 5-a shows that as the order of the FM used to model the sessions increases, the average number of topics associated to each meaningful cluster decreases. On the other hand, Figure 5-b illustrates that with increase in the FM order, the total number of the meaningful clusters generated decreases. Since higher order FM is more complete, and since with higher FM orders number of the dimensions of the feature vector space grows rapidly, a meaningful cluster of sessions is generated only when a group of sessions are very similar to each other; hence, it is more difficult to generate a meaningful cluster, however, meaningful clusters are more accurately associated with particular topics or user behaviors. One can think of using both a low-order and a high-order FM model to generate two cluster-sets for a web-site. Then, as a new session arrives, first it can be classified using the high-order clusters. If it is classified to a meaningful cluster, the user behavior, which is well oriented towards a particular interest, is accurately detected. Otherwise, the session is next classified using the low-order clusters to estimate the general characteristics of the user behavior as classified to the more general clusters.

6   Conclusions

In this chapter, we defined a framework for Web Usage Mining (WUM) that satisfies requirements of the web personalization applications. The framework comprises an accurate tracking technique, and a new model (the FM model) to analyze users access patterns. The FM model, which is a generalization of the Vector model, allows for a flexible, real-time, and adaptive WUM. We argued that these characteristics are not only useful for off-line and conventional WUM, but also critical for on-line anonymous web personalization. We demonstrated how flexibility of FM allows conceptualization of new navigation features as well as trading performance for accuracy by varying the *order*. For FM, we proposed a similarity measure, *PPED*, that can accurately classify partial sessions. This property is essential for real-time and anonymous WUM. We then utilized *PPED* within a dynamic clustering algorithm to make FM adaptable to short-term changes in user behaviors. Dynamic clustering is possible since unlike the Markov model, incremental updating of the FM model has a low complexity. Finally, we conducted several experiments that demonstrated the following:

- High accuracy of our tracking technique (40% improvement),
- Superiority of FM over the Vector model (at least by 25%),
- High precision of session classification when *PPED* is applied (above 98%),
- Tolerable accuracy of dynamic clustering as compared to K-Means (only 10% worse while being adaptable), and
- Capabilities of the FM model in identifying meaningful clusters with empirical datasets.

We intend to extend this study in several ways. First, we would like to design a recommendation system based on the WUM framework described in this chapter [41]. Running a real web personalization application in this framework will allow us to further enhance its capabilities. Second, since the parameter *TDC* in dynamic clustering algorithm (see Figure 3) is application-dependent, it should be learned through an optimization process. We are looking into various optimization techniques so that we can automatically determine the optimum value for *TDC*. Third, we plan to investigate other aggregation functions that might be more appropriate for certain features, as opposed to the simple averaging for all the features. Finally, for our cluster and session models, we want to compress the matrix even further, maybe through Singular Value Decomposition (SVD).

Appendix

```
import java.io.*;
import java.net.*;
import java.applet.*;
import java.lang.*;
import java.util.Date;

public class RemoteAgent extends Applet {
    // ID initialization
    private static long ID = -1 ;
    private static long startSession = System.currentTimeMillis() ;
    // Load and unload time for the page
    private long LoadTime, UnloadTime ;
    // "view-time" to be estimated
    private long Time ;
    // Acquisitor's port number
    private static final int Port = 21000

    // Setup the connection to the acquisitor, and
```

```java
// Get the unique ID (if agent is uploaded for the
//  first time to the client machine)
public void init(){
Socket sock ;
PrintWriter pwOut = null ;
BufferedReader brIn = null ;

try {
    if (ID < 0 || ((System.currentTimeMillis() - startSession) > 1530000)) {
        sock = new Socket(this.getCodeBase().getHost(), Port) ;
        pwOut = new PrintWriter(sock.getOutputStream(), true) ;
        brIn = new BufferedReader(new InputStreamReader(sock.getInputStream())) ;
        ID = -1 ;
        pwOut.println(ID) ;
        ID = Long.valueOf (brIn.readLine()).longValue() ;
        pwOut.close() ;
        brIn.close() ;
        sock.close() ;
        startSession = System.currentTimeMillis() ;
        }
} catch (UnknownHostException uhe){
    return ;
} catch (IOException ioe) {
    return ;
}

Time = 0;
}

// Record the load time for the page
public void start() {
LoadTime = System.currentTimeMillis() ;
}

// Record the unload time for the page,
// Compute the total view-time for the page, and
// Transfer the captured data to the acquisitor
public void stop() {
Socket sock ;
PrintWriter pwOut = null ;

UnloadTime = System.currentTimeMillis() ;
Time =  UnloadTime - LoadTime;

// Prepares information string about page.
String agentID = "<UID>" + ID + "<UID>" ;
String pageID = "<PID>" + this.getParameter("pageID") + "<PID>" ;
String T = "<T>" + java.lang.Long.toString(Time) + "<T>" ;
String outString = agentID + pageID + T ;

// Trying to send browsing information to Data Server.
try {
    if (ID > 0) {
    System.out.println(outString) ;
```

```
        sock = new Socket(this.getCodeBase().getHost(), Port) ;
        pwOut = new PrintWriter(sock.getOutputStream(), true) ;

        // Sends data to Data Server.
        pwOut.println(outString) ;
        pwOut.close() ;
        sock.close() ;
        }
    } catch (UnknownHostException uhe){
        return ;
    } catch (IOException ioe) {
        return ;
    }
    }
}
```

Acknowledgments

We are grateful for the assistance given to us by Jabed Faruque and Ming-Chang Lee in conducting the experiments. This research has been funded in part by NSF grants EEC-9529152 (IMSC ERC) and ITR-0082826, NIH-NLM grant nr. R01-LM07061, NASA/JPL contract nr. 961518, DARPA and USAF under agreement nr. F30602-99-1-0524, and unrestricted cash/equipment gifts from NCR, Microsoft, Intel and SUN.

References

1. Ackerman M., D. Billsus, S. Gaffney, S. Hettich, G. Khoo, D. Kim, R. Klefstad, C. Lowe, A. Ludeman, J. Muramatsu, K. Omori, M. Pazzani , D. Semler, B. Starr, and P. Yap. 1997. *Learning Probabilistic User Profiles: Applications to Finding Interesting Web Sites, Notifying Users of Relevant Changes to Web Pages, and Locating Grant Opportunities.* AI Magazine 18(2) 47-56, 1997.
2. Agrawal, R., and R. Srikant. 1994. *Fast algorithms for mining association rules.* Proceedings of the 20th VLDB conference, p.p 487-499, Santiago, Chile, 1994.
3. Ansari S., R. Kohavi, L. Mason, Z. Zheng. 2000. *Integrating E-Commerce and Data Mining: Architecture and Challenges.* Second International Conference on Electronic Commerce and Web Technologies, EC-Web 2000.
4. Armstrong R., D. Freitag, T. Joachims, and T. Mitchell. 1995. *WebWatcher: A Learning Apprentice for the World Wide Web.* AAAI Spring Symposium on Information Gathering from Heterogeneous, Distributed Environments, March 1995.
5. Baumgarten M., A.G. Bchner, S.S. Anand, M.D. Mulvenna, J.G. Hughes. 2000. *Navigation Pattern Discovery from Internet Data.* M. Spiliopoulou, B. Masand (eds.) Advances in Web Usage Analysis and User Profiling, Lecturer Notes in Computer Science, Vol. 1836, Springer-Verlag, ISBN: 3-540-67818-2, July 2000.
6. Borges J., M. Levene. 1999. *Data mining of user navigation patterns.* Proceedings of Workshop on Web Usage Analysis and User Profiling (WEBKDD), in conjunction with ACM SIGKDD International Conference on Knowledge Discovery and Data Mining, p.p 31-36, San Diego, California, August, 1999.

7. Breese J.S., D. Heckerman, C. Kadie. 1998. *Empirical Analysis of Predictive Algorithms for Collaborative Filtering.* Proceedings of Uncertainty in Artificial Intelligence, Madison, WI, July 1998. Morgan Kaufmann Publisher.

8. Büchner A.G., M.D. Mulvenna. 1998. *Discovering Internet Marketing Intelligence through Online Analytical Web Usage Mining.* ACM SIGMOD Record, ISSN 0163-5808, Vol. 27, No. 4, p.p 54-61, 1998.

9. Cadez I., Heckerman D., Meek C, Smyth P., and White S.: Visualization of Navigation Patterns on Web-Site Using Model Based Clustering. Technical Report MSR-TR-00-18, Microsoft Research, Microsoft Corporation, Redmond, WA,(2000)

10. Catledge L. and J. Pitkow. 1995. *Characterizing Browsing Behaviors on the World Wide Web.* Computer Networks and ISDN Systems, 27(6), 1995.

11. Chen M.S., J.S. Park, and P.S. Yu. 1998. *Efficient Data Mining for Path Traversal Patterns.* IEEE Transactions on Knowledge and Data Engineering, Vol. 10, No. 2, p.p 209-221, April, 1998.

12. Cohen W., A. McCallum, D. Quass. 2000. IEEE Data Engineering Bulletin, Vol. 23, No. 3. p.p 17-24, September 2000.

13. Cooley R., B. Mobasher, and J. Srivastava. 1999. *Data Preparation for Mining World Wide Web Browsing Patterns.* Journal of Knowledge and Information Systems, 1(1):5-32, Springer-Verlag, February, 1999.

14. Drott M.C. 1998. *Using Web server logs to improve site design.* Proceedings on the sixteenth annual international conference on Computer documentation, p.p 43-50, Quebec Canada, September, 1998.

15. Fu Y., K. Sandhu, and M. Shih. 1999. *Clustering of Web Users Based on Access Patterns.* International Workshop on Web Usage Analysis and User Profiling (WEBKDD'99), San Diego, CA, 1999.

16. Greenberg S. and A. Cockburn. 1999. *Getting Back to Back: Alternate Behaviors for a Web Browser's Back Button.* Proceedings of the 5th Annual Human Factors and Web Conference, NIST, Gaithersburg, Maryland, June, 1999.

17. Greenspun P. 1999. *Philip and Alex's Guide to Web Publishing.* Chapter 9, User Tracking; ISBN: 1-55860-534-7.

18. Henzinger M. 2000. *Link Analysis in Web Information Retrieval.* IEEE Computer Society, Vol. 23 No. 3, September, 2000.

19. Huberman B., Pirolli P., Pitkow J., and Lukos R.: Strong Regularities in World Wide Web Surfing. Science, 280, p.p 95-97 (1997)

20. Konstan J., B. Miller, D. Maltz, J. Herlocker, L. Gordon, and J. Riedl. 1997. *Applying Collaborative Filtering to Usenet News.* Communications of the ACM (40) 3, 1997.

21. Kuo Y.H., M.H. Wong. 2000. *Web Document Classification Based on Hyperlinks and Document Semantics.* PRICAI 2000 Workshop on Text and Web Mining, Melbourne, p.p 44-51, August 2000.

22. Leighton T. 2001. *The Challenges of Delivering Content on the Internet.* Keynote address in ACM SIGMETRICS 2001 Conference, Massachusetts, June 2001.

23. Levene L., and G. Loizou. 2000. *Zipf's law for web surfers.* Knowledge and Information Systems an International Journal, 2000.

24. Lieberman H. 1995. *Letizia: An Agent that Assists Web Browsing.* Proceedings of the International Joint Conference on Artificial Intelligence, Montreal, August 1995.

25. Lin I.Y., X.M. Huang, and M.S. Chen. 1999. *Capturing User Access Patterns in the Web for Data Mining.* Proceedings of the 11th IEEE International Conference Tools with Artificial Intelligence, November 7-9, 1999.

26. Mobasher B., R. Cooley, and J. Srivastava. 1997. *Web Mining: Information and Pattern Discovery on the World Wide Web.* Proceedings of the 9th IEEE International Conference on Tools with Artificial Intelligence (ICTAI'97), November 1997.

27. Mobasher B., H. Dai, T. Luo, M. Nakagawa, Y. Sun, J. Wiltshire. 2000. *Discovery of Aggregate Usage Profiles for Web Personalization.* Proceedings of the Web Mining for E-Commerce Workshop WebKDD'2000, held in conjunction with the ACM-SIGKDD Conference on Knowledge Discovery in Databases KDD'2000), Boston, August 2000.

28. Mobasher B., R. Cooley, and J. Srivastava. 2000. *Automatic Personalization Based on Web Usage Mining.* Special Section of the Communications of ACM on "Personalization Technologies with Data Mining", 43(8):142-151, August, 2000.

29. Mogul J, and P.J. leach. 1997. *Simple Hit-Metering for HTTP.* Internet draft-IETF-http-hit-metering-00.txt; HTTP Working Group. January, 1997.

30. Nasraoui O., R. Krishnapuram, A. Joshi. 1999. *Mining Web Access Logs Using a Fuzzy Relational Clustering Algorithm based on a Robust Estimator.* Proceedings of 8th World Wide Web Conference (WWW8), Torronto, May, 1999

31. Paliouras G., C. Papatheodorou, V. Karkaletsis, and C.D. Spyropoulos. 2000. *Clustering the Users of Large Web Sites into Communities.* Proceedings International Conference on Machine Learning (ICML), p.p 719-726, Stanford, California, 2000.

32. Pazzani M., L. Nguyen, and S. Mantik. 1995. *Learning from hotlists and coldists: Towards a WWW information filtering and seeking agent.* Proceedings of IEEE Intl.Conference on Tools with AI, 1995.

33. Perkowitz M., O. Etzioni. 1998. *Adaptive Web sites: Automatically Synthesizing Web Pages.* Fifth National Conference in Artificial Intelligence, p.p 727-732, Cambridge, MA, 2000.

34. Perkowitz M., and O. Etzioni. 2000. *Toward adaptive Web sites: Conceptual framework and case study.* Artificial Intelligence 118, p.p 245-275, 2000.

35. Pitkow J.E. 1997. *In Search of Reliable Usage Data on the WWW.* The Sixth International World Wide Web Conference, Santa Clara, California, 1997.

36. Schafer, J.B., J. Konstan, and J. Riedl. *Electronic commerce recommender applications.* Journal of Data Mining and Knowledge Discovery, 5:115–152, 2001.

37. Shahabi C., A. Zarkesh, J. Adibi, V. Shah. 1997.*Knowledge Discovery from Users Web-Page Navigation.* Proceedings of the IEEE RIDE97 Workshop, April, 1997.

38. Shahabi C., A. Faisal, F. Banaei-Kashani, J. Faruque. 2000. *INSITE: A Tool for Real-Time Knowledge Discovery from Users Web Navigation.* Proceedings of Very Large Databases (VLDB'2000), Cairo, Egypt, September, 2000.

39. Shahabi C., F. Banaei-Kashani, and J. Faruque. 2001. *A Reliable, Efficient, and Scalable System for Web Usage Data Acquisition.* WebKDD'01 Workshop in conjunction with the ACM-SIGKDD 2001, San Francisco, CA, August, 2001.

40. Shahabi C., F. Banaei-Kashani, J. Faruque, and A. Faisal. 2001. *Feature Matrices: A Model for Efficient and Anonymous Web Usage Mining.* EC-Web 2001, Germany, September, 2001.

41. Shahabi C., F. Banaei-Kashani, Y. Chen, D. McLeod. 2001. *Yoda: An Accurate and Scalable Web-based Recommendation System.* Sixth International Conference on Cooperative Information Systems (CoopIS 2001), Trento, Italy, September, 2001.

42. Shahabi C., F. Banaei-Kashani, J. Faruque. 2001. *Efficient and Anonymous Web Usage Mining for Web Personalization.* To appear at INFORMS Journal on Computing - Special Issue on Mining Web-based Data for e-Business Applications.

43. Spiliopoulou M., and L.C. Faulstich. 1999. *WUM: A Tool for Web Utilization Analysis*. In extended version of Proceedings of EDBT Workshop WebDB'98, LNCS 1590. Springer-Verlag, 1999.

44. Spiliopoulou M. 2000. *Web usage mining for site evaluation: Making a site better fit its users*. Special Section of the Communications of ACM on "Personalization Technologies with Data Mining", 43(8):127-134, August, 2000.

45. Srivastava J., R. Cooley, M. Deshpande, and P.N. Tan. 2000. *Web Usage Mining: Discovery and Applications of Usage Patterns from Web Data*. SIGKDD Explorations, Vol. 1, Issue 2, 2000.

46. VanderMeer D., K. Dutta, A. Datta, K. Ramamritham and S.B. Navanthe . 2000. *Enabling Scalable Online Personalization on the Web* . Proceedings of the 2nd ACM conference on Electronic commerce, p.p 185-196, 2000.

47. Yan T.W., Jacobsen M., Garcia-Molina H., Dayal U.: From User Access Patterns to Dynamic Hypertext Linking. Fifth International World Wide Web Conference, Paris, France, (1996)

48. Zhang T., R. Ramakrishnan, and M. Livny. 1996. *BIRCH: An Efficient Data Clustering Method for Very Large Databases*. SIGMOD '96, p.p 103-114, Montreal, Canada, June, 1996.

49. Zukerman I., D.W. Albrecht, and A.E. Nicholson. 1999. *Predicting users' requests on the WWW*. Proceedings of the Seventh International Conference on User Modeling (UM-99), Banff, Canada, p.p 275-284, June, 1999.

50. *http://www.personify.com*

51. *http://www.websidestory.com*

52. *http://www.bluemartini.com*

53. *http://www.webtrends.com*

54. *http://docs.yahoo.com/docs/pr/release634.html*

55. *http://www.javascript.com*

56. *http://java.sun.com/sfaq*

57. *http://msdn.microsoft.com/remotescripting*

58. *http://www.akamai.com*

Mining Indirect Associations in Web Data*

Pang-Ning Tan and Vipin Kumar

Department of Computer Science,
University of Minnesota
Minneapolis, MN 55455
{ptan,kumar}@cs.umn.edu

Abstract. Web associations are valuable patterns because they provide useful insights into the browsing behavior of Web users. However, there are two major drawbacks of using current techniques for mining Web association patterns, namely, their inability to detect interesting negative associations in data and their failure to account for the impact of site structure on the support of a pattern. To address these issues, a new data mining technique called indirect association is applied to the Web click-stream data. The idea here is to find pairs of pages that are negatively associated with each other, but are positively associated with another set of pages called the *mediator*. These pairs of pages are said to be *indirectly associated* via their common mediator. Indirect associations are interesting patterns because they represent the diverse interests of Web users who share a similar traversal path. These patterns are not easily found using existing data mining techniques unless the groups of users are known *a priori*. The effectiveness of indirect association is demonstrated using Web data from an academic institution and an online Web store.

1   Introduction

The unprecedented growth of the World Wide Web has revolutionized the way most commercial enterprises conduct their businesses today. It is now becoming increasingly common that the first point of interaction between a customer and an organization is at a Web site. As the number of online Web users grow, so does the volume of click-stream data collected at the Web servers. This has fueled a tremendous amount of interest in applying data mining techniques to discover hidden patterns in the click-stream data.

Association rules [1] and sequential patterns [3] are two notable types of Web patterns [9,24] that can bring added values to an e-commerce organization. These *Web association patterns* can provide useful insights into the browsing

---

* This work was partially supported by NSF grant # ACI−9982274 and by Army High Performance Computing Research Center contract number DAAD19−01−2−0014. The content of this work does not necessarily reflect the position or policy of the government and no official endorsement should be inferred. Access to computing facilities was provided by AHPCRC and the Minnesota Supercomputing Institute.

R. Kohavi et al. (Eds.): WEBKDD 2001, LNAI 2356, pp. 145–166, 2002.

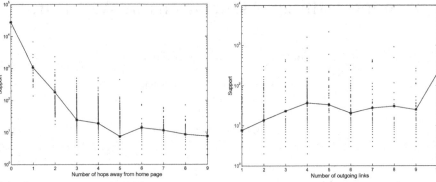

(a) Average support of a Web page against distance (measured in the terms of number of hops away) from the home page.

(b) Average support of a Web page against the number of outgoing links.

Fig. 1. Impact of site structure on the support of Web association patterns.

behavior of Web users. Previous work in mining association patterns has focused primarily on discovering patterns that occur frequently in the data, i.e., those with sufficiently high *support*[1]. Any patterns that do not satisfy some minimum support threshold are assumed to be statistically insignificant, and therefore, eliminated. However, there are situations in which such a filtering strategy may end up removing useful information. For example, patterns involving negatively-associated pages can be quite informative even though their support counts are low. These negatively-associated patterns may represent the navigational behavior of different groups of Web users, the different entry points to a Web page, etc.

Current techniques for mining Web association patterns also do not address the impact of Web site structure on the support of a pattern. For instance, Web pages that are located close to the home page are known to have higher hit rates compared to those located further away, as shown in Figure 1(a). In addition, Web pages that have many outgoing links, i.e., hub pages, also tend to have higher support, as shown in Figure 1(b). Thus, the bulk of the Web association patterns discovered using conventional approach would contain these *index pages* [17], i.e., the home page and hub pages. It is still unclear how to effectively handle patterns containing these pages. One trivial solution is to explicitly remove the index pages from each session during preprocessing. This is not a viable approach because some of the index pages can be quite informative. If the index pages are retained, then one must use a sufficiently low minimum support threshold to ensure that most of the interesting non-index pages are captured by the association patterns. However, a low support threshold may result in a large number of uninteresting patterns due to co-occurrences among the index pages. Some of these patterns can be filtered using objective measures, such as those

---

[1] The support of a pattern is the fraction of data set for which the pattern is observed.

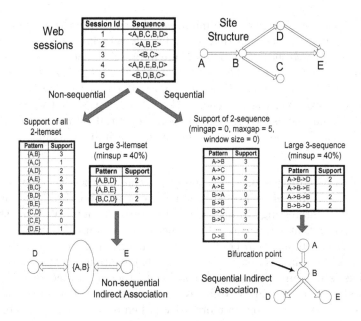

Fig. 2. Example of sequential and non-sequential indirect associations.

discussed in [29], but many would still remain. It may also be possible to eliminate the uninteresting patterns subjectively, if appropriate domain knowledge is available [21,10]. Alternatively, one can group together patterns that have a common set of index pages into higher order structures. This will not only reduce the number of patterns presented to an analyst, but also allow the analyst to have a better understanding of the patterns since the combined structure offers a wider perspective about the derived patterns.

In this paper, a new data mining technique called indirect association is applied to Web click-stream data. This technique was originally developed in [28] for market-basket type transactions. The key idea behind indirect association is to find interesting pairs of negatively associated items by combining association patterns that contain a common set of items. The main contribution of our current work is to extend this concept to sequential data. To illustrate the idea of indirect association, consider the example shown in Figure 2.

Example 1. The data set shown in Figure 2 contains five unique sessions. First, the frequent sequential and non-sequential association patterns are derived using standard association pattern discovery algorithms. By imposing a minimum support threshold of 40%, any patterns that appear in less than 2 sessions are discarded. The support of size-2 patterns and size-3 frequent patterns are shown in Figure 2. For the non-sequential case, page D appears frequently with both A and B. Similarly, E also appears frequently with both A and B. Without any prior knowledge about the structure and content of the Web pages, we would expect D and E to be visited together quite often. However, since the joint support of D and E is below the minimum threshold (and the pages are negatively correlated), we say that they are indirectly associated via the mediator set $\{A, B\}$. We can also show that A and C are indirectly associated via $\{B, D\}$. For the sequential case, $\{A\} \rightarrow \{B\} \rightarrow \{D\}$ and $\{A\} \rightarrow \{B\} \rightarrow \{E\}$ are frequent traversal paths. Since D and E do not appear together frequently, they are indirectly associated via the sequence $\{A\} \rightarrow \{B\}$. Notice that every sequential indirect association has a corresponding non-sequential indirect association[2], but not vice-versa. For example, there is no sequential indirect association between A and C via $\{B\} \rightarrow \{D\}$.

Sequential indirect associations allow us to characterize the behavior of different groups of Web users who share similar traversal subpaths. They can also be used to detect interesting bifurcation (splitting) points in the Web site structure, i.e., Web pages that serve as the divergence of various user interests. For example, page B is a bifurcation point for the sequential indirect association shown in Figure 2. In principle, every Web page that contains at least two outgoing hyperlinks is a bifurcation point according to the site structure. This include all the index pages at a given Web site. However, many of them are uninteresting, either because they are uninformative (when every visitor clicks on all or a random subset of the outgoing links) or unpopular (when the outgoing links are seldom traversed). In this study, a bifurcating Web page is considered interesting if each outgoing link is traversed by a distinct group of users. Knowledge about the different groups of Web users and pages that fork out the diverging interest can help analysts to take the appropriate actions for targeted marketing, placement of banner advertisement, etc., as well as to assist Web site administrators in re-organizing the structure of their Web site.

1.1   Related Work

There are several formulation to the Web association mining problem. Each formulation differs in terms of how *Web transactions* can be constructed from the original Web sessions. A naive approach is to simply ignore the sequential nature of the data and considers each transaction to be the set of pages accessed by a user in a given session.

A second formulation converts each session into a set of maximal forward references in order to filter out the effect of backward references [8]. For example, the first session of Figure 2 will generate two maximal forward references, $< A, B, C >$ and $< A, B, D >$.

A third formulation considers each individual page access as an event in the Web sequence [3,15,22,16,5,13]. Spiliopoulou et al.[22] and Pei et al.[16] combines the various sequences into a compact tree data structure to facilitate querying and mining of Web association patterns. Agrawal et al.[3] and Mannila et al.[15] uses a windowing approach to define elements of a sequence. Garofalakis et al.[13] uses regular expressions to specify constraints on items (events) that may appear

---

[2] except for sequences with repeating items.

as elements of a frequent sequence. The algorithms proposed in [3,15,13] are based on the generate-and-count paradigm, i.e. candidate patterns are initially generated prior to actual support counting.

A fourth formulation considers each session to be an alternating series of vertices (pages) and edges (hyperlinks) [20]. This approach assumes that knowing the vertices alone is insufficient because there could be more than one link connecting the same pair of pages and each link may contain different information.

The concept of indirect association proposed in this paper is applicable to any one of the transaction formulation above. For brevity, we describe indirect association only in the context of the first (for non-sequential indirect association) and third (for sequential indirect association) formulation.

Indirect association is somewhat related to the concept of negative association rules proposed by Savasere et al. in [19]. Both concepts deal with association patterns that have relatively low support counts. A negative association rule discovers what are the set of items a customer will not likely buy, given that he/she has bought a certain set of other items. Typically, the number of negative association rules in a sparse data set is prohibitively large, and the majority of them are uninteresting to the data analysts. In [19], Savasere et al. has proposed to use an item taxonomy to decide what constitutes an interesting negative association rule. Their intuition was that items belonging to the same product family are expected to have similar types of associations with other items. This suggests that the expected support of a pattern can be determined by the support of the parents of every item present in the pattern. If the actual support of a pattern is significantly lower than its expected support, then an interesting negative association rule exists among items in the pattern. Our work is similar in spirit to Savasere's approach because we also assume that negatively associated items are interesting if their joint support is significantly lower than their expected value. However, instead of computing the expected support from an item taxonomy, we assume that the expected support would be high if the negatively-associated items share a common mediator. This assumption is justified because for low support thresholds, many of the infrequent pairs of items do not have any mediators, and thus, finding one would be rather surprising.

Indirect association also provides a methodology to group together the discovered patterns according to the items they have in common. Even though the idea of grouping association patterns is not new, our work differs from others in terms of the types of patterns being grouped and how the combined patterns are represented. In [30], Toivonen et al. developed the notion of a rule cover, which is a small set of association rules that covers the entire database. Clustering was then used to group together similar rule covers. In [14], Liu et al. have used the χ^2 test to eliminate redundant association rules, and direction setting rules to summarize the surviving patterns. Both approaches are quite different from our work because they are intended to combine association rules that have the same rule consequent, whereas our approach is intended to combine frequent itemsets and sequential patterns.

The remainder of this paper is organized in the following way. In Section 2, we present a formal definition of non-sequential and sequential indirect associations. Next, we describe a level-wise algorithm for mining these patterns. We also describe how demographic data can be used to enrich the information conveyed by indirect associations. We then demonstrate the applicability of our technique on real-world data sets in Section 4. Finally, we conclude with a summary of our results and directions for future research.

2 Preliminaries

In this section, we describe some of the terminology used in this paper and present a formal definition of non-sequential and sequential indirect associations.

2.1 Definition

Let $I = \{i_1, i_2, \cdots, i_d\}$ denote the set of all items (or events, in the case of sequential data) in the database. Any non-empty subset of I is called an itemset. An itemset that contains k items is known as a k-itemset. For example, if $I = \{a, b, c, d, e\}$, then $C = \{b, e\}$ is an example of a 2-itemset defined on I.

We denote T as the set of all transactions, where each transaction $t \in T$ is a subset of I. The support of an itemset C, denoted as $sup(C)$, is defined as the fraction of all transactions that contain C. An itemset is said to be large, or frequent, if its support is greater than a user-specified minimum threshold t_f.

A sequence is an ordered list of itemsets, $s = s_1 \rightarrow s_2 \rightarrow \cdots \rightarrow s_n$, where each itemset s_j is called an element of the sequence. The length of a sequence s, denoted as $|s|$, corresponds to the number of elements in s. A sequence is called non-empty if it contains at least one element, i.e., $|s| > 0$. The number of items[3] contained in element s_j is denoted as $|s_j|$. While an item can appear only once in a given element, it can occur multiple times in different elements of a sequence. We also assume that items in an element are sorted according to lexicographic order. An item x_i that appears only once throughout a sequence s is called a *non-repeating* item. A k-sequence is a sequence that contains k items, where $k = \sum_j |s_j|$. For example, the sequence $s = \{a\} \rightarrow \{a, c\} \rightarrow \{a\}$ contains four items and three elements. Therefore, it is a 4-sequence with a sequence length equals to three.

A sequence $t = t_1 \rightarrow t_2 \rightarrow \cdots \rightarrow t_m$ is called a subsequence of s if each ordered element in t is a subset of an ordered element in s. Formally, we say that t is a subsequence of s if there exist integers $1 \leq j_1 < j_2 < \ldots < j_m \leq n$ such that $t_1 \subseteq s_{j_1}, t_2 \subseteq s_{j_2}, \cdots, t_m \subseteq s_{j_m}$. A sequence database D is a set of tuples $< sid, t >$ where sid is the sequence identifier and t is a sequence. A tuple $< sid, t >$ is said to contain a sequence s if s is a subsequence of t. The support of a sequence s, denoted as $sup(s)$, is defined as the fraction of all tuples in D that contain s.

---

[3] For sequences, we use the terminology item and event interchangeably throughout this paper.

The concatenation of two sequences s and t, denoted as st, is a sequence of length $|s| + |t|$, and consists of all elements of s immediately followed by the elements of t. A sequence w is a prefix sequence of s, denoted as $w \sqsubset s$, if there exists a non-empty sequence y such that $s = wy$. w is a minimal prefix sequence of s if $w \sqsubset s$ and its length is equal to one. Conversely, we define w as a maximal prefix sequence of s if $w \sqsubset s$ and its length is equal to $|s| - 1$. For example, $t = \{a\} \rightarrow \{a, c\}$ is a prefix sequence of $s = \{a\} \rightarrow \{a, c\} \rightarrow \{a\}$ because it contains the first two elements of s. Furthermore, it is a maximal prefix sequence of s since its sequence length is equal to $3 - 1 = 2$. We define y as a suffix sequence of s, denoted as $y \sqsupset s$, if there exists a non-empty sequence w, such that $s = wy$. It follows that the minimal and maximal suffix sequences of s correspond to the suffix sequences $y \sqsupset s$ such that the sequence length of y is 1 and $|s| - 1$, respectively. For example, $p = \{a\}$ is a minimal suffix sequence of $s = \{a\} \rightarrow \{a, c\} \rightarrow \{a\}$.

An item x is the *prefix item* for sequence s if x is the only item that belongs to the first element of s, i.e., $x \in s_1$ and $|s_1| = 1$. On the other hand, x is known as the *suffix item* of s if it is the only item in the last element of s, i.e., $x \in s_n$ and $|s_n| = 1$. x is called an *end item* of sequence s if it is a prefix item or suffix item of s.

2.2   Non-sequential Indirect Association

Definition 1. *A pair of items, a and b, is said to be indirectly associated via a mediator set M if the following conditions hold :*

1. *$sup(\{a, b\}) < t_s$ (Itempair Support condition)*
2. *There exists a non-empty set M such that :*
   (a) $sup(\{a\} \cup M) \geq t_f, sup(\{b\} \cup M) \geq t_f$ (Mediator Support condition).
   (b) $d(\{a\}, M) \geq t_d$, $d(\{b\}, M) \geq t_d$ where $d(P, Q)$ is a measure of the dependence between the itemsets P and Q (Mediator Dependence condition).

Condition 1 requires that the joint support between a and b is low. This is because indirect association is a meaningful concept only if both items rarely occur together in the same transaction. Otherwise, it makes more sense to characterize the pair in terms of their direct association. Alternatively, condition 1 can be modified to test for independence between a and b. However, it is often the case that itempairs that have very low support values are either independent or negatively correlated with each other [25]. Thus, it is often sufficient to use condition 1 to discover indirect association between independent or negatively correlated itempairs.

Condition 2(a) states that items that belong to the mediator set M must co-occur frequently with both a and b. This condition is necessary to guarantee the statistically significance of M. From a computational perspective, this condition can also be used to reduce the exponential number of candidate mediators between a and b.

Condition 2(b) requires that the indirect itempair, (a, b), must be highly dependent on items in the mediator set M. This condition is needed to prevent the use of spurious itemsets as mediators. For instance, suppose there is an item k that appears in every transaction. Without the mediator dependence condition, any infrequent itempair will automatically be indirectly associated via k. Thus, condition 2(b) is necessary to remove such spurious patterns. There are many interest measures we can use to represent the degree of dependencies among attributes of a dataset [29]. One such measure is the ϕ coefficient, which is analogous to Pearson's product-moment correlation coefficient for continuous variables. For pairs of binary attributes, it can be shown that within certain range of support values[4], the correlation between X and Y, $\phi_{X,Y}$, can be expressed in terms of their interest factor, $I(X,Y) \equiv \frac{P(X,Y)}{P(X)P(Y)}$ [7,6], and their support, $P(X,Y)$, i.e. :

$$\phi_{X,Y} \approx \sqrt{\mathrm{I(X,Y)} \times \mathrm{P(X,Y)}} \equiv IS(X,Y)$$

We use the right-hand side of the above expression, called the IS measure, to be the dependence measure for Condition 2(b) [25]. This measure is desirable because it takes into account both the statistical dependence and statistical significance of a pattern. We do not use $\phi_{X,Y}$ as the dependence measure because it treats both the co-presence and co-absence of items in the same way[29]. For many application domains involving sparse data sets such as Web click-stream data, co-presence of items is more important than co-absence[29].

Nonetheless, our indirect association formulation can accommodate other interest measures, such as Piatetsky-Shapiro's rule-interest, J-measure, mutual information and Gini index. This formulation can also be extended to a more general case where a and b are itemsets rather than individual items.

2.3   Sequential Indirect Association

Let a be a non-repeating, end item for the sequence $s_1 = a_1 \rightarrow a_2 \rightarrow \cdots \rightarrow a_n$, while b is a non-repeating, end item for the sequence $s_2 = b_1 \rightarrow b_2 \rightarrow \cdots \rightarrow b_n$. Furthermore, let a_i and b_j denote the elements of s_1 and s_2 that contain a and b respectively, i.e., $a_i = \{a\}$ and $b_j = \{b\}$.

Definition 2. *A pair of end items a and b are said to be indirectly associated via a mediator sequence w if $s_1 = a_i w$ or $s_1 = w a_i$, $s_2 = b_j w$ or $s_2 = w b_j$, and the following conditions are satisfied:*

1. *$sup(\{a,b\}) < t_s$ (Itempair Support condition).*
2. *There exists a non-empty sequence w such thtat:*
   (a) $sup(s_1) \geq t_f$ and $sup(s_2) \geq t_f$ (Mediator Support condition).
   (b) $d(a_i, w) \geq t_d$ and $d(b_j, w) \geq t_d$ (Mediator Dependence condition).

The first condition ignores the order in which a and b appears in the data sequences. By choosing t_s to be close to zero, we can ensure that a and b rarely occurs together in the same sequence. For Web data, this condition ensures that a and b are *mutually exclusive* pages, i.e., pages that are visited by distinct groups

---

[4] when $P(X) \ll 1$, $P(Y) \ll 1$ and $\frac{P(X,Y)}{P(X)P(Y)} \gg 1$.

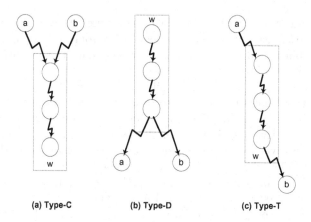

Fig. 3. Types of sequential indirect asssociation between a and b via a mediating sequence w: (a) Type-C (b) Type-D (c) Type-T.

of users. Condition 2(a) guarantees that only the frequent traversal paths are used in our analysis[5]. For condition 2(b), we use the IS measure to define the dependencies between an element and its mediator sequence.

In this paper, we are interested in three types of sequential indirect associations as shown in Figure 3:

1. **Type-C (Convergence)** - if a_i and b_j are the minimal prefix sequences for s_1 and s_2 respectively.
2. **Type-D (Divergence)** - if a_i and b_j are the minimal suffix sequences for s_1 and s_2 respectively.
3. **Type-T (Transitivity)** - if a_i is the minimal prefix sequence for s_1 and b_j is the minimal suffix sequences for s_2, or vice-versa.

Type-C indirect association represents the various ways to enter a frequent traversal path w. Finding the entry points into a Web site is a trivial task, by examining the first Web page accessed in each session. However, finding Type-C indirect associations is more complicated because the indirect itempair, (a, b), does not have to be directly connected to the first page of the frequent traversal path w. Type-D indirect association reflects the diverging interest of Web users from a bifurcation point. As previously noted, even though every Web page that have at least two outgoing hyperlinks can be considered a bifurcation point, not all such points are interesting. Type-D indirect association may unveil the location where the interest of Web users begin to diverge. Again, a and b do not have to be directly connected to their bifurcation point. Type-T indirect association is interesting because it shows that users who enter the frequent sequence w through page a rarely go to page b. An interesting example would

---

[5] Pitkow et al [18] observed that many paths occur infrequently, often as a result of erroneous navigation. By using the commonly traversed subpaths, one can preserve the benefits of sequential nature of the paths while being robust to noise.

be that b is an order confirmation page. This suggests that users who end up accessing page b must have entered the sequence through other pages. Sometimes, one may be able to find the corresponding type-C pattern to identify where does the users who visited page b come from.

Indirect association cannot be easily found using the standard association mining framework because one has to examine both the positive and negative dependencies between items. Although there have been attempts to mine both positive and negative associations simultaneously, such algorithms can be prohibitively expensive. Furthermore, the information conveyed by these patterns can be quite different from that of indirect association. For instance, a mixed itemset $\{A, B, \overline{C}\}$ or sequence $\{A\} \longrightarrow \{B\} \longrightarrow \{\overline{C}\}$ has a different meaning than an indirect association between A and C via B.

Clustering is another standard approach for finding the distinctive groups of Web users who are accessing a Web site [32,12,4]. Unless the number of clusters is sufficiently high, most clusters cannot be explained by a single frequent itemset or sequence. It is also more likely that several indirect associations are contained within a single cluster, rather than each indirect association connects between two separate clusters. Furthermore, there is no guarantee that any pair of clusters would share a common mediator, which is central to the concept of indirect association.

3   Implementation

3.1   INDIRECT Algorithm

An algorithm for mining (non-sequential) indirect association between pairs of items is shown in Table 1. There are two phases in this algorithm: (1) candidate generation and (2) candidate pruning. During the first phase, we use a standard frequent itemset generation algorithm such as Apriori [2] to generate the large itemsets. Next, we combine the large itemsets of size-k (L_k) to generate candidate indirect associations for pass $k + 1$ (C_{k+1}). Each candidate in C_{k+1} is a triplet, $< a, b, M >$, where a and b are the indirect itempairs associated via the mediator M. During the join step of this algorithm, i.e., step 4, a pair of large k-itemsets, $\{a_1, a_2, \cdots, a_k\}$ and $\{b_1, b_2, \cdots, b_k\}$, is merged together to produce a candidate indirect association $< a, b, M >$ if the two itemsets have exactly $k - 1$ items in common. Since C_{k+1} is generated from frequent itemsets, the mediator support condition is trivially satisfied. The candidate pruning phase, i.e., steps 5 through 7, is used to eliminate candidates that fail the itempair support and mediator dependence conditions (see Definition 1). One way to check the support of each itempair is to create an $|L_1| \times |L_1|$ support matrix for all pairs of frequent items. Thus, the itempair support condition can be easily verified using a matrix lookup operation. Alternatively, we may store the candidate indirect itempairs in a hash tree and performs an additional pass over the data set in order to count the actual support of each candidate itempair. The latter approach can be used to handle the case where a and b are itemsets rather than individual items. Both variants of this algorithm have been implemented.

Table 1. The INDIRECT algorithm.

---

1. Extract the large itemsets, $L_1, L_2, \cdots L_n$, using standard mining algorithms.
2. $P = \emptyset$
3. for $k = 2$ to n do
4. $C_{k+1} \leftarrow \text{join}(L_k, L_k)$
5.   for each $(a, b, M) \in C_{k+1}$ do
6.   if $(sup(\{a, b\}) < t_s$ and $d(\{a\}, M) \geq t_d$ and $d(\{b\}, M) \geq t_d$
7. $P = P \cup (a, b, M)$
8.   end
9. end

We now briefly describe the complexity of the above algorithm. The candidate generation phase can be quite expensive, because it requires at most $O(\sum_k |L_k| \times |L_k|)$ join operations. The join operation in Apriori is much cheaper because it only combines itemsets that have identical $k - 1$ prefix items, assuming the items are sorted in lexicographic order. This is not the case for indirect associations because the indirect itempair, (a, b), does not have to be the last items of each frequent itemset. Nonetheless, we have implemented other optimization strategies to reduce the number of join operations. For example, given a frequent itemset $\{a_1, a_2, \cdots, a_k\}$, we only need to perform the join operation with other frequent itemsets $\{b_1, b_2, \cdots, b_k\}$ for which the condition $a_2 \geq b_1$ is satisfied. This condition holds because all items within an itemset are kept in lexicographic order. The candidate pruning phase is inexpensive if the $|L_1| \times |L_1|$ itempair support matrix can fit into main memory. Otherwise, the complexity of this step can be as expensive as the candidate counting step of the Apriori algorithm.

Our algorithm for mining sequential indirect association is similar to the one given in Table 1. In this case, the L_k's correspond to frequent k-sequences generated using a sequential pattern discovery algorithm such as GSP [23]. During the join step, a pair of frequent sequences, $s^{(1)}$ and $s^{(2)}$, is combined to form a candidate indirect association (a, b, w) only if a and b are non-repeating, end items for $s^{(1)}$ and $s^{(2)}$, respectively. We have implemented several optimization strategies to reduce the number of join operations and candidate indirect associations. For example, since we are only interested in indirect relationship between end items, we can restrict the join operation to sequences of length ≥ 2 elements. Furthermore, the difference between their sequence lengths must be less than 2, i.e., $-1 \leq |s^{(1)}| - |s^{(2)}| \leq 1$. The join operation is also restricted to sequences whose first or last element contains only a single item. For example, the sequence $\{A\} \rightarrow \{C\} \rightarrow \{DE\}$ may join with another sequence $\{C\} \rightarrow \{DE\} \rightarrow \{F\}$ to create a candidate Type-T indirect association : $< A, F, \{C\} \rightarrow \{DE\} >$. However, we do not join the first sequence above with $\{FC\} \rightarrow \{DE\}$ nor $\{FG\} \rightarrow \{C\} \rightarrow \{DE\}$ because the indirect itempairs are not end items of their original sequences.

3.2   Post-processing

In this section, we describe various ways to extend our analysis of Web indirect associations. First, we may supplement the Web patterns with user demographic data to find the best features that characterize the different groups of users. For example, for each indirect association $< a, b, M >$, we compare the demographic distribution of users who access $(a \cup M)$ against the demographic distribution of users who access $(b \cup M)$. Any significant difference between the two distributions would indicate that the demographic features can characterize the users who visit the indirectly associated pages.

Second, the indirect associations can be merged together if they share a common mediator. For example, suppose (a, b) and (a, c) are indirectly associated via the mediator M. We can construct an association graph $G = (V, E)$, where V is the set of vertices, i.e., $V = \{a, b, c\} \cup M$, and E is the set of edges connecting the vertices. Each edge $e = (v_i, v_j) \in E$ indicates whether a direct or indirect association exists between v_i and v_j. An association graph is a compact representation of the interaction between all pairs of items (itemsets) that share a common mediator. We have implemented an indirect association viewer to visualize the association graphs for each mediator. Such a visualization tool allows an analyst to have a wider perspective about the derived patterns. Unlike other association pattern viewers [31], our technique uses both the support and dependence measures to analyze the interaction between various items. Furthermore, instead of constructing a global association graph for all items, our viewer is mediator-centric.

4   Experimental Evaluation

To demonstrate the effectiveness of indirect association, we tested our algorithm on Web server logs from the University of Minnesota Computer Science department (CS) and from an online Web store (ECOM). Table 2 summarizes the description of the data sets and threshold parameters used in our experiments.

Table 2. Summary of the data sets and threshold parameters.

Dataset	t_s	t_f	t_d	# items	# sequences
CS (Computer Science department)	0.02	0.1	0.1	91443	34526
ECOM (online Web store)	0.005	0.05	0.2	6664	143604

We first illustrate the relationship between the ϕ-coefficient and IS measure using Figures 4(a) and 4(b). These figures are generated by randomly selecting 100,000 pairs of pages from the data set. We then compute the ϕ-coefficient and IS value for each pair and generate a scatter plot of both measures. We observe that ϕ and IS are almost linearly correlated with each other when ϕ is greater than 0.1.

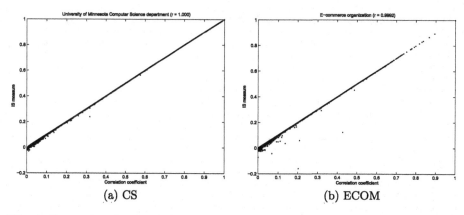

(a) CS   (b) ECOM

Fig. 4. Comparison between IS-measure and the ϕ-coefficient for the CS and ECOM data sets.

4.1   Non-sequential Indirect Association

Our non-sequential indirect association algorithm is applied to both CS and ECOM data sets. However, due to space considerations, we omit a detailed discussion about the non-sequential patterns generated from the ECOM data set and refer the reader to [27].

Initially, the Web logs are preprocessed to identify individual Web sessions. Noise due to accesses by Web robots are removed using the Web robot prediction models described in [26]. The sessions are then converted into market-basket type transactions by ignoring the order in which the Web pages appear in the session. After applying our non-sequential indirect association algorithm, the derived patterns are merged together and visualized.

There are 184,143 frequent itemsets found using Apriori, which is a well-known frequent itemset generation algorithm, out of which 44,598 of them are of size 6 or less. By combining the frequent itemsets of size 6 or less, we obtain 4,291 indirect associations, which is a 10-fold reduction in the total number of patterns. Note that for the thresholds given in Table 2, no indirect association is generated when combining frequent itemsets of size 7 or more. Finally, upon merging the indirect associations that share the same mediator, we are left with only 121 unique mediators to be presented to the analysts via the indirect association viewer.

We observe many interesting non-sequential patterns that reflect the diverse interests of different groups of Web users. Figure 5(a) illustrates one such example. The mediator set, i.e., the vertex in the middle of the graph, contains the Computer Science department homepage (/) and the graduate student information page (/grad-info). Solid edges indicate that the support between the two vertices is high while dashed edges indicate that there is an indirect association between the two vertices. By clicking on any vertex, the support and dependence value between the selected item and its mediator will be displayed in the bottom right panel of the viewer.

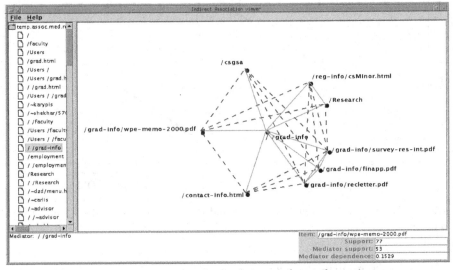

(a) Indirect associations via the graduate student information page.

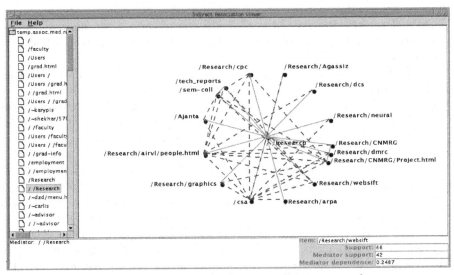

(b) Indirect associations via the Computer Science research page.

Fig. 5. Examples of Non-sequential Indirect Association.

From Figure 5(a), we observe that there are five distinct groups of users who frequently access the mediator pages. The first group contains users who access the pdf files /grad-info/recletter.pdf, /grad-info/finapp.pdf and /grad-info/survey-res-inf.pdf. These files are application materials, i.e., recommendation letters, financial aid applications and survey of research interest, for prospective graduate students. The second group corresponds to users who access /csgsa, which is the home page of the Computer Science graduate student association. Unlike the previous group, users who visit this page are mostly current graduate students who are interested in the activities of the student organization. The Web page /grad-info/wpe-memo-2000.pdf would be of interest to current graduate students who have not taken their Ph.D. preliminary written examination. The fourth group, which corresponds to users who access the /contact-info page, consists of visitors who are looking for the contact information of the Computer Science department. It is somewhat surprising that the first group of users, i.e., prospective graduate students who download the application materials, are indirectly associated with the fourth group, i.e., users who access the contact information page. One possible explanation is that some of the application materials, e.g., the financial aid form and the recommendation letter forms, contain the contact information of the Computer Science department. Therefore, the prospective graduate students do not have to search for the contact information immediately from the Web site. The last group of users, who access both the /reg-info/csMinor.html and /Research pages, represents undergraduate students who are currently taking Computer Science as their minor subject but are interested in the research activities of the department.

The above findings suggest that indirect association can capture the different groups of Web users who share a similar traversal path. In this example, the mediator pages, {/, /grad-info}, are frequently visited by different groups of Web users, including prospective graduate students, current graduate and undergraduate students. Each group has its own browsing agenda, which can be detected using our indirect association viewer. Figure 5(b) illustrates another example of different groups of Web users who are interested in the various research projects conducted by the faculty members of the Computer Science department.

We are also interested in using demographic features to explain some of the discovered patterns. To do this, we have identified several demographic features that may characterize the various groups of users who are traversing the Web site. These features include the hostname of the client (e.g., UMN, other EDU, GOV/MIL and ISP users), the type of browser used (e.g., Netscape or Internet Explorer) and the referrer field (which would indicate how the user arrives at the Web site, e.g via a search engine or other external Web sites).

Figure 6 shows an example of the demographic breakdown of Web users who visit the prospective graduate student page and the system staff contact information page. Both pages are indirectly associated with each other via the Computer Science department home page. This pattern is chosen because when we compute the difference between the demographic distribution of their Web users using an L_2-norm metric, we found their difference to be significantly higher than other patterns. Figure 6 supports this finding by showing that users who access the system staff contact information page mainly come from our own university, whereas those who are interested in the prospective graduate student page come from other universities, commercial organizations and countries outside of the United States.

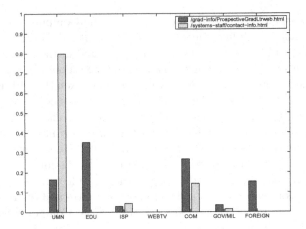

Fig. 6. Comparison between the demographic distribution of Web users who access the indirectly-associated pages `/grad-info/ProspectiveGradLtrweb.html` and `system-staff/contact-info.html`.

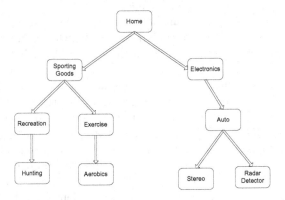

Fig. 7. A subgraph of the e-commerce Web site structure.

4.2 Sequential Indirect Association

This section describes the results of applying our sequential indirect association algorithm to the ECOM data set (see Table 3). We found that almost all of the indirect associations are of Type-D, indicating that there is a divergence in the interest of the Web users. For example, the third row in Table 3 indicates that users who visit the following sequence of pages {Home} → {Electronics} → {Auto} would either access the Stereos page or the Radar Detectors page, but not both. Thus, Auto is the bifurcation point for Web users who are interested in Stereos or Radar Detectors. Note that Auto has a direct hyperlink to both Stereos and Radar Detectors, as shown in Figure 7.

Another interesting sequential indirect association is between the Hunting page and the Aerobics page via the sequence {Home} → {Sporting Goods}.

Table 3. Examples of sequential indirect associations derived from ECOM.

Type	a	w	b	$d(a,w)$	$d(b,w)$
D	Camcorders	{Home} → {Electronics} → {Video}	13" TV and VCR Combo	0.29	0.21
D	Camcorders	{Electronics, Video}	27" TV	0.25	0.20
D	Stereo	{Home} → {Electronics} → {Auto}	Radar Detector	0.25	0.34
D	Hunting	{Home} → {Sporting Goods}	Aerobics	0.23	0.21
D	Scanner	Home → Electronics → Computer	Multimedia Computer	0.20	0.27
D	Shower curtains	{Domestics} → {Bath Shop}	Towel set	0.43	0.30
D	Bedroom furniture frame	{Home & accessories} → {Furniture}	Oak nightstand	0.22	0.20
D	Speakers	{Electronics} → {Stereo}	CD boombox	0.34	0.20
D	Women's gown set	{Home} → {Apparel}	Men's boots	0.22	0.21
D	Cordless phone	{Home} → {Telephones}	Answering device	0.30	0.34

Unlike the previous example, both indirectly associated pages are not directly linked to their bifurcation page, as shown in Figure 7. In fact, their parent nodes, i.e., the Recreation and Exercise pages, are not indirectly associated with each other. This suggests that visitors to the Hunting page may still be interested in the Exercise page, even though they are not quite as interested in the Aerobics page. Such information can potentially influence the type of action analysts should take on the various groups of Web users - actions such as where to strategically place a banner advertisement to target specific groups of Web users. If it is placed too close to the home page, this could be costly and ignored by most Web users. Conversely, if it is placed too far from the home page, some of the targeted Web audience may miss it.

A similar analysis has been performed on the CS data set. Again, we omit the detailed description of these results due to space considerations.

4.3 Performance

Our experiments were performed on a 700MHz Pentium III machine with 4 GB of RAM. The computational time for these experiments are 41.62 seconds (for extracting non-sequential indirect associations from the CS data set) and 3201.2 seconds (for extracting sequential indirect association from the ECOM data set), respectively. These computational times exclude the time for generating the frequent itemsets using the Apriori algorithm and frequent sequences using the GSP algorithm. An early stopping heuristic can also be used to avoid merging the larger-sized frequent itemsets. Below, we describe two scenarios under which the early stopping heuristic is applicable.

In Figure 8(a), we observe that if no non-sequential indirect association is produced during pass k, then combining itemsets of size $k+1$ and higher will not produce any new indirect associations. This is true for both the CS and ECOM data sets despite the fact that the dependence measure is not an anti-monotonic

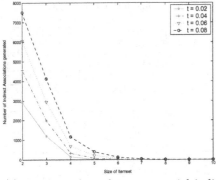

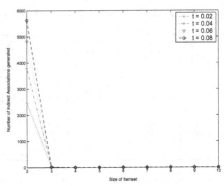

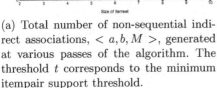

(a) Total number of non-sequential indirect associations, $< a, b, M >$, generated at various passes of the algorithm. The threshold t corresponds to the minimum itempair support threshold.

(b) Total number of new, non-sequential indirect itempairs, (a, b), generated at various passes of the algorithm. The threshold t corresponds to to the minimum itempair support threshold.

Fig. 8. Comparison between the number of indirect itempairs (a, b) and indirect associations $< a, b, M >$ generated from the CS data set.

function. For the CS data set, our algorithm can be terminated after combining frequent itemsets of size 7.

For the rest of the analysis in this section, we will distinguish between an indirect itempair (a, b), which ignores the composition of the mediator M, from an indirect association $< a, b, M >$. Figure 8(b) shows the total number of new indirect itempairs generated when combining itemsets of size 2 up to size 10. Although Figure 8(a) shows that combining itemsets of size 4 and higher can produce new indirect associations, Figure 8(b) indicates that no new indirect itempairs are generated. In other words, combining larger-sized itemsets tend to produce larger-sized mediators for indirect itempairs already discovered in the earlier passes of the algorithm. For practical reasons, it is often sufficient to terminate the algorithm early if no new indirect itempairs are generated. However, if completeness of the results is required, then the algorithm should be executed to its entirety at the expense of longer computational time.

4.4   Threshold Selection

To get an idea of how sensitive the indirect associations are to the choice of threshold parameters, we have repeated our experiments for the CS data set at various minimum itempair support, t_s, and minimum mediator dependence, t_d, thresholds. Figure 9(a) depicts the number of indirect associations and indirect itempairs generated at various t_s thresholds. Our results suggest that although the number of indirect associations grows quite rapidly with increasing t_s, the number of indirect itempairs does not grow quite as fast. This is because increasing t_s will bring in new itempairs (a, b) that barely fail its previously chosen t_s threshold. The number of indirect associations that correspond to these new

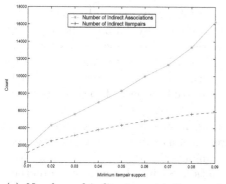

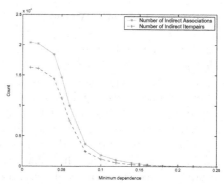

(a) Number of indirect associations and indirect itempairs generated at various t_s thresholds (with $t_f = 0.1\%$ and $t_d = 0.10\%$).

(b) Number of indirect associations and indirect itempairs generated at various t_d thresholds (with $t_f = 0.1\%$ and $t_s = 0.01\%$).

Fig. 9. The effect of using different thresholds on the number of patterns generated by the indirect association algorithm.

itempairs can be quite large because each indirect itempair can have multiple mediators. This explains the rapid rise in the number of indirect associations $< a, b, M >$ when t_s increases.

Figure 9(b) shows a similar plot when different minimum mediator dependence thresholds, t_d, are used. In this case, lowering the value of t_d increases both the number of indirect associations and indirect itempairs since more mediators can pass the mediator dependence condition (condition 2(b) of Definition 1). However, if t_d is set too low, then some of the indirect associations could be spurious due to the presence of uninformative mediators.

We can use the statistical χ^2 test to determine what is an appropriate lower bound for t_d. For pairs of binary attributes, the χ^2 measure is closely related to the ϕ-coefficient via the following equation, $\phi = \sqrt{\chi^2/N}$. For example, the χ^2 cutoff value at 95% confidence level with one degree of freedom is 3.84. For the data sets used in our experiments, with $N = 34526$ and $N = 143604$ (see Table 2), this cutoff value corresponds to ϕ values of 0.0207 and 0.0101, respectively. Using the IS-ϕ plots of Figure 4(a) and 4(b), any choice of t_d above, say, 0.1, would pass the χ^2 significance test.

5   Conclusions

In this paper, we have applied a novel technique called indirect association on Web click-stream data. This technique looks for interesting negatively associated itempairs by combining association patterns that have similar substructures. Our experiments using Web logs from an academic institution and an e-commerce organization reveal many interesting patterns. For non-sequential indirect associations, we were able to identify the different groups of Web users who share a similar traversal path. We show how demographic features can be used to characterize the different user groups found by indirect associations. The number of patterns are significantly reduced after merging indirect associations that have the same mediator. For sequential indirect associations, we found many of the patterns are of Type-D, which suggests that the patterns may contain potentially interesting bifurcation points. However, more study is needed to subjectively select interesting indirect associations from uninteresting ones.

For future research, we are investigating the possibility of deriving indirect association using compact data structures such as FP-trees or aggregate trees. For instance, leaf nodes that share a common subpath to the root may form candidate mediators for the indirect association. Such techniques can potentially improve the performance of our algorithm especially when dealing with indirect association between itemsets or elements with more than one item. We are also interested in evaluating the use of bifurcation points for predictive modeling. Currently, Markov models have been used quite extensively to predict the access behavior of Web users [18,11]. However, higher order Markov models are often needed to achieve better prediction accuracy. We will investigate the possibility of using bifurcation points to truncate some of the states in high-order Markov models, without losing much of their predictive accuracy.

References

1. R. Agrawal, T. Imielinski, and A. Swami. Database mining: a performance perspective. *IEEE Transactions on Knowledge and Data Eng.*, 5(6):914–925, December 1993.
2. R. Agrawal and R. Srikant. Fast algorithms for mining association rules. In *Proc. of the 20th VLDB Conference*, pages 487–499, Santiago, Chile, September 1994.
3. R. Agrawal and R. Srikant. Mining sequential patterns. In *Proc. of the Eleventh Int'l Conf. on Data Engineering*, pages 3–14, Taipei, Taiwan, March 1995.
4. A. Banerjee and J. Ghosh. Clickstream clustering using weighted longest common subsequences. In *Workshop on Web Mining at the First SIAM Int'l Conf. on Data Mining*, pages 33–40, Chicago, IL, 2001.
5. J. Borges and M. Levene. Mining association rules in hypertext databases. In *Proc. of the Fourth Int'l Conference on Knowledge Discovery and Data Mining*, pages 149–153, New York, NY, August 1998.
6. T. Brijs, G. Swinnen, K. Vanhoof, and G. Wets. Using association rules for product assortment decisions : A case study. In *Proc. of the Fifth Int'l Conference on Knowledge Discovery and Data Mining*, pages 254–260, San Diego, August 1999.
7. S. Brin, R. Motwani, and C. Silverstein. Beyond market baskets: Generalizing association rules to correlations. In *Proc. of 1997 ACM-SIGMOD Int. Conf. on Management of Data*, pages 255–264, Tucson, Arizona, June 1997.
8. M.S. Chen, J.S. Park, and P.S. Yu. Efficient data mining for path traversal patterns. *IEEE Transactions on Knowledge and Data Eng.*, 10(2):209–221, 1998.
9. R. Cooley, B. Mobasher, and J. Srivastava. Web mining: Information and pattern discovery on the world wide web. In *International Conference on Tools with Artificial Intelligence*, pages 558–567, Newport Beach, CA, 1997.

10. R. Cooley, P.N. Tan, and J. Srivastava. Discovery of interesting usage patterns from web data. In M. Spiliopoulou and B. Masand, editors, *Advances in Web Usage Analysis and User Profiling*, volume 1836, pages 163–182. Lecture Notes in Computer Science, 2000.

11. M. Deshpande and G. Karypis. Selective markov models for predicting web page access. In *Proc. of First SIAM Int'l Conf. on Data Mining*, Chicago, 2001.

12. Y. Fu, K. Sandhu, and M. Shih. A generalization-based approach to clustering of web usage sessions. In B. Masand and M. Spiliopoulou, editors, *Web Usage Analysis and User Profiling*. Springer-Verlag, 2000.

13. M.N. Garofalakis, R. Rastogi, and K. Shim. Spirit: Sequential pattern mining with regular expression constraints. In *Proc. of the 25th VLDB Conference*, pages 223–234, Edinburgh, Scotland, 1999.

14. B. Liu, W. Hsu, and Y. Ma. Pruning and summarizing the discovered associations. In *Proc. of the Fifth Int'l Conference on Knowledge Discovery and Data Mining*, pages 125–134, San Diego, CA, August 1999.

15. H. Mannila, Toivonen H., and A.I. Verkamo. Discovery of frequent episodes in event sequences. *Data Mining and Knowledge Discovery*, 1(3):259–289, 1997.

16. J. Pei, J. Han, B. Mortazavi-Asl, and H. Zhu. Mining access patterns efficiently from web logs. In *4th Pacific-Asia Conference (PAKDD 2000)*, pages 396–407, Kyoto, Japan, April 2000.

17. P. Pirolli, J.E. Pitkow, and R. Rao. Silk from a sow's ear: Extracting usable structures from the web. In *Proc. of the CHI '96 Conference on Human Factors in Computing Systems*, pages 118–125, Vancouver, BC, April 1996.

18. J.E. Pitkow and P. Pirolli. Mining longest repeating subsequences to predict world wide web surfing. In *USENIX Symposium on Internet Technologies and Systems*, Boulder, CO, October 1999.

19. A. Savasere, E. Omiecinski, and S. Navathe. Mining for strong negative associations in a large database of customer transactions. In *Proc. of the Fourteenth Int'l Conf. on Data Engineering*, pages 494–502, Orlando, Florida, February 1998.

20. C. Shahabi, A.M. Zarkesh, J. Adibi, and V. Shah. Knowledge discovery from users web-page navigation. In *Workshop on Research Issues in Data Engineering*, Birmingham, England, 1997.

21. A. Silberschatz and A. Tuzhilin. What makes patterns interesting in knowledge discovery systems. *IEEE Trans. on Knowledge and Data Engineering*, 8(6):970–974, 1996.

22. M. Spiliopoulou, L.C. Faulstich, and K. Winkler. A data miner analyzing the navigational behaviour of web users. In *Proc. of the Workshop on Machine Learning in User Modelling of the ACAI'99 Int. Conf.*, Creta, Greece, July 1999.

23. R. Srikant and R. Agrawal. Mining sequential patterns: Generalizations and performance improvements. In *Proc. of the Fifth Int'l Conf. on Extending Database Technology (EDBT)*, pages 3–17, Avignon, France, March 1996.

24. J. Srivastava, R. Cooley, M. Deshpande, and P.N. Tan. Web usage mining: Discovery and applications of usage patterns from web data. *SIGKDD Explorations*, 1(2):12–23, 2000.

25. P.N. Tan and V. Kumar. Interestingness measures for association patterns : A perspective. In *KDD 2000 Workshop on Postprocessing in Machine Learning and Data Mining*, Boston, MA, August 2000.

26. P.N. Tan and V. Kumar. Discovery of web robot sessions based on their navigational patterns. *Data Mining and Knowledge Discovery*, 6(1):9–35, 2001.

27. P.N. Tan and V. Kumar. Mining association patterns in web usage data. In *International Conference on Advances in Infrastructure for e-Business*, L'Aquila, Italy, January 2002.

28. P.N. Tan, V. Kumar, and J. Srivastava. Indirect association: Mining higher order dependencies in data. In *Proc. of the 4th European Conference on Principles and Practice of Knowledge Discovery in Databases*, pages 632–637, Lyon, France, 2000.

29. P.N. Tan, V. Kumar, and J. Srivastava. Selecting the right interestingness measure for association patterns. Technical report, AHPCRC, 2002.

30. H Toivonen, M. Klemettinen, P. Ronkainen, K. Hatonen, and H. Mannila. Pruning and grouping discovered association rules. In *ECML-95 Workshop on Statistics, Machine Learning and Knowledge Discovery in Databases*, pages 47–52, Heraklion, Greece, April 1995.

31. A. Wexelblat. An environment for aiding information-browsing tasks. In *Proc. of AAAI Symposium on Acquisition, Learning and Demonstration: Automating Tasks for Users*, Birmingham, UK, 1996.

32. T. Yan, M. Jacobsen, H. Garcia-Molina, and U. Dayal. From user access patterns to dynamic hypertext linking. In *Fifth International World Wide Web Conference*, Paris, France, 1996.

Author Index

Banaei-Kashani, Farnoush   113
Berendt, Bettina   1

Cheung, David   48
Ching, Wai-Ki   48

Geyer-Schulz, Andreas   25

Hahsler, Michael   25
Huang, Joshua Zhexue   48

Jahn, Maximillian   25

Katsaros, Dimitrios   68
Krishnamoorthy, Mukkai S.   88

Kumar, Vipin   145

Manolopoulos, Yannis   68

Nanopoulos, Alexandros   68
Ng, Joe   48
Ng, Michael   48

Punin, John R.   88

Shahabi, Cyrus   113

Tan, Pang-Ning   145

Zaki, Mohammed J.   88

Lecture Notes in Artificial Intelligence (LNAI)

Vol. 2250: R. Nieuwenhuis, A. Voronkov (Eds.), Logic for Programming, Artificial Intelligence, and Reasoning. Proceedings, 2001. XV, 738 pages. 2001.

Vol. 2253: T. Terano, T. Nishida, A. Namatame, S. Tsumoto, Y. Ohsawa, T. Washio (Eds.), New Frontiers in Artificial Intelligence. Proceedings, 2001. XXVII, 553 pages. 2001.

Vol. 2256: M. Stumptner, D. Corbett, M. Brooks (Eds.), AI 2001: Advances in Artificial Intelligence. Proceedings, 2001. XII, 666 pages. 2001.

Vol. 2258: P. Brazdil, A. Jorge (Eds.), Progress in Artificial Intelligence. Proceedings, 2001. XII, 418 pages. 2001.

Vol. 2275: N.R. Pal, M. Sugeno (Eds.), Advances in Soft Computing – AFSS 2002. Proceedings, 2002. XVI, 536 pages. 2002.

Vol. 2281: S. Arikawa, A. Shinohara (Eds.), Progress in Discovery Science. XIV, 684 pages. 2002.

Vol. 2293: J. Renz, Qualitative Spatial Reasoning with Topological Information. XVI, 207 pages. 2002.

Vol. 2296: B. Dunin-Kęplicz, E. Nawarecki (Eds.), From Theory to Practice in Multi-Agent Systems. Proceedings, 2001. IX, 341 pages. 2002.

Vol. 2298: I. Wachsmuth, T. Sowa (Eds.), Gesture and Language in Human-Computer Interaction. Proceedings, 2001. XI, 323 pages.

Vol. 2302: C. Schulte, Programming Constraint Services. XII, 176 pages. 2002.

Vol. 2307: C. Zhang, S. Zhang, Association Rule Mining. XII, 238 pages. 2002.

Vol. 2308: I.P. Vlahavas, C.D. Spyropoulos (Eds.), Methods and Applications of Artificial Intelligence. Proceedings, 2002. XIV, 514 pages. 2002.

Vol. 2309: A. Armando (Ed.), Frontiers of Combining Systems. Proceedings, 2002. VIII, 255 pages. 2002.

Vol. 2313: C.A. Coello Coello, A. de Albornoz, L.E. Sucar, O.Cairó Battistutti (Eds.), MICAI 2002: Advances in Artificial Intelligence. Proceedings, 2002. XIII, 548 pages. 2002.

Vol. 2317: M. Hegarty, B. Meyer, N. Hari Narayanan (Eds.), Diagrammatic Representation and Inference. Proceedings, 2002. XIV, 362 pages. 2002.

Vol. 2321: P.L. Lanzi, W. Stolzmann, S.W. Wilson (Eds.), Advances in Learning Classifier Systems. Proceedings, 2002. VIII, 231 pages. 2002.

Vol. 2322: V. Mařík, O. Stěpánková, H. Krautwurmová, M. Luck (Eds.), Multi-Agent Systems and Applications II. Proceedings, 2001. XII, 377 pages. 2002.

Vol. 2333: J.-J.Ch. Meyer, M. Tambe (Eds.), Intelligent Agents VIII. Revised Papers, 2001. XI, 461 pages. 2001.

Vol. 2336: M.-S. Chen, P.S. Yu, B. Liu (Eds.), Advances in Knowledge Discovery and Data Mining. Proceedings, 2002. XIII, 568 pages. 2002.

Vol. 2338: R. Cohen, B. Spencer (Eds.), Advances in Artificial Intelligence. Proceedings, 2002. XII, 373 pages. 2002.

Vol. 2356: R. Kohavi, B.M. Masand, M. Spiliopoulou, J. Srivastava (Eds.), WEBKDD 2002 – Mining Web Log Data Across All Customers Touch Points. Proceedings, 2002. XI, 167 pages. 2002.

Vol. 2358: T. Hendtlass, M. Ali (Eds.), Developments in Applied Artificial Intelligence. Proceedings, 2002 XIII, 833 pages. 2002.

Vol. 2366: M.-S. Hacid, Z.W. Raś, D.A. Zighed, Y. Kodratoff (Eds.), Foundations of Intelligent Systems. Proceedings, 2002. XII, 614 pages. 2002.

Vol. 2371: S. Koenig, R.C. Holte (Eds.), Abstraction, Reformulation, and Approximation. Proceedings, 2002. XI, 349 pages. 2002.

Vol. 2375: J. Kivinen, R.H. Sloan (Eds.), Computational Learning Theory. Proceedings, 2002. XI, 397 pages. 2002.

Vol. 2377: A. Birk, S. Coradeschi, T. Satoshi (Eds.), RoboCup 2001: Robot Soccer World Cup V. XIX, 763 pages. 2002.

Vol. 2381: U. Egly, C.G. Fermüller (Eds.), Automated Reasoning with Analytic Tableaux and Related Methods. Proceedings, 2002. X, 341 pages. 2002 .

Vol. 2385: J. Calmet, B. Benhamou, O. Caprotti, L. Henocque, V. Sorge (Eds.), Artificial Intelligence, Automated Reasoning, and Symbolic Computation. Proceedings, 2002. XI, 343 pages. 2002.

Vol. 2389: E. Ranchhod, N.J. Mamede (Eds.), Advances in Natural Language Processing. Proceedings, 2002. XII, 275 pages. 2002.

Vol. 2392: A. Voronkov (Ed.), Automated Deduction – CADE-18. Proceedings, 2002. XII, 534 pages. 2002.

Vol. 2393: U. Priss, D. Corbett, G. Angelova (Eds.), Conceptual Structures: Integration and Interfaces. Proceedings, 2002. XI, 397 pages. 2002.

Vol. 2403: Mark d'Inverno, M. Luck, M. Fisher, C. Preist (Eds.), Foundations and Applications of Multi-Agent Systems. Proceedings, 1996-2000. X, 261 pages. 2002.

Vol. 2407: A.C. Kakas, F. Sadri (Eds.), Computational Logic: Logic Programming and Beyond. Part I. XII, 678 pages. 2002.

Vol. 2408: A.C. Kakas, F. Sadri (Eds.), Computational Logic: Logic Programming and Beyond. Part II. XII, 628 pages. 2002.

Vol. 2413: K. Kuwabara, J. Lee (Eds.), Intelligent Agents and Multi-Agent Systems. Proceedings, 2002. X, 221 pages. 2002.

Lecture Notes in Computer Science

Vol. 2370: J. Bishop (Ed.), Component Deployment. Proceedings, 2002. XII, 269 pages. 2002.

Vol. 2371: S. Koenig, R.C. Holte (Eds.), Abstraction, Reformulation, and Approximation. Proceedings, 2002. XI, 349 pages. 2002. (Subseries LNAI).

Vol. 2372: A. Pettorossi (Ed.), Logic Based Program Synthesis and Transformation. Proceedings, 2001. VIII, 267 pages. 2002.

Vol. 2373: A. Apostolico, M. Takeda (Eds.), Combinatorial Pattern Matching. Proceedings, 2002. VIII, 289 pages. 2002.

Vol. 2374: B. Magnusson (Ed.), ECOOP 2002 – Object-Oriented Programming. XI, 637 pages. 2002.

Vol. 2375: J. Kivinen, R.H. Sloan (Eds.), Computational Learning Theory. Proceedings, 2002. XI, 397 pages. 2002. (Subseries LNAI).

Vol. 2377: A. Birk, S. Coradeschi, T. Satoshi (Eds.), RoboCup 2001: Robot Soccer World Cup V. XIX, 763 pages. 2002. (Subseries LNAI).

Vol. 2378: S. Tison (Ed.), Rewriting Techniques and Applications. Proceedings, 2002. XI, 387 pages. 2002.

Vol. 2379: G.J. Chastek (Ed.), Software Product Lines. Proceedings, 2002. X, 399 pages. 2002.

Vol. 2380: P. Widmayer, F. Triguero, R. Morales, M. Hennessy, S. Eidenbenz, R. Conejo (Eds.), Automata, Languages and Programming. Proceedings, 2002. XXI, 1069 pages. 2002.

Vol. 2381: U. Egly, C.G. Fermüller (Eds.), Automated Reasoning with Analytic Tableaux and Related Methods. Proceedings, 2002. X, 341 pages. 2002. (Subseries LNAI).

Vol. 2382: A. Halevy, A. Gal (Eds.), Next Generation Information Technologies and Systems. Proceedings, 2002. VIII, 169 pages. 2002.

Vol. 2383: M.S. Lew, N. Sebe, J.P. Eakins (Eds.), Image and Video Retrieval. Proceedings, 2002. XII, 388 pages. 2002.

Vol. 2384: L. Batten, J. Seberry (Eds.), Information Security and Privacy. Proceedings, 2002. XII, 514 pages. 2002.

Vol. 2385: J. Calmet, B. Benhamou, O. Caprotti, L. Henocque, V. Sorge (Eds.), Artificial Intelligence, Automated Reasoning, and Symbolic Computation. Proceedings, 2002. XI, 343 pages. 2002. (Subseries LNAI).

Vol. 2386: E.A. Boiten, B. Möller (Eds.), Mathematics of Program Construction. Proceedings, 2002. X, 263 pages. 2002.

Vol. 2387: O.H. Ibarra, L. Zhang (Eds.), Computing and Combinatorics. Proceedings, 2002. XIII, 606 pages. 2002.

Vol. 2388: S.-W. Lee, A. Verri (Eds.), Pattern Recognition with Support Vector Machines. Proceedings, 2002. XI, 420 pages. 2002.

Vol. 2389: E. Ranchhod, N.J. Mamede (Eds.), Advances in Natural Language Processing. Proceedings, 2002. XII, 275 pages. 2002. (Subseries LNAI).

Vol. 2391: L.-H. Eriksson, P.A. Lindsay (Eds.), FME 2002: Formal Methods – Getting IT Right. Proceedings, 2002. XI, 625 pages. 2002.

Vol. 2392: A. Voronkov (Ed.), Automated Deduction – CADE-18. Proceedings, 2002. XII, 534 pages. 2002. (Subseries LNAI).

Vol. 2393: U. Priss, D. Corbett, G. Angelova (Eds.), Conceptual Structures: Integration and Interfaces. Proceedings, 2002. XI, 397 pages. 2002. (Subseries LNAI).

Vol. 2396: T. Caelli, A. Amin, R.P.W. Duin, M. Kamel, D. de Ridder (Eds.), Advances in Pattern Recognition. Proceedings, 2002. XVI, 863 pages. 2002.

Vol. 2398: K. Miesenberger, J. Klaus, W. Zagler (Eds.), Computers Helping People with Special Needs. Proceedings, 2002. XXII, 794 pages. 2002.

Vol. 2399: H. Hermanns, R. Segala (Eds.), Process Algebra and Probabilistic Methods. Proceedings, 2002. X, 215 pages. 2002.

Vol. 2401: P.J. Stuckey (Ed.), Logic Programming. Proceedings, 2002. XI, 486 pages. 2002.

Vol. 2402: W. Chang (Ed.), Advanced Internet Services and Applications. Proceedings, 2002. XI, 307 pages. 2002.

Vol. 2403: Mark d'Inverno, M. Luck, M. Fisher, C. Preist (Eds.), Foundations and Applications of Multi-Agent Systems. Proceedings, 1996-2000. X, 261 pages. 2002. (Subseries LNAI).

Vol. 2404: E. Brinksma, K.G. Larsen (Eds.), Computer Aided Verification. Proceedings, 2002. XIII, 626 pages. 2002.

Vol. 2405: B. Eaglestone, S. North, A. Poulovassilis (Eds.), Advances in Databases. Proceedings, 2002. XII, 199 pages. 2002.

Vol. 2407: A.C. Kakas, F. Sadri (Eds.), Computational Logic: Logic Programming and Beyond. Part I. XII, 678 pages. 2002. (Subseries LNAI).

Vol. 2408: A.C. Kakas, F. Sadri (Eds.), Computational Logic: Logic Programming and Beyond. Part II. XII, 628 pages. 2002. (Subseries LNAI).

Vol. 2409: D.M. Mount, C. Stein (Eds.), Algorithm Engineering and Experiments. Proceedings, 2002. VIII, 207 pages. 2002.

Vol. 2412: H. Yin, N. Allinson, R. Freeman, J. Keane, S. Hubbard (Eds.), Intelligent Data Engineering and Automated Learning – IDEAL 2002. Proceedings, 2002. XV, 597 pages. 2002.

Vol. 2413: K. Kuwabara, J. Lee (Eds.), Intelligent Agents and Multi-Agent Systems. Proceedings, 2002. X, 221 pages. 2002. (Subseries LNAI).